Europe Since 1989

Transitions and transformations

William Outhwaite

Routledge
Taylor & Francis Group

LONDON AND NEW YORK

First published 2016 by Routledge

2 Park Square, Milton Park, Abingdon, Oxfordshire OX14 4RN
52 Vanderbilt Avenue, New York, NY 10017

Routledge is an imprint of the Taylor & Francis Group, an informa business

First issued in paperback 2019

British Library Cataloguing-in-Publication Data
A catalogue record for this book is available from the British Library

Library of Congress Cataloging-in-Publication Data
Outhwaite, William.
    Europe since 1989 : transitions and transformations / by William Outhwaite. — 1 Edition.
        pages cm
    1. European Union countries—Economic integration. 2. Europe—Foreign relations. 3. Europe—Politics and government. I. Title.
    HC241.O926 2015
    940.56—dc23
    2015017541

ISBN: 978-1-138-84706-4 (hbk)
ISBN: 978-0-367-87066-9 (pbk)

Typeset in Times New Roman
by Apex CoVantage, LLC

Europe Since 1989

Europe Since 1989 charts the development of Europe east and west since the 1989 revolutions. It analyses the emergent European society, the development of a European public sphere, and civil society. Most books on Europe are heavily biased to the West, and *Europe Since 1989* takes the opposite approach. It argues that the transformation of the postcommunist world has implications for the whole of Europe and explores the interplay between long-term fundamental tendencies and chance events and the possible futures which confront contemporary Europe.

With close attention to political, economic, and other social transformations, and an appendix which gives special attention to European macro-regions (Nordic/Baltic Europe, Mediterranean Europe), it offers a sociology of Europe with a strong interdisciplinary emphasis.

William Outhwaite is professor of sociology (emeritus) at Newcastle University. His recent books in this area include *European Society* (Polity, 2008), *Critical Theory and Contemporary Europe* (Continuum, 2012), and (with Larry Ray) *Social Theory and Postcommunism* (Blackwell, 2005).

Contents

Acknowledgements

My greatest debt is to the Leverhulme Trust, whose Major Research Fellowship (2008–2011) made possible the bulk of the work behind this book. My new colleagues at Newcastle, where I had moved in 2007, were also unfailingly supportive. Several friends there or elsewhere have commented on parts or all of earlier drafts – notably Frane Adam, Valentina Feklyunina, Luke Martell, Peter Phillimore, Larry Ray, Darrow Schecter, Richard Sakwa, and Simon Susen. (Any errors are, of course, mine.) Laura Marcus, whom I accompanied to Edinburgh and followed to Oxford, where I was an undergraduate, and Daniel Outhwaite have watched the project develop over the years.

An earlier version of Chapter 2 was presented at the International Consortium of Social Theory Programs Conference at Cork in summer 2011. Some of the material in Chapter 4 was presented at a work-in-progress seminar at Newcastle, the International Consortium of Social Theory Programs Conference at Sussex in summer 2010, and a Citizenship in South-East Europe (CITSEE) seminar at Edinburgh in December 2010. An earlier version of parts of this chapter is in the *Journal of Democratic Socialism* 1(1), 2011, and I presented an earlier version of the appendix at the Conference of Europeanists in Barcelona, also in 2011. Some of the material in the later chapters was presented at workshops at Lancaster University and the Hansa-Wissenschaftskolleg, Delmenhorst, in June 2009 and appears in a similar form in my chapter 'Towards a European Society' in the *Routledge Handbook of European Sociology*, edited by Sokratis Koniordos and Alexandros-Andreas Kyrtsis (2015). While finalising the manuscript I benefited also from comments on an overview of the whole project from Mihaela Mihai, Werner Bonefeld, and others at a politics seminar at York in early 2015.

Abbreviations

ASEAN	Association of South-East Asian Nations
ÁVH	Államvédelmi Hatóság (State Protection Authority)
CAP	Common Agricultural Policy
CDU	Christlich–Demokratische Union (Christian Democratic Union)
CEE	Central and Eastern Europe
CEEC(s)	Central and Eastern European Countries
CIS	Commonwealth of Independent States (Russian: SNG)
CMEA	(Comecon) Council for Mutual Economic Assistance
ČSR, ČSSR	Czechoslovak (Socialist) Republic
CSU	Christlich–Soziale Union (Christian Social Union)
DDR	Deutsche Demokratische Republik (German Democratic Republic)
EB	Eurobarometer
EBRD	European Bank for Reconstruction and Development
EC	European Community/ies
ECB	European Central Bank
ECJ	European Court of Justice; now Court of Justice of the European Union (CJEU)
ECSC	European Coal and Steel Community
EFTA	European Free Trade Area
FPÖ	Freiheitspartei Österreichs (Austrian Freedom Party)
gal/tan	green/alternative/libertarian versus traditionalism/authority/nationalism.
GDP	gross domestic product
IMF	International Monetary Fund
KGB	Committee for State Security (Komitet gosudarstvennoy bezopasnosti)
MEP	Member of the European Parliament
MfS	Ministerium für Staatssicherheit (Stasi)
NAFTA	North American Free Trade Association
NATO	North AtlanticTreaty Organization
NGO	non-governmental organisation
OECD	Organisation for European Cooperation and Development
OMC	Open Method of Coordination
PDS	Partei des demokratischen Sozialismus
PHARE	Pologne, Hongrie: Activité pour la Restructuration Économique

TACIS	Technical Assistance to the Commonwealth of Independent States
SCO	Shanghai Cooperation Organisation
SdRP	Social Democracy of the Polish Republic
SED	Sozialistische Einheitspartei Deutschlands/Socialist Unity Party of Germany
SVP	Schweizerische Volkspartei (Swiss People's Party)

1 Introduction

Two alternative prefaces to the second edition, 2030?[1]

Version 1

In 2015, a quarter of a century after the end of communism in Eastern Europe, the end state, or *finalité*, of United Europe was still more or less as open as when Andrew Shonfield (1973) had described it as a 'journey to an unknown destination'. Two 'Eastern enlargements' had been completed, more or less smoothly, in 2004 and 2007, with Croatia joining the European Union (EU) in 2013, and the rest of the Western Balkans lined up to follow sooner or later. There were, however, still massive uncertainties about the definitive accession of Turkey and several former Soviet territories to the west and south of Russia. The term 'accession fatigue' had been current for some time, and there were increasing fears that the EU might have overreached itself. The dreary squabbles over the constitutional treaties which cast a shadow over the end of the first decade of the new century for the European Union were, however, soon superseded by a more rational federal structure and now seem as remote as the agitation over 'states' rights' in the history of the United States. The situation stabilised in the second decade of the twenty-first century, culminating in the presidency of David Miliband, Europe's first directly elected president, whose family history symbolised the rapprochement between East and West and between Russia, at last enjoying genuine democracy, and the EU.

Version 2

In 2015, a quarter of a century after the end of communism in Eastern Europe, the future of Europe was still open. The term 'accession fatigue' had been current for some time, and there were increasing fears that the EU might have overreached itself. These fears proved all too realistic, as the Union spiralled towards stagnation and its eventual meltdown, beginning with the collapse of the eurozone and the abandonment of the Schengen border-free space in the later 2010s. The parallels drawn in the early years of the century with the Ottoman Empire came home to roost in the 2010s for the new 'sick man Europe'. In retrospect, the long half-century from 1951 to 2004 marks a golden age for European federalists, and despite the initial successes of the common currency and the first two eastern enlargements, it became clear that the European project had run out of steam. The decline of democracy in the EU member states, pioneered by Berlusconi in Italy and Orbán in Hungary, matched the excesses of presidentialism and managed or 'sovereign' democracy further east. If the original dreams of a federal Europe had, in part, followed a Modell Deutschland, Europe in the 2030s experiences a Modell Russland and a race to the bottom by increasingly authoritarian regimes.

Introduction

Over sixty years since the beginnings of postwar West European integration, and twenty-five years since Europe as a whole experienced a first wave of unification with the fall of the Iron Curtain, its future seems as open as when Andrew Shonfield (1973) described it as being on a journey to an unknown destination. Political union, break-up, or the persistence of something like what we have known up to the present: a spread bet would want to cover all three possibilities.

What we do have are two big negative certainties. One is that we did not have a nuclear war between the North Atlantic Treaty Organization (NATO) and the Warsaw Pact. Historians will continue to argue how likely it was, and contemporary commentators discuss the danger of a new Cold War (including Mikhail Gorbachev, who ended the previous one), but this much is certain. The second is that we did not, for better or worse, experience a gradual rapprochement between the eastern and western halves of the subcontinent, but rather, an abrupt adaptation of much of the former to the political and economic systems of the latter. This has been reflected in the continuing marginalisation of postcommunist Europe in much of the current academic literature – something which this book aims to counter.

Whereas the gradual 'widening' and 'deepening'[2] of what has become the European Union was a linear process, advancing by fits and starts, 1989 was a real caesura, in which what was barely conceivable in midsummer was a fait accompli for much of communist Europe by the following midwinter. By the new year of 1990, it seemed possible that EUrope, the Europe of the European Union, would one day absorb a good part of the rest of the subcontinent[3] – even if it could not do this at a stroke, as it was to do with eastern Germany. There was needless delay, but the 2004 and 2007 enlargements came in the end. For a time, it seemed that the EU might have bitten off more than it could chew, but then the problems turned out to be, for the moment at least, in the older member states of the south and west. Now widening is pretty much on hold, but paradoxically, the threat of partial or total collapse of the eurozone has led to calls for greater centralisation, impotently encouraged in the early 2010s by a free-riding UK government sneering from the sidelines.

Most books on Europe are heavily biased to the West. This one takes the opposite approach, starting with the 1989 revolutions and examining the implications of postcommunist transition for the region and for Europe as a whole. The underlying argument is one which Larry Ray and I made in our book *Social Theory and Postcommunism* (Outhwaite and Ray, 2005), that the transformation of the postcommunist world has implications for the whole of Europe. Although I would not endorse Habermas's early characterisation of the 1989 revolutions as essentially a matter of 'catching up' (Habermas, 1990), it is at least true that much of postcommunist Europe has caught up with the process of European integration begun in the west in the 1950s. I also focus in particular on an issue which has been central to modern social theory since its earliest beginnings with Montesquieu: the interplay of long-term fundamental tendencies and chance events.

This long-standing theme of social theory has been transformed by globalisation and the long-overdue marriage between sociology and international relations. When I began to teach about Europe in the mid-1970s, my approach was strongly comparative but also methodologically nationalist. (The term had just been invented by Herminio Martins and it caught on some considerable time later.) The comparisons were essentially within and between the two blocs, with divided Germany as a convenient microcosm of the division of Europe. The European Communities were a special topic which I tended to avoid for lack of expertise and which seemed only marginally relevant to the social scientific study of Europe. It would now be unthinkable to set things up in this way, though the discourses of international relations and European integration studies remain curiously distinct. The revival of state-centred, as opposed to society-centred, theories in sociology, following Theda Skocpol (1979, 1985) was also a vital contribution: whether or not the emergent EU could be called a state, it was clearly the source of very substantial processes of social change, as well as a site in which they were reflected upon and responded to. This book is about Europe as a whole, not just the EU, but the EU inevitably becomes increasingly prominent in the course of the book.

* * *

The two 'prefaces' remind us that, just as our futures are open, within certain limits, our past could also have taken a different form. The rest of this introduction explores in more detail some events which might not have happened.

The first is the Bolshevik victory in 1917. As Archie Brown (2009: 46) writes, 'An entirely possible alternative to the victory of the Communists was the development of an extremely right-wing nationalist regime'. Without the Bolshevik victory and its enormous demonstration effect on the rest of the world, communism might well have remained a minority current in European politics and, more specifically, in European socialism, as, of course, it mostly did in Western Europe. The Bolshevik victory was only possible because of the world war. Michael Glenny and Norman Stone pointed out that Russia was, of course, on a steep growth curve before WW1, close to overtaking France as the world's fourth-largest economy (Glenny and Stone, 1990: 324). They suggest that 'the very advance of Russia before 1914 virtually caused Germany to attack her in that year' (Glenny and Stone, 1990: 443–4).

Another is the Nazi victory in 1933. At the time Hitler slipped into power, support for the Nazis appeared to have peaked and they, too, could have declined into a minority position. And without a Nazi Germany, it is quite likely that Italian fascism and its mostly southern European relatives would have mutated into something more like the Spanish and Portuguese dictatorships, without launching what we know as the Second World War.

Michael Mann (2011: 29) suggests a similar range of counterfactual possibilities: 'Without the two world wars, probably no fascist or communist regimes (only failed revolutions), no massive American Empire, no single reserve currency, less variable rhythms in the development of social citizenship in the liberal countries. . . . '

Without World War II, then, we would probably not have had the division of Europe. However, *given* the military outcome of World War II, the division of Europe and its partial Stalinisation were probably more or less inevitable. Stalin certainly seems to have thought so, if we take seriously his famous observation to the Yugoslav communist and later dissident Milovan Djilas that 'everyone imposes their own [social] system as far as their army can reach'.

Yet even within the contours of the second half of the twentieth century in Europe, the Europe of the Cold War, there were surely many possibilities. The most dramatic is again that the Cold War might develop into a nuclear war which extinguished all human and most other animal life on the planet. We should never forget that this was a possibility: as late as 1983-84 the USSR was nervous about the prospect of a NATO first strike, and a NATO exercise was modified to allay Soviet fears (Brown, 2009: 477). A full-blown nuclear exchange of this kind now seems unlikely, though we may see smaller-scale wars involving the use of nuclear weapons in the present century.[4]

Less dramatically, with the Cold War remaining cold, we might have seen more communist regimes (Greece being a likely candidate in the immediate postwar period) or, more probably, fewer. (Czechoslovakia could have escaped communism: in the event, local communist strength made up for the absence of Soviet troops or serious external pressure.) In their different ways, Austria and Finland offer models of liberal capitalist neutral regimes which might have been more widespread and would certainly have been more welcome to almost everyone except Stalin. In Germany in the early 1950s, even the Soviets seriously considered the prospect of 'liquidating' the recently established and unpopular East German state in order to negotiate a neutralised unified Germany (Brown, 209: 268–9) – essentially the Austrian solution, though, of course, on a much larger and therefore riskier scale. It was the June 1953 uprising in Berlin, Brown (2009: 270) suggests, which decided the issue in favour of their continuing, instead, to prop up the German Democratic Republic (GDR).

With Yugoslavia, there are again two alternative scenarios. In one, the Soviet Union is sufficiently panicked by the prospect of the Titoist heresy spreading to the rest of the socialist bloc to launch an invasion – possibly preceded by the assassination of Tito which they seriously considered and do seem to have attempted (Brown, 2009: 206–7). In the alternative scenario, of what we might call premature Gorbachevianism, more regimes might have been allowed to adopt the Yugoslav road of a neutral and substantially liberalised communist regime.

The Yugoslav regime was, of course, relatively popular; elsewhere in the bloc, there was little active support, as distinct from acquiescence. A liberalisation strategy might well have led to a 1989, the implosion of the communist order, in the early 1950s. Realistically, since even counterfactual historical speculation has limits, we should not have expected this until Stalin was dead and, though not buried, at least a stuffed dummy alongside Lenin in the Red Square mausoleum. There were significant protests in Plzeň, in Western Czechoslovakia, and then, more substantially, in Berlin in June 1953, where the Soviet Union used military force, as it was entitled to do under the postwar occupation agreement. The next round, in 1956, was more problematic, since it followed the propaganda's own goal (again prefiguring Gorbachev's policy of glasnost, or openness) of Khrushchev's 'secret' speech to the Party denouncing Stalin's rule. Protest in 1956 was much more widespread, and the situation in Poland and Hungary could have developed very differently from the way it did.

In the event, of course, the 'Polish October' of protest was swiftly defused by the installation of Gomułka, who had been in prison from 1951 to 1954 and only recently readmitted to the Communist Party. Without this, however, the situation might easily have provoked military intervention by the USSR and its allies in the ironically named *Warsaw* Pact. Mark Kramer (1998: 172) quotes Khrushchev as saying at a Presidium meeting that, although there were plenty of reasons for military intervention, 'finding a way to end such a conflict later on would be very hard'.

Conversely, in Hungary, the peaceful solution to the crisis which the Soviet Presidium had voted for at the end of the same month, following the replacement of Gerő by Kádár (who, just like Gomułka, had been in prison until 1954), was immediately abandoned after incidents including the killing of some secret policemen and a local politician. Mikoyan, who had negotiated with the Hungarian Party, condemned the intervention and apparently nearly resigned over the issue (Brown, 2009: 285–6).[5] Whether a peaceful resolution in Hungary would have speeded up the reform process in the communist bloc or initiated a collapse of 1989 dimensions is anyone's guess. Brown (2009: 270) is, no doubt, right that this crack-down, like the others, strengthened the position of hard-liners in the ruling parties.

What about the 'Prague' Spring of 1968? Its gradualism and the fact that it was led by reformist communists might have counted in its favour, but again the USSR and its allies cracked down. (Romania refused to participate in the invasion, and the GDR was kept in the background, with only some troops in Western Bohemia and at some airfields, probably in order to avoid embarrassing analogies on the twentieth anniversary of Hitler's invasion in 1938.) Again the brakes were put on economic as well as political reform across the bloc, except in Hungary and to some extent Germany. Most people outside the system, including many western communists, concluded that it was unreformable; the more cautious view turned out to be right: that if it was to be fundamentally changed, this could only be from what John Le Carré called Moscow Centre. Gorbachev's rise to power was a lucky fluke; his predecessors had been too old to launch what were widely recognised as necessary reforms of the system. Once initiated, however, the momentum of perestroika turned out to be unstoppable and ironically illustrated Gorbachev's other buzzword: 'acceleration'. What was less certain was which of the satellites would follow suit. In the GDR, where the party was now embarrassed by its slogan that 'learning from the Soviet Union means learning to win', the rather feeble response was that just because the neighbours are redecorating, there's no need for everyone to do it. As things turned out, almost everyone had done it, in one way or another, by the end of 1989, leaving the Soviet Union with the German question to resolve and a string of internal territorial problems. Almost the only blood on the wall was in Romania.

There was on the face of it nothing particular about the first half of 1989. Reformers in Hungary were making substantial headway, but the surprise success of Solidarity in the semi-free elections on June 4 coincided with the Tiananmen massacre in Beijing.[6] It was not clear until early November that the Soviet Union would not support a similar crackdown in the European satellites. At least three of the revolutions began with what, in the technical vocabulary of social science, are generally known as cock-ups: the confusion over just which day the Berlin border was to be opened, the faking by the secret police of the death of an apparent Czech demonstrator, and the, with hindsight, ill-advised decision by Ceausescu to organise a large demonstration, where the cheers turned to boos (and, of course, on live television).

An orthodox Marxist could cite the interaction of long-term tendencies with short-term contingencies in the collapse of communism as a demonstration of the 'law' of the transformation of quantity into quality. Less formally, it illustrates Göran Therborn's lesson that social scientists should be 'very alert, like all good historians, to the important, and often lasting, impact of contingency and chance' (Therborn 2011: 208). If the great biologist Jacques Monod had not used the title, I would have been tempted to call this book *Chance and Necessity*. The theme was central to the concerns of one of the founding fathers of social science: Montesquieu. In his major work, *The Spirit of the Laws*, Montesquieu had clearly expressed in 1748 the basic idea of the dependence of political and legal arrangements on broader social processes, in what we would now call a holistic and multi-causal approach.[7] At the same time, he was conscious of the mutability of human laws[8] and the influence of contingencies and what he called 'les exemples des choses passées'.[9]

This may be one of the first references to what we would now call path dependence, a concept which, for good reason, has played a key role in the analysis of postcommunist transition and is the subject of Chapter 3. Although there was a tendency among many observers and some protagonists to assume the inevitability of a standard transition model, there remained the question of whether it could be expected to succeed to different degrees in different parts of the former bloc, as well as the key issue of the pace of transition. What were the positive and negative legacies of communism, and how important were they? Were the birthmarks of postcommunist societies likely to persist or to be effaced by later developments? Would policy decisions taken in the first weeks and months have lasting effects? The next chapter examines some of these issues.

Before closing this introduction, I should say something more about counter-factuals in relation to the two main themes of this book: postcommunist transition and the expansion of the European Union. I can be briefer here since they turn around a single big question: Was there ever a possible 'third way', economically and geopolitically, between the capitalist and the socialist world? In more institutional terms, was the polarisation between the EU and/or NATO and 'the rest' an inevitability? Anticipating my later discussion, I suggest that, with hindsight, it was unlikely that postcommunist states would choose an economic *via media*, and equally unlikely that a geopolitical compromise of the kind outlined by Mary Sarotte (2009) and discussed in the next chapter would have stuck. Second, although the 'Copenhagen Criteria' for accession had not yet been formulated, it was clear that EU membership required a capitalist economy and a liberal democracy, meaning that there were criteria of political and economic viability for accession candidates.

Was the expansion of the EU inevitable? Clearly not in its details, but there were strong push and pull factors making it likely. On the push side, a major theme of the 1989 revolutions, along with democracy and 'normality', had been the idea of 'Europe', whatever that meant in practice. On the pull side, the EU was committed to considering all European liberal democracies as candidates for accession, and it embodies a strong internal dynamic, well described by Georg Vobruba (2005) in his image of concentric circles, towards enlargement. (Briefly, those 'inside' have, other things being equal, an interest in their immediate neighbours also coming in.) How these various pressures worked themselves out is the subject of the following chapters.

Notes

1 These alternative prefaces were inspired by some comments on an earlier paper by my former colleague, Peter Phillimore.
2 Widening means enlargement; deepening refers to the qualitative extension of integration between member states.
3 It had, however, spurned Morocco in 1987 and has continued to procrastinate about Turkey.
4 More optimistically, we might remember that poison gas, widely used in combat in the First World War, was later mostly used 'only' against civilians, massively in the Holocaust but rarely thereafter (by Saddam Hussein against the Iraqi Kurds, for example, and in a terrorist attack in Japan).
5 Mikoyan's Teflon quality (there were jokes about him dodging between raindrops – see Brown, 2009: 286), in a career lasting forty years, raises interesting questions about whether he might have reached the top and acted as a liberalising force. In the event, he was pensioned off by Brezhnev in 1965.
6 The 'Chinese road', combining Communist Party rule (and repression) with economic reform, is another counterfactual possibility for the Soviet Union; see, for example Walder 1997 and Tucker 2010, and my discussion in chapters 4 and 6, below.
7 As well as *The Spirit of the Laws*, see also Montesquieu (1976). My recent book on social theory (Outhwaite, 2015) opens with Rousseau and Montesquieu.

8 'The nature of human laws is to be subject to all the accidents which occur, and to vary according to changes in human wishes' (*L'esprit des lois*, book 26, chapter 2; my translation.)

9 *L'esprit des lois*, book 19, chapter 4. Jadwiga Staniszkis (1999: 9, 25) uses the same image of 'History and Chance' in dealing with the related issue of 'continuity in change'.

References

Brown, Archie (2009) *The Rise and Fall of Communism*. London: Bodley Head.

Glenny, Michael and Norman Stone (1990) *The Other Russia*. London: Faber and Faber.

Habermas, Jürgen (1990) *Die nachholende Revolution*. Frankfurt, Suhrkamp. Title essay translated as 'What Does Socialism Mean Today? The Rectifying Revolution and the Need for New Thinking on the Left', *New Left Review* I/183, September-October 1990, pp. 3–21.

Kramer, Mark (1998) 'The Soviet Union and the 1956 Crises in Hungary and Poland: Reassessments and New Findings', *Journal of Contemporary History* 33(2): 163–214.

Mann, Michael (2011) *Power in the 21st Century. Conversations with John A. Hall*. Cambridge: Polity.

Montesquieu, Charles Secondat (1976) 'Essay on the Causes That May Affect Men's Minds and Characters', translated and annotated by Melvin Richter, *Political Theory* 4(2): 132–62.

Outhwaite, William (2015) *Social Theory*. London: Profile.

Outhwaite, William, and Larry Ray (2005) *Social Theory and Postcommunism*. Oxford: Blackwell.

Sarotte, Mary (2009) *1989. The Struggle to Create Post-Cold-War Europe*. Princeton: Princeton University Press.

Shonfield, Andrew (1973) *Europe: Journey to an Unknown Destination*. Harmondsworth: Penguin.

Skocpol, Theda (1979) *States and Social Revolutions*. Cambridge: Cambridge University Press.

Skocpol, Theda (1985) 'Bringing the State Back In: Strategies of Analysis in Current Research', in Peter B. Evans, Dietrich Rueschemeyer and Theda Skocpol (eds.), *Bringing the State Back In*. Cambridge: Cambridge University Press, pp. 3–42.

Staniszkis, Jadwiga (1999) *Post-Communism. The Emerging Enigma*. Warsaw: Institute of Political Studies, Polish Academy of Sciences.

Therborn, G. (2011) *The World. A Beginner's Guide*. Cambridge: Polity.

Tucker, Aviezer (2010) 'Restoration and convergence: Russia and China since 1989', in George Lawson, Chris Armbruster and Michael Cox (eds.), *The Global 1989. Continuity and Change in World Politics*. Cambridge University Press, pp. 157–178.

Vobruba, Georg (2005) *Die Dynamik Europas*. Wiesbaden: VS Verlag für die Sozialwissenschaften.

Walder, Andrew (1997) 'The State as an Ensemble of Economic Actors: Some Inferences from China's Trajectory of Change', in Nelson, Joan, Charles Tilly and Lee Walker (eds), *Transforming post-Communist Political Economies*. Washington, DC: National Academy Press, pp. 432–452.

2   After 1989

This chapter sets the scene for the more analytical discussion in later chapters of the postcommunist transition in East Central Europe and Russia. New Year's Day 1990 seems the obvious date to begin this flashback and Prague the obvious place. Havel had been elected president of Czechoslovakia by the old communist parliament on December 29 and had orchestrated a New Year's Eve service in St. Vitus' Cathedral. His New Year's Day speech reminded his audience that their acceptance of the inescapability of the communist regime had 'helped to perpetuate it'.[1] Although the fall of the Berlin Wall has become the iconic image of 1989, it was really Czechoslovakia which saw the most striking reversal. The post-1968 Czechoslovak regime was one of the most repressive in the bloc and its demise one of the most abrupt. Even here, of course, there was not an immediate handover of the kind which used to be familiar in British politics, where one set of ministers moved out in the morning after a general election defeat and another moved in that afternoon. There was a period of negotiation, documented in its early stages by Timothy Garton Ash from his vantage point in the Civic Forum headquarters, the Magic Lantern Theatre. He provides a superb vignette of the dissident physicist Pavel Bratinka working out his exile in his stoker's hut on December 1, 1989, and saying that, 'On the whole I favour a bicameral legislature'. In the new parliament he was to become deputy chair of the foreign affairs committee and Jiri Dienstbier, also working as a stoker, would be foreign minister.[2] Czechoslovakia, then, also provides the starkest example of the transformation of dissidents, or more or less 'loyal' oppositionists, into politicians on the one hand, or relatively powerless observers on the other. Garton Ash (1990: 98) quotes Dienstbier's prediction on November 24, a mere week since the crucial events of the November 17: 'Either the counter-revolution or . . . a Western consumer society.' No bullshit, no third way.

Elsewhere in the bloc, the pattern was already well set. In Poland, the semi-free elections of June 4 had produced a Solidarity government and, by December 17, Balcerowicz's legislative package for economic transition. In October 1989, Hungary had set the programme for the free elections eventually held in May 1990. In Germany, where the border had only been open since November 9, the Round Tables were already being overtaken by the prospect of reunification, and emigration from East to West was running in January 1990 at 2000 people a day.

Romania had just got rid of the Ceauşescus in a Christmas Day execution whose brutality matched that of their long rule, and the real transition would take a good deal longer, as it would also in Bulgaria, where Mladenov, Zhivkov's successor and former foreign minister, had had to promise elections in the coming spring. In the Baltic States and Yugoslavia, the situation was still open, though the Baltics were impressed by the opposition success in Poland and even more so by the fact that the USSR had not intervened there or in the other 'satellites' (Kramer, 2003). Ukraine, which is often overlooked in discussions of 1989, was even more strongly influenced by Poland; the opposition movement Rukh received Adam Michnik and others at its founding conference in September. On January 21, 1990, the official day commemorating the unification of the state, it organised a human chain from Lviv to Kiev – a form of demonstration used the previous August in the Baltic States.[3]

By the beginning of 1990, there had already been an implicit rejection of what a few months earlier might have seemed alternatives. Before going further, I should rapidly mention two paths not taken.[4] The first is that of a 'third way' between capitalism and state socialism; the second is that of a new type of democracy reflecting and building on the civil society activism of the 1980s. There are three prime sites in which an observer in late 1989 or early 1990 might have looked for signs of a third way. One is Germany, where it seemed for a time that there was the option of a confederation of the two German states and, at least for the East, an intermediate economic path. We know how quickly that was overtaken by events: the slogan 'We are one people', whether or not it began as an appeal to the East German security forces not to shoot their fellow citizens, rapidly became a demand for reunification under Kohl's ample wings. A second candidate is Poland, where the transformation had, after all, been driven by what started off as a trade union. Here, too, however, the incoming Solidarity government rapidly initiated capitalist shock therapy and called on what remained of the union to bring the working class into line with the new course. Finally, Hungary, like Poland, but more substantially and over a longer period, had already gone some distance towards a form of market socialism of a Yugoslav kind. Was socialist self-management without communist monopoly rule (the latter had already gone in Hungary by the summer of 1989) a possibility? No one much seemed to think so, and local analyses probably paralleled that of Nigel Swain (1992: 31–2): 'The reintroduction of capitalist economic relations in Hungary . . . was probably inevitable'. In Hungary and Yugoslavia, as in Germany, a bird in the hand (Western capitalism) looked a better prospect than a pig in a poke (Kornai, 1992).

As for democracy, a striking feature of dissident activity in the 1980s had been an approach which György Konrád (1984) called anti-political. Havel's 'living in truth' and the practice of operating openly *as if* under conditions of freedom were also far removed from the instrumentalism of conventional politics. The eclipse of civil society movements and of the broad anti-communist alliances which had been such a feature of 1989 was as rapid, by Western standards, as had been their rise. In part, this was intended. As Havel (2008: 78) put it, '[T]he Civic Forum was a body created for a single purpose: to peacefully push aside the previous regime and mediate the transition to democracy. It was meant to exist for a couple of weeks and then dissolve into normal political parties'. There was disappointment both inside and outside the region at the rapid disappearance of innovative movements and their replacement by something like a 'Western' party system, distinguished only by its volatility and the understandable intensity of political antagonisms rooted in the old regime. The process was, however, inevitable.[5]

What were, then, the options confronting the new regimes of East Central Europe? The most obvious were negative, at least formally: to abolish the leading role of the Communist Party and its penetration of the media and the rest of the state, to abolish or neutralise the secret police, and to remove restrictions on private economic activity. Václav Klaus, in a retrospective speech of 1994, distinguished between the passive aspect (deregulation and liberalisation, including that of the political system) and 'positive actions' such as privatisation.[6]

These are, however, lagged processes. It was communist parliaments that had begun the reforms in the summer of 1989 in Hungary and elected Havel president in December. As Valerie Bunce and Mária Csanádi noted (1993: 248), '[L]iberalization of politics – at least in the initial stages of making politics more competitive – tended to precede other changes in the system. What this has meant, most ironically, is that politics is once again "in command" in Eastern Europe'.

Of the reforms listed earlier, several, as we have seen, had already been secured earlier in 1989 in Poland and Hungary. In Poland, the Round Table talks from February to April had produced an agreement on the legalisation of Solidarity, which unexpectedly won the June elections, and further extensions of electoral freedom and parliamentary rights. On December 29 a new constitution was introduced and Balcerowicz's economic reform package for 1990 was launched: as two foreign but inside advisers wrote, 'it aims to create during the course of 1990 the legal, economic, financial and administrative conditions needed for a market economy'.[7] By then, against a background of economic crisis, a process of 'nomenklatura privatisation' was already well advanced, with the outvoted Communist Party setting up thirty-six companies by the time of its last congress in January 1990; these were taken over by one of its successor parties, the Social Democracy of the Polish Republic (SdRP). As Wojciech Roszkowski (2003: 46) writes, 'In 1990 most of the Communist party companies went miraculously bankrupt and their assets were taken over by private creditors, mostly from the Communist *nomenklatura*'.

In Hungary, economic liberalisation, in the form of the 'law on business associations', had also already allowed a kind of wild privatisation in 1988, when Kádár was replaced as party leader by Grósz and the opposition movement Fidesz had achieved de facto recognition (Bayer, 2003: 173). In Czechoslovakia there had been nothing like this reform process before the implosion of the regime in the last weeks of 1989. As Havel (2008: 55) puts it, '[W]e had no entr'acte of perestroika or reform communism, but we started directly, after a few days of revolution, to build a normal democratic society'. On the other hand, however, as Wheaton and Kavan (1992: 117) point out, in Czechoslovakia

The existence of networks and a more or less ready-made leadership contrasts with the situation in Romania and East Germany, where the party provided the leaders for the revolutions. Further, the Czech dissidents had contacts and sympathizers, even as high as the upper echelons of the party.

Even in Czechoslovakia, then, there was considerable continuity, notably at the very top, where Deputy Prime Minister Marian Čalfa became transitional prime minister in the 'government of national understanding' set up on December 10, 1989, just three weeks after the November 17 rally (and was later reappointed by Havel after free elections). As Havel (2008:72) recalls it,

> Ultimately, it was Čalfa who taught the new government how to govern. There was not a lot that was specifically communistic in what you call the 'technology of power' once the leading role of the Communist Party no longer applied, and things were no longer decided first in the Politburo. The government simply meets on certain days; there's an agenda, there are procedural rules, the ministers have to receive their briefing materials in time, and so on.

There could be no question of just 'dismantling' the existing structures. Instead,

> We tried to fill existing posts with new, uncompromised people and then, by democratic means – that is, by passing constitutional and ordinary laws – to carry out the systemic changes we were able to agree on as the most necessary and the most important.
>
> (Havel 2008: 69–70)[8]

If the two obvious options in 1989–1990 were the abolition of the secret police and of central planning of the economy, even the first of these took a month or more and, in the case of the German Stasi, a massive demonstration (Sarotte, 2009: 96–7). In the Czechoslovak case, interestingly, Havel (2008: 106) explains the fact that it took a month to disband the state security (StB) by the lack of information and reliable forces:[9]

> We talked a lot at the time about setting up a kind of 'ethical tribunal' to render a verdict on the moral and political responsibility for conditions under the previous regime, but there obviously wasn't the appetite, or even the energy, for that. The saddest thing of all is our miserable record in successfully prosecuting actual crimes. The state of our judiciary was clearly a factor here.
>
> (Havel 2008: 62)

In Germany the beginnings were also extremely slow. The first Round Table meeting with the communist government had taken place on December 7, and as well as calling for elections by May, it demanded the dissolution of the Ministerium für Staatssicherheit, the Stasi. This had been renamed the Amt für Nationale Sicherheit, with a new head installed on November 21; the ineptitude of this step is well reflected in the unfortunate acronym NaSi. *Spiegel* commented on the issue on December 18,[10] and when the Round Table met again on January 8 it learned of a conspiracy launched on December 9 by the state security in the provincial town of Gera. Unimpressed by the government's proposal for a second name change to imitate the West German 'Office for the Protection of the Constitution' (Verfassungsschutz), New Forum organised a demonstration on January 15 at the Stasi Berlin headquarters which ended in a break-in and, two days later, the sealing of the files in the building (Sarotte, 2009, pp. 92–8).

Turning to countries with a more gradual transition in 1989, the same lengthy process can be seen in Poland (Roszkowski, 2003: 44). Hungary is unusual in that the pre-1956 state security agency, the ÁVH, was disbanded in that year by the revolutionary government. After the suppression of the revolution, it was not formally reinstated, but its personnel were vetted and, according to two leading historians, 98% were approved for employment in the departments of the interior ministry which replaced it (Scheibner 2008). Hungary has lagged behind other countries in allowing researchers access to the archives; the historian János Kenedi obtained a judgement against Hungary in the European Court of Human Rights in 2009 for denying him access. More recently, the FIDESZ government has repeatedly blocked proposals to open the files.[11]

In Germany, the Ministerium für Staatssicherheit /Ministry for State Security (MfS) was abolished, with a small number of its personnel finding employment in the West German security and espionage services and rather more in security agencies and other newly founded private firms, often based on previous technical and service branches of the MfS (*Spiegel*, 1990). Mary Sarotte (2009: 98) reports that Stasi employees continued to destroy documents: '[A]s late as September 1990, [Bärbel] Bohley and [Robert] Havemann's widow would find it necessary to occupy a main Stasi archive building, to force access to the files'. Two of those who carried out the dissolution of the MfS, David Ulrich and Gill Schröter (1991: 183–4), pointed out that the citizens' committees which took over the Stasi headquarters in regional centres in the course of December showed considerable courage in occupying the premises of 'what was really still an intact secret service'. Its files, apart from those destroyed in late 1989 and early 1990, are held by a state agency generally known by the name of its director, originally the priest and democratic activist Joachim Gauck. Anyone with a file is entitled to see it.

On the second issue, the replacement of central planning by a market economy, there were more open choices over the speed and modalities of the transition.[12] At the beginning of 1990, the process was well under way in Hungary and about to be launched officially in Poland. A perceived economic imperative, articulated by local and foreign experts, coincided with a perceived political imperative. Wydra (2000: 93) quotes Jacek Kuroń's recollection of a speech by the US economist Jeffrey Sachs in an article in 1991:

When Jeffrey Sachs spoke in the OKP [Civic Parliamentary Club] . . . Rysiek Bugaj, sitting next to me, said: what rubbish is this guy saying! And I said: I don't know much of what he is talking about, but listening to him I know

that this solution has a political value. The programme could be economically worse, or better. But it must have a political value, i.e. you present this
programme to the people and they support it.[13]

The Hungarian economist Janos Kornai provided a ten-year retrospective on a
programmatic book which he had published in 1989, *The Road to a Free Economy*. There he had brushed aside talk of market socialism but argued for an
'organic' development of the private sector, combined with a cautious strategy
of privatisation of state companies, as opposed to a 'give-away'. The latter, as
practised in Czechoslovakia and, most disastrously, Russia, was, he argued, mis-
taken, especially since it allowed the preservation of a 'soft budget constraint'
on companies. Arguments that voucher privatisation was morally just and would
produce a 'property-owning democracy' rapidly faded as shares were bought up
by banks and/or oligarchs. Companies privatised in this way were not, as had been
promised, more efficient than new creations. The only real benefit was political,
securing for the Czech government a second term which at the time was unique in
the region (Kornai, 2000: 18). In Poland and Hungary, by contrast, governments
resisted the temptation of a give-away privatisation and paid the electoral cost. In
both countries, however, insider, or nomenklatura, privatisation was already far
advanced by the end of 1989.[14] Kornai concedes that he 'did not predict the deep
recession that followed; I was too optimistic in my expectations of future growth'
(2000: 21).

   Jean-Luc Delpeuch (1994) provides valuable insight into the early years of
Czech transition. Working from September 1990 until July 1992 in Vladimír
Dlouhý's economic ministry, he participated in the debates between gradualists
and radicals, known as *razantní* (racers) in Czech. As he points out, the opposition between the two strategies often took a paradoxical form: for example, the
severe devaluation of the crown 'delayed the opening of the economy to foreign
competition' and therefore operated de facto as a protectionist policy (Delpeuch,
1994: 146–7). His criticism, he recalls,

> was sometimes interpreted as hostility to reform [and] made me realise that
> for Czech citizens this was something fundamental and almost solemn.
> Reform is the symbol of a rediscovered identity and dignity, the materialisa-
> tion of a route which resolutely turned away from an absurd and degrading
> period.
>
> (Delpeuch 1994: 156)

   This climate of opinion encouraged the over-hasty adoption of inappropriate
economic models (Delpeuch, 1994: 150).

   Polish 'shock therapy' was particularly harsh (Hardy, 2009: 29; Ost, 2005),
with real wages falling by as much as half for peasants in early 1990; as a result,
'their enthusiasm about the free market rapidly abated' (Kowalski, 1993: 349,
quoted by Epstein, 2005: 193). There has been a long debate about the rival merits
of speed and gradualism (Åslund et al, 1996; Popov, 2007; Frye, 2010: 106–7).
Popov argues that 'the debate about the speed of the liberalisation (shock therapy

versus gradualism) was to a large extent misfocused, whereas the crucial importance of strong institutions for good performance was overlooked'. In the absence
of such institutions to redirect investment, 'there is a general reduction of output –
a typical supply-side recession that could have been avoided with a slower pace of
liberalisation' (Popov, 2007: 18; for an earlier theoretical argument, see van Ees
and Garretsen, 1994). In the long run, however (in which, as Keynes famously
said, we are all dead), the outcomes seem to have been rather similar. States which
cut harder at the beginning enjoyed higher growth rates later on and caught up
with those which had taken a more gradualist approach. By then, however, many
postcommunist citizens *were* dead, victims of soaring mortality rates, particularly
men in the former USSR (Haerpfer, Wallace and Abbott, 2013).

In the economic reform area, the picture rapidly becomes complicated by the
intrusion of outside 'experts' and, eventually, of the European Union. We are
entering, in other words, a terrain well mapped by analysts such as Janine Wedel
(1998) for the 'advice industry' of what were known in Poland as the 'Marriott
men' and Wade Jacoby's analyses of processes of imitation or 'ordering from
the menu' (Jacoby, 2000, 2002, 2004).[15] Jeffrey Sachs was undoubtedly the most
prominent (see Sachs, 1990; Sachs and Lipton, 1990; an interview with Sachs
(1992) and Sachs 1993). In a much-quoted passage in his *Economist* article, Sachs
(1990) wrote that there was no viable alternative to the market economy:

> Eastern Europe will still argue over . . . whether to aim for Swedish-style
> social democracy or Thatcherite liberalism. But that can wait. Sweden and
> Britain alike have nearly complete private ownership, private financial mar-
> kets and active labour markets. Eastern Europe today has none of these insti-
> tutions; for it, the alternative models of Western Europe are almost identical.

Sachs, who had refused to advise the Polish communist government (Sachs, 1992:
441 n.16; Sachs 2000: 13–4) and became an adviser to Solidarity when it was
re-legalised, also later worked in Russia for the Yeltsin government. Kornai, who
had co-organised a conference with Sachs in the spring of 1990,[16] declined any
political role or official advicery position, but served for the second half of the
1990s on the Hungarian Central Bank Council, as well as writing influential books
and articles, including, perhaps, the definitive political economy of *The Socialist
System* (1992). With the eventual prospect of European Union (EU) accession
for much of the region, as discussed in later chapters, the role of experts was, of
course, greatly extended.

A related issue forms a kind of bridge between these two: the question of the
restitution of property taken by the communist regimes or, crucially, *before*, by
the Nazi or puppet regimes which preceded them. In Warsaw, for example, such
prominent sites as those of the Wedel chocolate factory, the Marriott Hotel, the
French and US embassies, and even the Palace of Justice had been expropriated
by one regime or both (Chodakiewicz and Currell, 2003: 173–4).

In Poland and Czechoslovakia this was not just a matter of individual properties
or even categories of property such as factories or large land holdings, but entire
territories such as the Sudetenland, the former East Prussia, and Western Poland.

One of the many stones on the road to German reunification was the question of whether a future united Germany would renounce any claim to Silesia: Chancellor Kohl, with an eye on supporters expelled from there in the postwar years, both procrastinated and prevaricated. Garton Ash (1993: 227–8) cites an anonymous source for the claim that, as long ago as 1970, Kohl was already thinking that the Federal Republic should formally accept that the Oder-Neisse boundary was definitive, but after consulting colleagues refrained from making any public statement. Nearly twenty years later, in autumn 1989, and now as federal chancellor rather than prime minister of a federal state on the western fringe of the country, he reassured Bronisław Geremek that the border was indeed a dead issue but that he could not say so publicly for domestic political reasons. As well as 'sitting out' the tricky issue, something for which he was famous, Kohl could stir up enough hostile reaction abroad to show the *revanchist* expellees that their demands endangered German unity (Garton Ash, 1993: 229–30). Across Central Europe, the prevailing compromise seems to have become that whatever happened in the immediate postwar period was accepted as a fait accompli, and only seizures by the communist governments established in the late 1940s were open to legal challenge. In Poland, where the issue dragged on for a decade, a law passed in 2001 provided for shared ownership or compensation of 50% of the value of property seized between 1944 and 1962 (Chodakiewicz, 2003: 177).

Two further and related issues should be mentioned here, although they point forward into the later 1990s. First, it is worth examining the production of new constitutions. In the Polish case, although the parliament democratically elected in October 1991 began work on a new constitution, it was not until April 1992 that an act was passed to prepare it. Even then,

> The attitude of the parliamentary elite to the creation of the constitution is illustrated by the fact that the Constitutional Commission was established as late as half a year after the law came into effect, namely on October 30, 1992.
>
> (Stavrowski, 2003: 79–80)

Ulrich Preuss, the legal and political theorist who had been writing on constitutional and democratic politics throughout the 1980s (Preuss 1984), had immediately become involved in work on a commission drafting a proposal for a new German constitution and analysing the 1989 revolutions and their outcome (Preuss, 1992–3, 1995a, 1995b). He emphasised in particular the fact that although 'in the years since 1989 the European continent has undergone social and political changes which are hardly less radical and far-reaching than those in the last quarter of the eighteenth century' (Preuss 1995a: 3),

> the elimination of the communist regimes and the erection of profoundly new economic, social, and political structures happened, with few exceptions, within the framework of the existing constitution of the respective country. Before the revolutionaries overturned the old regimes, they amended the communist constitutions according to the amendment procedures of those

very constitutions. Thus, for example, the leading role of the communist Party, which in fact meant the dictatorship of the *nomenklatura*, or the category of the people's property were not abolished until the pertinent articles of the constitution had been repealed. Having been forced to listen to hypocritical revolutionary phraseology and having experienced an all-pervasive legal nihilism for the preceding forty years, the anticommunist opposition wanted to be neither revolutionary nor negligent of the rule of law.

(Preuss 1995a: 8)[17]

Preuss notes that initially what occurred throughout the bloc was 'a process of repeated amendment of the old constitutions according to the prescribed procedures by majorities of the people's deputies elected under the old system.' (Preuss 1992–3: 94)[18]

In the early 1990s Claus Offe and Preuss worked with the Norwegian political theorist Jon Elster and others on a major project on transformation (Elster et al, 1998).[19] The focus on constitutional politics[20] reflects Elster's earlier work on constitutionalism and democratic transition and on the 'Round Table Talks' which were a feature of almost all the transitions, as well as the interests of all three senior authors (see Elster and Slagstad, 1986; Elster, 1991, 2004).[21] The book traced the details behind the creation of formal constitutions in the four countries studied (Hungary, Bulgaria, and what became the Czech and Slovak Republics), since 'the choices which the relevant actors – the *pouvoir constituant* – make are likely to have long-lasting effects' (Elster et al, 1998: 63). The authors concluded:

it appears that it is the formative impact of new institutions – i.e. their capacity to shape the frames, habits, routines, and expectations (and even memories) of citizens in convergent ways and thereby to render inherited fears, hostilities, and suspicions groundless – that is the critical determination of consolidation.

(Elster et al, 1998: 296)

Meanwhile in New York, Andrew Arato, who had been extremely active writing on and with the Hungarian opposition in the 1980s,[22] was completing, with Jean Cohen, their major theoretical study *Civil Society and Political Theory* (Cohen and Arato, 1992). Arato was also becoming more closely concerned with constitutional theory and the practice of constitution making in the postcommunist context. In a retrospective postscript to a volume of essays from the 1990s, he writes of the much-discussed eclipse of civil society in postcommunist Europe:

Recognizing the empirical phenomena of the depoliticization of civic initiatives and social movements at the time of the Round Tables and the first competitive elections, I was nevertheless deeply concerned about the neglect of autonomous associations and publics in the emerging political designs and in the policy process. I came to the conclusion . . . that civil society had to be securely institutionalized before becoming a key terrain of participatory politics in the long term.

I have always stressed fundamental civil and political rights as the neces-sary conditions for the institutionalization of a modern civil society. These rights, however, could be established only in a setting that satisfies the demands of liberal constitutionalism. This is how I can explain my shift in interest to the study of constitution making, constitutional adjudication, and constitutional politics.

(Arato, 2000: ix–x; see also 168)

The outcomes in most of postcommunist Eastern Europe, 'where formerly legal nihilism and paper constitutions were the rule'(Arato, 2000: x) demonstrate this (Arato, 2000: xiii).

Like Preuss, who took up his earlier stress on the 'self-limiting' character of the 1989 revolutions and their constitutional aftermath, Arato considers 'the efforts of Central European constitution makers, especially the architects of Round Tables, to postulate the fiction of legal continuity with a past without legality . . . highly innovative and worthy of imitation'.[23] The political ideas at the back of 'self-limiting' opposition movements of civil society and their continuation by oth-ers in the postcommunist transition to genuine constitutionalism mean that Arato was irritated by Habermas' (1990) notion of a 'catching-up' revolution and also with Habermas and Offe's claim that 1989 failed to produce any theoretical pro-gramme (Arato, 2000: 271–2). As he wrote in an earlier essay, 'None of [these] interpretations . . . really grasp the meaning of what is potentially new in the transformation of the East, the option of a self-democratizing civil society'(Arato, 2000: 4; see also 260 n.23). And as he notes later in the same article, civil society theory experiences 'a distinct innovation when thinkers like Jacek Kuron, Adam Michnik, Claude Lefort, and Alain Touraine begin to include social movements in the concept' (Arato, 2000: 44).[24]

The evaluation of the early months of transition has, of course, been a massive topic of discussion, not least in memoirs by and interviews with the protagonists. Communist memoirs display a full spectrum from the upbeat ('we lost, but we played a good game') to replays of the earlier Western motif of 'the god that failed'.[25] Harry Willetts wrote in his introduction to the English version of Teresa Torańska's classic volume of interviews with Stalinists at the beginning of the 1980s that 'Fallen communists do not publish apologias' (Torańska, 1987: 9–12). They certainly do now. Most interesting, perhaps, are books like Torańska's or the post-1989 volume by Mink and Szurek (1999), based on multiple interviews which display varied responses by people previously holding similar positions in the nomenklatura. Two motifs stand out in the hundred interviews conducted by Mink and Szurek. One, among the continuing believers, is the theme that commu-nism had failed to perform its basically well-founded historical task and therefore had to be 'let go' like an underperforming worker.[26] The other is the more purely practical and technocratic theme that working for the Party was just an obvious career move, and a valuable source of practical experience, as one Polish respondent (Mink and Szurek 1999: 126) put it.

Some of these themes will reappear in the next section on decommunisation and lustration. For the moment it is enough to note what Mink and Szurek (1999: 214) call a 'successful conversion' of former communists which remains in part 'mysterious'.

To lustrate or not?

Along with, and related to, constitution making, the second major dilemma which confronted all postcommunist states was that of 'decommunisation', restitution and 'lustration'. It is no accident that it was two of the countries where the transition had been most abrupt, Czecho-Slovakia[27] and Germany, that were most systematic in addressing these issues; conversely, where the transition had been more a matter of agreement, as in Poland and Hungary, they were seen as less pressing.[28] Claus Offe (1996) was one of the first to examine these issues: a main section of *Varieties of Transition* is concerned with questions of restitution and retribution. Once again, as in 1989, the question is not so much 'What is to be done?' but 'Should/can *anything* be done?'[29] Whatever one thinks of the rather simple slogan that these just *were* 'regimes of injustice', it is clear that they made possible, and even required, all sorts of individual and collective acts of injustice against all sorts of individual and collective victims. One response is to say that because everyone was both a victim of and to some degree complicit with the past regimes, it is pointless and/or unjust to single out only some perpetrators of abuses. Offe cites a paper by Elster which argues:

> Because nobody is innocent, nobody should be put on trial. Because everybody suffered, nobody should be compensated . . . One might imagine a kind of public autodafé of the pre-communist property records as well as the archives of the secret police and those of the communist party.

But this, Offe comments, would involve 'a sweeping disregard for matters of degree'. Nevertheless, it can be argued that informal retribution might be preferred and would be less costly. Perhaps more importantly, retroactive justice focuses on violations of rights but not on other damage such as 'the ruined economy, the spoiled environment or broken and alienated personalities' (Offe, 1996: 84).

Germany is one of the countries which has been most active in prosecuting abuses of power and other crimes; two others, rather improbably in view of their otherwise slow pace of reform and democratisation, are Albania and Bulgaria (Borneman, 1997: 9–10). It was in Germany that the most thorough attempts were made to remedy injustices and to expose and, in some cases punish, those responsible. In particular, anyone who had a state security file on them is entitled to see it (if it still exists), though not before the names of other victims or third parties are removed for the sake of their privacy.[30] As Offe points out, 'it is only Germany that is in command of the political resources to effectively enforce whatever rules and principles have been derived from the intense theoretical and moral debate about how to come to terms with the past' (Elster et al, 1998: 86). The three relevant options, which he says usually need to be combined, are disqualification (deprivation of jobs or individual or collective resources), retribution via the criminal law, and restitution (or compensation).

> Disqualification cannot be excluded because there are many functionaries whose acts made up the old regime and whose further presence in, or access to, important positions in society is therefore unlikely to be tolerated . . . even though they have not committed criminal acts according to the laws of the old regime.
> Retribution also cannot be excluded, as key protagonists in the old regime seem to have regularly violated their own legality in the service of the regime . . . And nor can restitution be excluded, as victims of the old regime will generate pressure for re-privatization and compensation.
>
> (Elster et al, 1998: 89)

Offe brilliantly analyses the practical (including legal and moral) difficulties with all these measures and the ways in which Germany and other postcommunist states have handled them. Given these complexities, he favours an approach which, as he put it in the chapter mentioned earlier, 'keeps in focus the similarity of problems in the individual countries as well as the presence of social and cultural traditions, not to mention institutional and economic resources, typical only for particular nations' (Elster et al, 1998: 138). In practice, this amounts to an emphasis on restitution (the topic of his Chapter 6), where diverse local conditions determine, for example, the dates of expropriations for which compensation can be sought.[31] Even here, however, Offe addresses the 'suspicion . . . that underneath the proclamation of lofty principles of justice all kinds of arbitrary interests, privileges and resentments govern the actual practice of restitution' (Elster et al, 1998: 125).

It is in fact this theme which came to predominate. Even in Germany, there was considerable dispute over who should be prosecuted. It seemed unjust to prosecute border guards for shooting people, as they were trained to do, when the entire regime, or at least the politburo of the central committee, was responsible for the policy, which had been written into law in 1982 and was repeated to the guards at the beginning of each watch. In the end it proved possible in 1997 to convict three of the surviving leaders: Egon Krenz, Günter Schabowski, and Günter Kleiber, and in 2004 another two. The 1992 trial of Erich Honecker had been stopped on health grounds, although three of the five co-defendants were in fact sentenced, and another, Erich Mielke, the former minister for state security, was sentenced for another crime: the murder of two police officers in 1931. These trials took place according to principles of GDR law and the 1948 Declaration of Human Rights which had been determined to override the legality of the 'order to shoot', first by the Federal Court in 1994 and subsequently by the European Court of Human Rights in 2001. This whole protracted and messy process can perhaps be held to demonstrate the primacy of the rule of law over justice (Bräutigam, 2004: 976).

Germany was able to conduct an extremely thorough purge of the GDR's nomenklatura and other public officials, including, for example, half of all judges and prosecutors (Offe, 1996: 95), though in a way which differed widely from one sector to another. By and large one can assume that most senior public-sector employees were dismissed or retired if they could be shown to have worked for or collaborated with the Stasi, though this was not true, as we have seen, of the newly emergent private sector,[32] nor of those in less elevated positions such as schoolteachers, especially in Berlin (Borneman, 1997: 171; Appel, 2005: 384). Among the perverse effects were the employment of West Germans often seen as 'second-raters' and the opportunity for employers to use a record as a pretext to sack superfluous employees. GDR politicians, where they were not suspected of Stasi collaboration, were often able to recycle themselves in the notionally 'corresponding'[33] liberal and Christian parties of the Federal Republic, or in the Sozialistische Einheitspartei Deutschlands/Socialist Unity Party of Germany (SED's) successor party, the Partei des demokratischen Sozialismus/Party of Democratic Socialism (PDS). Kohl was justifiably suspicious of the East German Christian Democrats, but by February 1990 he had overcome his scruples and incorporated them into his 'Allianz für Deutschland' (Teltschik, 1991: 113, 118, 129). However, the two Christian Democratic parties were not merged until the eve of reunification, and the decision remained controversial, not just for members of the former opposition groupings, but also from some Eastern members who had wanted a less conservative and more centrist programme than that in the West (Thumfart, 2002: 218–28).

Elsewhere in the bloc, 'decommunisation' was necessarily more patchy and slower to be implemented.[34] As Havel (2008: 71) said in his memoirs,

> Suppose we had wanted to demote or fire everyone who was a member of the Communist Party? We'd have had to dissolve the entire Academy of Sciences and strip most of the universities of their faculties. We wouldn't have had a single higher-ranking officer in the armed forces, nor a single criminal investigator; a single CEO, a single diplomat, and maybe not even a single air traffic controller.

The Czechoslovak programme of 'lustration' of those who had collaborated with the state security was the most prominent. Although a senior politician, Josef Bartončik, had been exposed in the 1990 elections, the systematic programme of lustration was not initiated until late 1991, against President Havel's opposition and partly in response to the attempted coup in the Soviet Union and anxieties about a possible communist comeback, as well as a year and a half of on-going controversy (Keane, 1999: 428–35). The lustration law, which John Keane (1999: 431) describes as 'the most ethically dubious and politically controversial purging legislation in all of central and eastern Europe', required any candidate for a senior position in the public service or an enterprise in which the state owned a controlling share to obtain a certificate confirming that there was no evidence that he or she had collaborated with the communist state security or held a senior position in the party. The programme was a substantial one, delivering over a third of a million certificates in the first two years, of which only around 3% were positive (David, 2003: 414; Appel, 2005: 386). It was, however, less actively pursued in Slovakia, where Mečiar put the law on ice after the breakup of the federation at the beginning of 1993. The Czecho-Slovak law was itself modified in November 1992 in favour of 'candidate informers' against whom there was no evidence of actual collaboration (Karajkov, 2009).

Havel's reservations seem to have been based partly on the view he had controversially stated in his first presidential address – that everyone had gone along with the regime to some extent – and also that it would 'affect the small fish. The big ones are laughing at us. They have become capitalists; the act does not affect them' (quoted from Keane, 1999: 433–4). He also foresaw that lustration would become a political football and generate an atmosphere of paranoia. Delpeuch (1994: 164) declines to comment on the principle, having not lived (except as a short-term resident) under the communist system. 'I merely note that most of the senior people in the economic ministry whom I considered competent and motivated were affected by the "lustration law" and had to leave their jobs'.

The Czech lustration programme, along with the related measures in Germany, was the most substantial and consistent in the bloc. Elsewhere, although the question was actively discussed throughout the 1990s, a formal programme was not introduced until 1994 in Hungary (revised in 1996), 1995 in Albania (after a law of 1993 was declared unconstitutional), and 1997 in Poland, where it did not take effect until 1999. In the Baltic States the issue tended to be linked with questions of citizenship in relation to the Russian minorities; in Bulgaria and Romania there was a similar political to-and-fro throughout the 1990s. Since 2007 in Poland, lustration has been overseen by the Institute of National Remembrance (IPN) and increasingly politicised. It may have been necessary, as Borneman and others have argued, but it seems inevitably messy. In a context where trust in politicians is already low, Horne and Levi (2004: 63) write: 'We suspect that lustration, over time, adversely affects citizen confidence in politicians'.[35]

What did citizens of the countries concerned think of lustration? Czech, Polish, and Hungarian surveys in the early 1990s suggest a public opinion broadly in favour of some such measures, while concerned that it should not distract attention from more urgent and important issues (Williams, Szczerbiak and Fowler, 2003: 14–5; see also Szczerbiak, 2014). In an argument which is relevant to the discussion of path dependence in the next chapter, the authors suggest that the fact that lustration was also pursued in Poland and Hungary as well as in Czecho-Slovakia and the Czech Republic shows that the harshness of the preceding regime and the form of transition should not be given as much explanatory weight as they often have been in the literature. More important, they argue, are short-run political contingencies:

[I]n all three states, proponents of the toughest lustration regimes have been on the political right, at both elite and mass level, while centrists and centre-right forces have had far more difficulty with the issue.

[W]here governments rejected an explicit lustration policy, as in Hungary and Poland after 1990, they unwittingly encouraged opponents to demand lustration in the process of creating a distinct political identity for themselves while addressing a perceived cause of post-Communist ills (Williams, Szczerbiak and Fowler, 2003: 12–13).

[Thus] . . . the passage of each lustration bill . . . reflected not the country's political history but rather the parliamentary arithmetic of fluid party systems, the actual or anticipated response of veto players such as the presidency or the constitutional court, trial and error, and learning from neighbours' recent experiences (Williams, Szczerbiak and Fowler, 2003: 20; see also David, 2013).

There were important principles of both formal and informal justice at stake,[36] but they tended to point in contradictory directions. Lustration, and more broadly 'decommunisation' policies, therefore, illustrate the overall fluidity of the post-communist condition, which coexisted uneasily with the search for blueprints for economic and political reconstruction.

Notes

1 'From a New Year's Day Speech', *New York Review of Books*, February 15, 1990. In a similar vein, Jacek Kuroń is reported to have said 'Communist Poland was us' (Roszkowski, 2003: 25).
2 Garton Ash (1990: 115). The Hungarian economist János Kornai (2006: 363) recalls a conference he organised with Jeffrey Sachs in March 1990: 'Toward the end of the second session, a Czech economist announced that he could not stay any longer and had to hurry home. Half ironically and half seriously he added, "Anyone not in Wenceslaus Square now will not be a minister." His haste paid off; he was soon made a minister.'
3 Possibly the first human chain was a peace demonstration in England in 1983 against the deployment of short-range US nuclear missiles in West Germany.
4 A third is the neutralisation of the postcommunist region as opposed to its polarisation between the EU/NATO and Russia (Sarotte, 2009). For the economic dimension, see Lane (2007: 462).
5 The weakness of civil society, in the sense of associational life, remains a striking feature of the postcommunist world. See, for example, Howard (2003: 13–4).
6 See also Balcerowicz's claims, cited by Elizabeth Dunn (2004: 4, 35) on the 'naturalness' of a market economy. Dunn (2004: 35) comments that, 'The problem with the Balcerowicz plan was that most state-owned enterprises, including Alima [the baby food producer on which her book is based], simply could not compete in an environment of unconstrained international competition'.
7 Sachs and Lipton (1990: 48).
8 He goes on to point out (p. 71) something documented by many later surveys, notably those conducted by Richard Rose and summarised in Rose (2009), that where

Communist Party membership was so widespread, it does not mark a significant difference in political attitudes.

 9 See also Wheaton and Kavan (1992: 136–7).

10 'Arbeit für 10000 Staatsanwälte. Die Auflösung des Stasi-Überwachungsapparates
stellt die DDR-Regierung vor kaum lösbare Probleme', *Spiegel* 51, pp. 35–42.

11 www.politics.hu/20140219/fidesz-again-torpedos-law-on-communist-era-spying/.
Accessed February 9, 2014.

12 On privatisation programmes across the bloc, see Frydman et al (1993a, 1993b). For
the Czechoslovak case, see Wheaton and Kavan (1992: 154–64).

13 Somewhat later, Sachs (2000: 16) presented his own account of a meeting with Kuroń.
See also Stenning et al (2010: 40–9).

14 For a relatively benign account of this, see Mink and Szurek (1999). Where others have
seen a deliberate move by communist political and economic elites to move into private economic activity, the authors stress the reactive aspect of people losing their jobs
and looking for alternatives. Their account, based on interviews in Poland, Hungary,
and the Czech Republic, needs to be balanced by closer attention to the machinations
of party and secret police managers, as in the German cases mentioned earlier. Conversely, defenders of the purges and lustration discussed in more detail in the next section can reasonably point out that there was little or no screening in the private sector.
And, of course, it was only a minority of the vast army of unemployed people who had
these recycling opportunities.

15 But this was not a one-way street: see also Bockman and Eyal (2002: 310–52 and
Stenning et al (2010: chapter 2, esp. pp. 38–40). See also Ganev (2005) for a sceptical
account of the impact of neoliberalism. Bohle and Greskovitz (2012: 212–13) note that
Slovenia had the same advisers as Estonia but did not follow their advice.

16 See note 2 earlier. Kornai (2006: 355) claims that 'Most experts ten to fifteen years
later agree, in hindsight, that the gradualists were right'. He adds in a footnote: 'Jeffrey
Sachs agreed with me initially, but then became an advocate of acceleration. I remember the conversations in which we tried in vain to persuade each other. Much later,
when he saw the developments in Russia, he conceded that I had been right'.

17 See also Chapter 5, pp. 91–107, and de Raadt (2009).

18 Preuss noted that, although some West German legal scholars suggested that the communist constitutions had 'simply become obsolete as a result of the revolution', this
view was not accepted in the GDR or the other states in the bloc.

19 See also Bönker, Wolmann and Wiesenthal (1995) and Bönker, Müller and Pickel
(2002).

20 The running head of the book is 'Constitutional Politics and Economic Transformation', suggesting that this may have been an earlier title.

21 Elster worked at, and became director of, the Center for the Study of Constitutionalism in Eastern Europe, set up in 1989 at the University of Chicago Law School, which
played an important part in analysing and advising on the production of new constitutions. (The other major institutional resource was the *East European Constitutional
Review*, published by the New York University School of Law from 1992 to 2003, and
its rubric Constitutional Watch.)

22 See also Arato and Fehér (1989) and Fehér and Arato (1991).

23 p. xiv. On the practice of the Hungarian Constitutional Court and its rationale, see Kis
(2003).

24 On the rejection of the concept of civil society, see Arato (2000: 68).

25 As Mink and Szurek (1999: 209–10) point out, it is interesting that there is nothing,
or very little, comparable among ex-fascists. There *are*, however, many memoirs by

former Wehrmacht officers; see the interview with Wolfram Wette ('Zähe Legenden') in *Die Zeit* 23, June 1, 2011, p. 22.

26 See, for example, the interviews with Mieczysław Rakowski (pp. 245–6) and Jerzy Urban (p. 256). A sub-theme here is the bizarre notion that the opposition was 'unconstructive' and did not allow time for the regimes to make necessary reforms. See in particular the interview with Miroslav Stepan, the former mayor of Prague (p. 290).

27 This hyphenated name was the short-lived compromise term for the state which replaced the Czechoslovak Socialist Republic, replaced in turn by the Czech and Slovak Federative Republic and, soon afterwards, by the break-up of the federation.

28 As Marcin Król (2002: 73) put it, 'Even in politics you do not shoot the partner of a major agreement'.

29 See the Introduction to Elster et al (1998: 25) on the '*tabula rasa of 1989*'.

30 See Garton Ash (1997). Garton Ash, whose book is based on his own file, notes that in Germany the thoroughness of the surveillance apparatus is parallelled by that of its subsequent exposure (p. 21).

31 In Germany, for example, there is compensation for expropriations carried out by the German Democratic Republic (GDR) after its establishment in 1949, but not for those in the previous years of the Soviet occupation which had included not just reparations but a major land reform programme. In Hungary and Czechoslovakia, the dates were set to include communist expropriations but not those of property owned by Germans in the immediate postwar years. In some countries only land is considered; sometimes only citizens and residents are eligible for compensation. Backward-looking questions of justice intersect with more practical concerns about the likely use of restituted resources.

32 See the *Spiegel* article cited earlier.

33 The GDR had, largely for cosmetic reasons, a system of 'block parties' – Christian, liberal, agrarian, and even nationalist – allied with the communist SED. They were known informally as the 'block flutes' because they all played the same tune. People who, for professional reasons, were expected to join the SED – such as judges, of whom 97.6 % were members (Borneman, 1997: 170) – could sometimes get away with joining one of these instead.

34 Mink and Szurek's nomenklatura interviewees were uniformly contemptuous of it. See also Tarifa and Weinstein (1995–6).

35 On Hungary, see Barrett et al (2007: 300–1).

36 David and Choi (2009: 185) conducted a survey of the attitudes of former political prisoners in the Czech Republic, which produced the interestingly counterintuitive finding that, while there was a strong demand for material or symbolic compensation and recognition, 'The longer the victim's jail sentence, the less intense his or her desire to see his/her former enemy imprisoned'. On lustration, see David (2011, esp. chapter 3, 2003).

References

Appel, Hilary (2005) 'Anti-Communist Justice and Founding the Post-Communist Order: Lustration and Restitution in Central Europe', *East European Politics and Societies*, 19(3): 379–405.

Arato, Andrew and Ferenc Fehér (eds.) (1989), *Gorbachev: The Debate*. Cambridge: Polity Press.

Arato, Andrew (2000) *Civil Society, Constitution and Legitimacy*. Lanham: Rowman and Littlefield.

Åslund, Andres, Peter Boone, Simon Johnson, Stanley Fisher and Barry W. Ickes (1996) 'How to Stabilize: Lessons from Post-Communist Countries', *Brookings Papers on Economic Activity*, 1: 217–313.

Barrett, Elizabeth, Péter Hack and Ágnes Munkácsi (2007) 'Lustration as Political Competition: Vetting in Hungary', in A. Mayer-Rieckh and P. De Greiff (eds.), *Justice as Prevention. Vetting Public Employees in Transitional Societies*. New York: Social Science Research Council, chapter 7, pp. 261–307.

Bayer, József (2003) 'The Process of Political System Change in Hungary', *Begegnungen. Schriftenreihe des Europa-Instituts Budapest*, Band 22: 171–85.

Bockman, Johanna and Gil Eyal (2002) 'Eastern Europe as a Laboratory for Economic Knowledge: The Transnational Roots of Neoliberalism', *American Journal of Sociology* 108(2): September, 310–52.

Bohle, Dorothee and Greskovits, Béla (2012) *Capitalist Diversity in Europe's Periphery*. Ithaca and London: Cornell University Press.

Bönker, Frank, Hellmut Wollmann and Helmut Wiesenthal (eds.) (1995) *Transformation sozialistischer Gesellschaften: Am Ende des Anfangs*, Leviathan Sonderheft 15. Opladen: Westdeutscher Verlag.

Bönker, Frank, Klaus Müller and Andreas Pickel (eds.) (2002) *Postcommunist Transformation and the Social Sciences*. Lanham: Rowman and Littlefield.

Borneman, John (1997) *Settling Accounts. Violence, Justice, and Accountability in Postsocialist Europe*. Princeton: Princeton University Press.

Bräutigam, Hansgeorg. (2004) 'Die Toten an der Berliner Mauer und an der innerdeutschen Grenze und die bundesdeutsche Justiz', *Deutschland-Archiv* 37, 6: 969–976. www.chronik-der-mauer.de/index/php/de/Common/Document/field/file/id/39851. Accessed July 27, 2015.

Bunce, Valerie and Mária Csanádi (1993) 'Uncertainty in the Transition: Post-communism in Hungary', *East European Politics and Societies* 7(2): 240-275.

Chodakiewicz, Marek Jan and Dan Currell (2003) 'Restitucja: Property Restitution in Poland', in Marek Jan Chodakiewicz,, John Radziłowski and Dariusz Tołczyk (eds.), *Poland's Transformation. A Work in Progress*. Charlottesville: Leopolis Press, pp. 159–93.

Cohen, Jean, and Andrew Arato (1992) *Civil Society and Political Theory*. Cambridge: MIT Press.

de Raadt, Jasper (2009) 'Contested Constitutions: Legitimacy of Constitution-Making and Constitutional Conflict in Central Europe', *East European Politics and Societies* 23(3): 315–38.

David, Roman (2003) 'Lustration Laws in Action: The Motives and Evaluation of Lustration Policy in the Czech Republic and Poland', *Law and Social Inquiry* 28(2): 387–439.

David, Roman (2011) *Lustration and Transitional Justice: Personnel Systems in the Czech Republic, Hungary, and Poland*, Philadelphia: University of Pennsylvania Press.

David, Roman (2015) 'Transitional Justice and Changing Memories of the Past in Central Europe'. *Government and Opposition*, 50(1): 24-44.

David, Roman and Susanne Y. P. Choi (2009) 'Getting Even, or Getting Equal? Retributive Desires and Transitional Justice.' *Political Psychology*, 30(2: 161–92.

Delpeuch, Jean-Luc (1994) *Post-communisme: L'Europe au défi. Chronique pragoise de la réforme économique au coeur d'une Europe en crise*. Paris: L'Harmattan.

Dunn, Elizabeth (2004) *Privatizing Poland. Baby Food, Big Business and the Breaking of Labor*. Ithaca: Cornell University Press.

Elster, Jon and Rune Slagstad (eds.) (1986) *Constitutionalism and Democracy*. Cambridge: Cambridge University Press.

Elster, Jon (1991) 'Constitutionalism in Eastern Europe: An Introduction', *University of Chicago Law Review* 58(2) Spring: 447–82.

Elster, Jon, Claus Offe and Ulrich Preuss, with Frank Boenker, Ulrike Goetting and Friedbert W. Rueb (1998) *Institutional Design in Post-Communist Societies: Rebuilding the Ship at Sea*. Cambridge: Cambridge University Press.

Elster, Jon (2004) *Closing the Books. Transitional Justice in Historical Perspective*. Cambridge: Cambridge University Press.

Epstein, Rachel (2005) 'Diverging Effects of Social Learning and External Incentives in Polish Central Banking and Agriculture', in Frank Schimmelfennig and Ulrich Sedelmeier (eds.), *The Europeanization of Central and Eastern Europe*. Ithaca: Cornell University Press,, pp. 178–98.

Fehér, Ferenc and Andrew Arato (eds.) (1991) *Crisis and Reform in Eastern Europe*. New York: Transaction Books.

Frydman, Roman et al (1993a) *The Privatization Process in Central Europe*. Budapest and London: Central European University Press.

Frydman, Roman et al (1993b) *The Privatization Process in Russia, Ukraine and the Baltic States*. Budapest and London: Central European University Press.

Frye, Timothy (2010) *Building States and Markets after Communism. The Perils of Polarized Democracy*. Cambridge: Cambridge University Press.

Ganev, Venelin (2005) 'The "Triumph of Neoliberalism" Reconsidered: Critical Remarks on Ideas-Centered Analyses of Political and Economic Change in Post-Communism', *East European Politics and Societies* 19(3): 343–78.

Garton Ash, Timothy (1990) *The Magic Lantern*. New York: Random House.

Garton Ash, Timothy (1993) *In Europe's Name. Germany and the Divided Continent*. London: Jonathan Cape.

Garton Ash, Timothy (1997) *The File. A Personal History*. New York: Random House.

Habermas, Jürgen (1990) *Die nachholende Revolution*. Frankfurt, Suhrkamp. Title essay translated as 'What Does Socialism Mean Today? The Rectifying Revolution and the Need for New Thinking on the Left', *New Left Review* I/183, September-October: 3–21.

Haerpfer, Christian, Claire Wallace and Pamela Abbott (2013) 'Health Problems and the Transition from Communism in the Former Soviet Union: Towards an Explanation'. *Perspectives on European Politics and Society* 14(4): 460–79.

Hardy, Jane (2009) *Poland's New Capitalism*. London: Pluto.

Havel, Václav (1990) 'From a New Year's Day Speech', *New York Review of Books* 15(2).

Havel, Václav (2008) *To the Castle and Back*. London: Portobello Books, 2008. First published 2006.

Horne, Cynthia M. and Margaret Levi (2004) 'Does Lustration Promote Trustworthy Governance? An Exploration of the Experience of Central and Eastern Europe', in János Kornai and Susan Rose-Ackerman (eds.), *Building a Trustworthy State in Post-Socialist Transition*. New York: Palgrave Macmillan, pp. 52–74.

Howard, Marc Morjé (2003) *The Weakness of Civil Society in Post-Communist Europe*. Cambridge: Cambridge University Press.

Jacoby, Wade (2000) *Imitation and Politics: Redesigning Modern Germany*. Ithaca: Cornell University Press.

Jacoby, Wade (2002) 'Talking the Talk and Walking the Walk: The Cultural and Institutional Effects of Western Models', in Frank Bönker, Klaus Müller and Andreas Pickel (eds.), *Postcommunist Transformation and the Social Sciences*. Boulder: Rowman & Littlefield, pp. 129–52.

Jacoby, Wade (2004) *The Enlargement of the European Union and NATO. Ordering From the Menu in Central Europe*. New York: Cambridge University Press.

Karajkov, Risto (2009) 'Lost in Lustration: Transitional Justice at 20', *Transitions Online* 28(8) www.tol.cz. Accessed July 27, 2015.

Keane, John (1999) *Václav Havel. A Political Tragedy in Six Acts*. London: Bloomsbury.

Kis, Janos (2003) *Constitutional Democracy*. Budapest: Central European University Press.

Konrád, György (1984) *Antipolitics*. New York: Harcourt.

Kornai, János (1992) *The Socialist System. The Political Economy of Communism*. Oxford: Oxford University Press.

Kornai, János (2000) 'Ten Years After *The Road to a Free Economy*: The Author's Self-Evaluation'. Paper for the World Bank 'Annual Bank Conference on Development Economics – ABCDE'. Washington, D.C.: World Bank.

Kornai, János (2006) *By Force of Thought. Irregular Memoirs of an Intellectual Journey*. Cambridge : MIT Press.

Kowalski, Zbigniew (1993) 'Back to Market: Polish Family Farming in the 1990s', *Canadian Journal of Agricultural Economics* 41(3) November: 349–56.

Kramer, Mark (2003) 'The Collapse of Eastern European Communism and the Repercussions within the Soviet Union' (Part 1), *Journal of Cold War Studies* 5(4): 178–256.

Król, Marcin (2002) 'Democracy in Poland', in Mary Kaldor and Ivan Vejvoda (eds), *Democratization in Central and Eastern Europe*, pp. 67–77.

Lane, David (2007) 'Post-Communist States and the European Union', *Journal of Communist Studies and Transition Politics* 23(4): 461–77.

Mink, Georges and Jean-Charles Szurek (1999) *La grande conversion. Le destin des communistes en Europe de l'Est*. Paris: Seuil.

Offe, Claus (1996) *Varieties of Transition. The East European and East German Experience*. Cambridge: Polity.

Ost, David (2005) *The Defeat of Solidarity. Anger and Politics in Postcommunist Europe*. Ithaca: Cornell University Press.

Popov, Vladimir (2007) 'Shock Therapy versus Gradualism Reconsidered: Lessons from Transition Economies after 15 Years of Reforms', *Comparative Economic Studies* 49: 1–31.

Preuss, Ulrich (1984) *Politische Verantwortung und Bürgerloyalität: Von den Grenzen der Verfassung und des Gehorsams in der Demokratie*. Frankfurt: Fischer.

Preuss, Ulrich (1992–93) 'Constitutional Powermaking for the New Polity: Some Deliberations on the Relations between Constituent Power and the Constitution' *Cardozo Law Review* 14: 639–60.

Preuss, Ulrich (1995a) *Constitutional Revolution. The Link between Constitutionalism and Progress*, Atlantic Highlands: Humanities Press. Earlier version published in 1990 as *Revolution, Fortschritt und Verfassung*. Berlin: Klaus Wagenbach.

Preuss, Ulrich (1995b) 'Patterns of Constitutional Evolution and Change in Eastern Europe', in Joachim Jens Hesse and Nevil Johnson (eds.), *Constitutional Policy and Change in Europe*. Oxford: Oxford University Press, pp. 95–126.

Rose, Richard (2009) *Understanding Post-Communist Transformation: A Bottom Up Approach*. London: Routledge.

Roszkowski, Wojciech (2003) 'Points of Departure', in Marek Jan Chodakiewicz, John Radziłowski and Dariusz Tołczyk (eds.), *Poland's Transformation. A Work in Progress*, Charlottesville: Leopolis Press.

Sachs, Jeffrey and David Lipton (1990) 'Poland's Economic Reform', *Foreign Affairs* 3: 47–66.

Sachs, Jeffrey (1990) 'What Is to Be Done?', *The Economist* January 13, p. 21 (US edn.), 23 (UK edn.).

Sachs, Jeffrey (1992) 'Privatization in Poland: An Interview with Jeffrey Sachs, *Suffolk Transnational Law Journal* XV(2) Spring: 440–67.

Sachs, Jeffrey (1993) *Poland's Jump to the Market Economy*. Cambridge: MIT Press.

Sachs, Jeffrey (2000) Interview for PBS Commanding Heights. www.pbs.org/wgbh/com mandingheights. Accessed July 27, 2015.

Sarotte, Mary (2009) *1989. The Struggle to Create Post-Cold-War Europe*. Princeton: Princeton University Press.

Scheibner, Tamás (2008) Review of Gábor Tabajdi and Krisztián Ungváry, *Elhallgatott múlt* [Silenced Past] (Budapest: Corvina, 2008), in *ECE Journal*, 40(1–2): 198–200.

Stavrowski, Zbigniew (2003) 'The Constitutional Debate in Poland after 1989', in Marek Jan Chodakiewicz, John Radziłowski and Dariusz Tołczyk (eds.), *Poland's Transformation. A Work in Progress*. Charlottesville: Leopolis Press, pp. 77–88.

Stenning, Alison, Adrian Smith, Alena Rochovská and Dariusz Świątek (2010) *Domesticating Neo-Liberalism. Spaces of Economic Practice and Social Reproduction in Post-Socialist Cities*. Chichester: Wiley.

Szczerbiak, Aleks (2014) 'Explaining Patterns of Lustration and Communist Security Service File Access in Post-1989 Poland', Working Paper No. 133. Sussex European Institute, Falmer, Brighton.

Swain, Nigel (1992) *Hungary. The Rise and Fall of Feasible Socialism*. London: Verso.

Tarifa, Fatos and Jay Weinstein (1995–6) 'Overcoming the Past: De-Communization and Reconstruction of Post-Communist Societies', *Studies in Comparative International Development* 30(4): 63–77.

Teltschik, Horst (1991) *329 Tage*. Berlin: Siedler.

Thumfart, Alexander (2002) *Die Politische Integration Ostdeutschlands*. Frankfurt: Suhrkamp.

Torańska, Teresa (1987) *Oni. Stalin's Polish Puppets*. New York: Harper Collins.

Ulrich, David and Gill Schröter (1991) *Das Ministerium für Staatssicherheit. Anatomie des Mielke-Imperiums*, Reinbek: Rowohlt.

van Ees, Hans and Harry Gerretsen (1994) 'The Theoretical Foundation of the Reforms in Eastern Europe: Big Bang Versus Gradualism and the Limitations of Neo-classical Theory', *Economic Systems* 18(1) March: 1–13.

Wedel, Janine (1998) *Collision and Collusion. The Strange Case of Western Aid to Eastern Europe 1989–1998*. New York: St. Martin's Press.

Wheaton, Bernard and Zdenek Kavan (1992) *The Velvet Revolution. Czechoslovakia 1988–1991*. Boulder: Westview.

Williams, Kieran, Aleks Szczerbiak and Brigid Fowler (2003) 'Explaining Lustration in Eastern Europe: 'A Post-Communist Politics Approach'.' Working Paper No. 62. Sussex European Institute.

Wydra, Harald (2000) *Continuities in Poland's Permanent Transition*. Basingstoke: Macmillan.

3   Path dependence

Causal models of postcommunist transition

The previous chapter sketched out the dilemmas and trajectories of the early years of postcommunist transition in Europe. This chapter continues the discussion in a more analytic framework, looking at ways in which observers have attempted to explain transition. The notion of path dependence, the idea that the past constrains the present and the future, is a core reference point here. As Horváth and Szakolczai (1992: 211–212) wrote:

> The key question in . . . [revolutionary] . . . situations is whether something is possible, and what will be realised out of the enormous range of possibilities. A small factor, a minuscule event, an accident may well have a profound and lasting impact, establishing for a long time . . . the limits and range of future possibilities.

There are two rather different ideas behind the concept of path dependence. The first stresses the idea of irreversible choices. If there are two alternative routes from A to B, with little to choose between them, it usually makes sense to stick with your initial choice, and it may even be impossible to switch routes without returning to your starting point. The other image is closer to the way paths are more or less unconsciously formed by humans or other animals: taking a route which is easier because others have already used it and trodden down the grass or other obstacles.

It is easy to see why the concept of path dependence, which had played a big role in the 1980s, should have seemed particularly suited to the postcommunist condition. In many versions, at least, it relies on a notion of branching points, or 'critical junctures'.[1] It is ironic that the Norwegian philosopher Jon Elster, who could claim to be the father of the concept of path dependence, in his analysis of causality at the end of the 1970s made no explicit use of it when he came to work in the 1990s on postcommunist transition.[2] Elster's model of 'branching points' in history was part of his analysis of counterfactual conditionals: to say that someone or something was causally efficacious is to commit oneself to the claim that in the absence of that thing or person, matters would have been significantly different. As Elster (1978: 175) points out, the philosophical and historical discussions of counterfactuals have taken a different form. In philosophy, they appear as a criterion for differentiating causation from correlations: '[T]he former warrants the statement that if the cause had not occurred, then the effect would not have occurred, whereas no such counterfactual is implied by the latter.'

Philosophers have disagreed over the question whether, as Elster argues, this helps in analysing causation: historians have more often questioned the point of such speculation.[3] It is not clear, however, how anyone can

> discuss the relative importance of causes without engaging in some sort of thought experiment where one removes successively and separately each of the causes in question and evaluates what difference the absence of this cause would have made to the phenomenon in question.
>
> (Elster, 1978: 176)

Although one might not want to do a *lot* of this sort of thing, one could hardly avoid it altogether. 'What has troubled the historians, viz. the idea that statements about causation implies (sic) statements about counterfactuals, has been taken for granted by the logicians' (Elster, 1978: 176).

As Öberg and Hallberg Adu (2009: 132) note in a sceptical review of the issues, 'Researchers that *presume* that there has been a critical juncture somewhere along the path will most likely find one.' It could, however, hardly be denied that 1989/1991 *were* critical junctures. Furthermore, the notion of path dependence went to the heart of the questions confronting observers of and, of course, participants in the early years of postcommunism: how far were the prospects for these societies shaped by, first, the communist past (and, for that matter, the precommunist past) and, second, the form of the handover of power and the initial decisions taken?

To cut a long story very short, there were two extreme diagnoses. The first was that all postcommunist countries required the same neoliberal medicine, even if they might respond differently to it. (Srubar, 1996) They all suffered from the same political and economic disease: Communist Party dictatorship and central planning; They might, with luck, become successful capitalist democracies and, though this was less discussed in the early stages, some of them might end up in the European Union – to paraphrase Yeats, as 'rough beasts slouching towards Brussels to be reborn'. The second might be called the Dublin diagnosis, following the well-known joke in which a traveller asking the way to Dublin is told that you shouldn't try to get there from here.[4] The lasting effects of communism, the mode of transition, and other aspects of the situation made meaningful change a massively difficult prospect. Ken Jowitt (1992), who had worked on state socialism through the 1970s and 1980s, coined the twin terms of the 'Leninist extinction' and the 'Leninist legacy'.[5] He suggested pessimistically that 'it will be demagogues, priests and colonels more than democrats or capitalists who will shape Eastern Europe's institutional identity' (Jowitt, 1992: 300). As Jowitt recognised, legacies can be positive and negative, but the emphasis among those who picked up the term was more often on the latter: poisoned chalices for English and French writers or poisoned pralines for Germans.

At the risk of reifying disciplinary identities in this highly interdisciplinary field, it makes sense to link the first approach with economists,[6] aiming to apply a neoliberal blueprint on a tabula rasa, and the second with political scientists, with their attention particularly focussed on the demise or, at the very least, drastic mutation of the communist parties. As Bunce and Csanadi (1992: 14, cited in Stark, 1995: 67) put it, 'When communist hegemony died, institutions died and, with that, roles and rules'. Stark (1995: 68) presented his alternative path dependency approach in these disciplinary terms:

> The political scientists' alarms are a strong antidote to the economists' utopian projects. But from a third, more sociological perspective, the question is not whether the way is cleared for designer capitalism or the floodgates of disaster are opened but whether the metaphor of collapse and the concept of institutional vacuum accurately depict the contemporary societies of Eastern Europe.[7]

Stark had been working in the late 1980s in Hungary, where economic reform had, of course, gone further than anywhere else in the bloc and where there was an active public debate around reform, the informal 'second economy', and related issues. Elsewhere, things were also moving, contrary to the public, and to some extent also academic, image of monolithic communism (Stark, 1995: 70; see also Bruszt and Stark, 1991: 204).

In the introduction to their fully developed analysis, Stark and Bruszt (1998) set it in opposition to 'neoliberals who portray economic transformation as a project of social imitation' and 'involutionists', who foresee the persistence of the worst features of state socialism in a condition of permanent under-development (Stark and Bruszt, 1998: 5, citing Burawoy and Krotov, 1992).[8]

> In contrast to the imitationists, who see in the present only the absent features of an ideal future, we are interested in what the present holds for the future. In contrast to the involutionists, who see in the present the dead weight of the past, we see that the past can provide institutional resources for change in the present. In contrast to the transition problematic that is common to both, we see social change not as transition from one order to another but as transformation – rearrangements, reconfigurations and recombinations that yield new interweavings of the multiple social logics that are a modern society.
>
> Thus, in contrast to the involutionists' theory of past dependency, we analyze processes of path dependency as we explore how strategic choices, often highly contingent, shape further policy courses.
>
> (Stark and Bruszt, 1998: 7)

Running alongside these differences in analytic approach were policy controversies over the merits of shock therapy in which, as Balcerowicz put it, 'everything should be done as quickly as possible', or Sachs' image that you cross a chasm in one jump or not at all, and a more gradualist approach to 'rebuilding the ship at sea'.[9]

Before looking more closely at how these approaches panned out in the 1990s, I should mention a general feature of the literature on path dependence. Particularly in the economic literature, 'dependence' has a pejorative edge, as when an essay is marked down for 'lacking an independent argument' or being 'excessively dependent on a limited range of sources'. The assumption, briefly, is that the 'lock-in' to a particular trajectory may discourage or prevent recourse to better alternatives. Increasing returns in the short run may divert attention from strategies with a higher long-run pay-off; the well-trodden path is not likely to be the best way. The political and sociological literature, especially that focussing on postcommunism, less often takes this line. Here, in what Paul Pierson (2000, 2004) aptly calls the 'murkier' environment of more historical studies, the focus is more often on describing the alternative paths and explaining how they came to be 'chosen', with notions such as 'legacies' describing the more pathological aspects.[10]

Pierson (2000: 265; 2004: 52) also warns against a deterministic interpretation of path dependence:

> Nothing in path-dependent analyses implies that a particular alternative is permanently 'locked in' following the move onto a self-reinforcing path . . . Douglass North (1990: 98–99) summarizes the key point well: 'At every step along the way there are [are choices] – political and economic – that provide . . . real alternatives'.[11]

It should be clear that the discussion of path dependence both in Russia (Hedlund) and in East Central Europe (Stark and Bruszt) is very much in the spirit of what Pierson describes here. Two other elements prominent in the early discussion of postcommunism should be noted; both turn out with hindsight to be less significant than was assumed at the time. The first is the apparent difficulty of combining economic reform with political democratisation. This still appears in the first sentences of Stark and Bruszt (1998: 1):

> Can the transformation of property regimes and the extension of citizenship rights be achieved simultaneously? This is the postsocialist challenge. Can the governments of postsocialist Eastern Europe successfully pursue economic reform when the citizens who bear its costs acquire the means to replace political incumbents and choose among competing political programs? This is the postsocialist experiment.

Claus Offe (1996: 34) had coined in 1991, in similar terms, what became one of the dominant motifs of the literature on postcommunism: the notion of a 'triple transition' involving, first, the territorial shape and/or ethnic composition of the states concerned; second, controversies over their constitutional form; and finally their other political characteristics, 'the "normal politics" of the allocation and distribution of positive rights and resources through legislatures and executives'.[12] With hindsight, the territorial transitions may not have been as substantial as they threatened to be,[13] but Offe was undoubtedly right to point to the way in which such territorial and constitutional issues interwove with other aspects of politics and that the context meant that copying of Western institutions produced something very different. It became clear, however, that in one way or another economic and political transformation mostly went together and complemented rather than undermined one another.

The other widely held assumption was that the character of the pre-1989 regimes and the mode of their replacement would have lasting effects on the process of transformation. Thus, Czechoslovakia, which had hardly any private economic activity and with a highly repressive regime which meant that civil society was mostly underground, could be expected to have a more difficult transition than Poland and Hungary, where private-sector economic activity was relatively well developed, counter-elites were already active and tolerated, and the transition was negotiated rather than revolutionary. In practice, these differences seem to have been largely without long-lasting effects. Stark and Bruszt (1998: 16) themselves stressed that

> Despite the observation that the relative strength of civil society seems a good predictor of the timing and sequencing of upheavals in Eastern Europe in 1989, we would argue that the preoccupation with the strength/weakness of civil society (however reformulated) remains misplaced . . . the degree of organization of civil society should be analyzed not simply relative to that of other cases but, more important, in relation to the forces obstructing (or promoting) change inside the ruling elite.

Stark and Bruszt focussed on the economy, which is, of course, one of the policy areas where one would expect to find the greatest degree of continuity. However drastic the privatisation programmes, they would not systematically abolish one productive structure to replace it with another, even if neoliberal rhetoric sometimes flirted with this possibility. Their four cases, Germany, Czechoslovakia, Poland, and Hungary, displayed four distinct strategies. In East Germany a single state agency, the Treuhand, set up shortly before unification, privatised or closed the bulk of state enterprises and property, including land. By the summer of 1991 it had already privatised some 2000 of the German Democratic Republic's (GDR's) 7000 state enterprises, selling almost all to West Germans (Stark and Bruszt, 1998: 89). At the other extreme, Czechoslovakia ran a voucher privatisation scheme in 1992 in which all citizens had an option to acquire shares in state property. In practice, the bulk of shares ended up in the hands of large investment funds. As Stark and Bruszt (1998: 158) note, 'The outcome . . . has not been a people's capitalism but a strange kind of finance capitalism'. Poland and Hungary adopted more mixed and flexible strategies of privatisation, corresponding, Stark argued, to their more gradual decommunisation process: the Polish programme began in fact under the communist government (Stark and Bruszt, 1998: 94) and there were similar continuities in Hungary (Bruszt, 1995: 282). Stark argued that these choices also reflected different attitudes to state, society, and the market.

The Federal Republic relied on its enlarged state, mistrusting the capacities of what was left of East German society. The Czecho-Slovak, and particularly the Czech regime, was strongly pro-market, whereas the Hungarian government was more suspicious of it. In Poland, the regime privatised with a view to legitimating the market in the eyes of a strong civil society (Stark and Bruszt, 1998: 102–103).

Two further elements of Stark and Bruszt's analysis should be noted. First, these strategies have important implications for the fate of existing interenterprise networks, where these existed. The Treuhand, predictably, paid little attention to such 'residues' of the past, whereas the Czech and Hungarian contexts of interlocking relations of ownership were much more favourable to them. 'In both cases, property relations are being transformed – but *within structures whose network features exhibit continuity even as their ownership content is altered*' (Stark and Bruszt, 1998: 165, original emphasis). Secondly, and in contrast to pejorative conceptions of path dependence in which it is contrasted with the decisive and optimising choices of an ideally unconstrained executive, Stark and Bruszt (1998: 187) argue that

> ... where institutional structures placed the strongest constraints on executive authority, there policies were more coherent. Relatively unconstrained executives (in Hungary, throughout the period, under conservatives and Socialists alike; in Germany during the immediate aftermath of unification) were more likely to produce policies whose unanticipated consequences created crises and provoked policy reversals (recklessly in Hungary, modulated in Germany). Relatively constrained executives (in Czechoslovakia from 1990 to 1992; in the Czech Republic after separation; in Germany after the institutions of federalism and corporatism took effect) were more likely to produce coherent policies that could be adjusted rather than abandoned.

Accountability, as they argue in their concluding chapter, can be beneficial.

Coming between Stark and Bruszt's earlier papers and their *summa* of 1998 (and incorporating a chapter by Stark), the volume edited by Hausner, Jessop, and Nielsen (1995: 4) took a judicious view of the literature on path dependence.[14]

> State socialism's collapse created what one can reasonably term a 'systemic vacuum', i.e., a situation where there was no overall systemic logic ... A systemic vacuum ... should not, however, be confused with an 'institutional vacuum', that is, an absence of institutions. On the contrary, post-socialist trajectories are heavily dependent on a dense and complex institutional legacy such that the (often invisible) remnants of previous economic and political orders still shape expectations and patterns of conduct ... This is why the transformation process cannot but be 'path-dependent'.

This is not, however, a deterministic approach. 'The dynamics of the transformation process result from actual strategic choices made in a context of path dependency' (Hausner, Jessop, and Nielsen, 1995: 4). The editors stress the dimension of choice and what they call path *shaping*: 'in contrast to the "snakes and ladders" approach of path dependency analysts, the path-shaping approach implies that, within specific, historically given, and potentially malleable limits, social forces can redesign the "board" on which they are moving and reformulate the rules of the game' (Hausner, Jessop, and Nielsen, 1995: 7).

Although the term path dependence may be largely absent from the book by Elster et al (1998), the underlying idea substantially shapes the authors' analyses. Their conception of forward and backward linkages is probably intended as a more precise reformulation of the issue.

> A balanced account of the transition and the determinants of its outcomes in terms of consolidation will probably have to assess the relative weight of . . . three . . . factors – the residues of the past, the configuration of rule-making actors that emerges at the moment of transition, and future-oriented strategic decision making of key political and economic actors.
>
> The challenge is to arrive at a more synthetic approach. Rather than opting for one of the three types of independent variables, such an approach would have to allow for backward and forward linkages and other forms of complex interaction. Forward linkages occur when structures select agents and institutional settings, and the latter in turn select choices and decisions. Backward linkages would be cases in which choices put agents and institutional rules in their place, and these new arrangements alter or nullify the determining force of structural legacies or replace them with newly created legacies.
>
> (Elster et al, 1998: 295–296)

Offe, in the introduction, poses the issue graphically:

> What the regime had left behind . . . was the atomized and politically decapitated mass of ex-clients of state socialism, accustomed to the authoritarian (as well as largely egalitarian) provision of the means of subsistence and the rules according to which life had to be conducted.
>
> (Elster et al 1998: 25)

He concludes pessimistically with the expectation 'that "new" regimes are likely to get involved in a never-ending process of rule making and rule revision without ever reaching a state of stability' (Elster et al, 1998: 29). The second chapter of the book, authored by Boenker, Goetting, and Preuss, is specifically concerned with the effects of the past, stressing that postcommunist societies have at least three relevant pasts: 'the communist period, the more remote pre-communist period, and the very immediate period of extrication from communist regimes' (Elster et al, 1998: 35). Boenker adds in Chapter 5 that the 'rather sterile' debate between rapid and gradualist strategies of economic reform 'has tended to hide the underlying dilemmas of the structure. Yet it is precisely those dilemmas which have given rise to the muddy strategies, the oscillations between strategies, and the massive differences between areas of reforms that can be observed in Eastern Europe' (Elster et al, 1998: 161).

The concept of path dependence was, then, an important feature of the discussion of postcommunist transition in the 1990s. It was taken up, for example, by Bernard Chavance and Eric Magnin (1997), who provided a useful table, reproduced next from the reprint of their chapter in Hodgson (2002: 170). They list four 'forces of identity and difference in postsocialist countries.

Factors of similarity

Postsocialist common features (systemic family path-dependence)
Institutional mimetism toward the West, desire to join the European Union[15]
Influence of international organizations (IMF) and of their conditions
Globalization trends

Factors of dissimilarity

Diversity in initial conditions resulting from the past evolution of socialist economies

National specific paths, after 1989 (unique political, social, and economic conditions and events: individual path-dependence)

Variety of institutional external influences (for example, Anglo-Saxon vs. West European, or German vs. British or French)

Idiosyncratic institutional bricolage, spontaneous adaptation and transformation of imitated institutions according to nationally specific societal contexts

A model of this kind, they suggest, needs to be set against notions of convergence on a single 'Western' model of capitalism.

> In place of a (difficult but) simplistic 'transition to a market economy' we see in Central Europe the emergence of various path-dependent mixed economies.
>
> While an evolutionary approach stressing path-dependence gives some clues as to the emerging shape of post-socialist capitalisms and the formation of systemic irreversibilities, the middle-and long-term dynamic perspectives of these economies remain partially uncertain and relatively open.
>
> (Chavance and Magnin, in Hodgson, 2002: 195–196)

In a more critical approach, Michel Dobry (2000) provides a lengthy critique of theories of transition and path dependence. For him, path dependence, though conceived as an antithesis to transitology, shares its teleological focus[16] and its 'fascination' with 'extrication paths', whether out of dictatorship in Latin America or out of post-totalitarian communism.

In 2001, two researchers working on a project based at Humboldt University on 'Preemptive Institution Building' also launched a substantial attack on Stark's model. They focus on Stark, they explain, for two reasons:

> [F]irst, in contrast to the widespread practice of using the term without speci-fying its conceptual function, Stark has applied his concept of path depend-ency in a well elaborated and inspiring manner. Second . . . he explains different privatization strategies as path-dependent outcomes of particular modes of transition.
>
> (Beyer and Wielgohs, 2001: 357–358)

Their critique focuses especially on the latter aspect. The Czech and Slovak Republics, they point out, diverged from a shared transition, while Estonia, despite its very different initial conditions, adopted a similar Treuhand-style approach to privatization as Germany. More informal and flexible privatization transfer strate-gies, which Stark identifies particularly with Poland, are also found elsewhere, whereas Hungary, Stark's paradigm case, actually displays dramatic changes in policy. 'Considering the frequent policy shifts and changing strategies, one can hardly interpret the mode of transition as having long-lasting influence on privati-zation policy choices' (Beyer and Wielgohs, 2001: 378–379). Their analysis of fif-teen European countries supports Stark's emphasis on the importance of the first free elections, but shows, contrary to a strong version of path dependence, that later political shifts were also important. (Beyer and Wielgohs, 2001: 379) Thus, although there are continuities in postcommunist social and political change, there is no case for embracing a *theory* of path dependence:

> [T]he matters of original path-dependency theories are always *long-term outcomes* of historical development – the long-lasting predominance of a particular technological solution or the persistence of divergent institutional orders. The case of postsocialist privatization strategies is the opposite: in terms of history, they are *short-run* phenomena by nature.
>
> (Beyer and Wielgohs, 2001: 387)

Stark did not, as far as I am aware, reply to this critique or to the more detailed analyses provided by the authors in the book based on the Humboldt project.[17] He and Bruszt did, however, reply to Michael Burawoy's review article in the *American Journal of Sociology* (Burawoy, 2001; Stark and Bruszt, 2001). In a review covering their book and that by Eyal, Szelényi, and Townsley (1998), Burawoy (2001: 1101) criticised both books for 'an overestimation of the importance of elites, patterns of privatization, and political democracy, and an underestimation of the importance of capital accumulation, class relations, and global forces'. On the specific issue of path dependence, Burawoy (2001: 1108) argues that Stark and Bruszt place too much emphasis on the moment of transition, or 'extrication', and too little on longer-term conditions.

Hungary and (at that time) Russia, he suggests, have similar patterns of economic network connections and political centralisation. However, 'these national economies are worlds apart: in the one a dramatic and unprecedented disintegration while in the other stuttering growth' (Burawoy, 2001: 1109). In any case, he concludes,

> [H]ow much does it matter that Hungarian companies own one another, that Czech companies are more likely to be owned by banks, that Polish companies are likely to be owned by investment companies, or that German companies are likely to be owned by the Treuhandanstalt?
>
> (Burawoy, 2001: 1110)

In their reply, Stark and Bruszt (2001: 1132–1133) point out that they do not neglect the communist (and procommunist) past, especially the ways in which resources from the past are used in the present. Burawoy, they suggest, is too dismissive of legal and political 'superstructures', which appear to have had a significant impact on levels of inequality (Stark and Bruszt, 2001: 1133–1135).

Behind this exchange are, of course, the usual debates over action and structure, base and superstructure, and so on. Looking back, I suggest the rather boring conclusion that path dependence has a place as one element of the complex picture of postcommunist reality and that the processes usually discussed under this label need to be put in a broader geo-historical context (Møller, 2009).[18]

At the same time we have in any case to recognise the importance of unpredictable contingencies (Koselleck, 1998; Ebbinghaus, 2009: conclusion). As Harald Wydra (2000: 195–196) writes of the Polish case, a path-dependence approach would find it hard

> . . . to explain why and how Solidarity – after its disintegration and the momentary loss of effective influence in Polish politics since 1993 – rose from ashes. By the same token, there would also be difficulties in explaining why a feeling such as anti-communism assumed such a pervasive identity-creating dynamics and institutional impact from the mid-1990s onwards. Similarly, in path-dependent terms it would be paradoxical to argue that the round-table community as a consensual social contract could be causally connected with the missing rupture-point in the transition. Yet what the round-table community did . . . was to reinforce continuities such as perpetual politics of reform or the desire to return to the start. Furthermore, path dependence has serious flaws when it comes to explain why the politics of memory in Poland, in the last resort, is not so much about the prosecution of former communists and retribution or disqualification, but rather, amounts to a belated and futile attempt to stage a cathartic purge.[19]

A focus on 'how we became what we are' will always tend towards seeing inevitabilities where there were really accidents. What looks like a lock-in may be more like inertia, or what Pareto called the persistence of aggregates, or simply a contingent repetition of a previous state. A related danger is that of identifying too closely with the transition process in the role of back-seat driver, 'seeing like a state' (Scott, 1998). And yet it is a feature of postcommunist transition that it did embody what Alain Touraine would call a societal *project* – one which was very

widely understood even by its opponents or those who criticised its implementation. The critics of transitology were right that there was no in-built mechanism
guaranteeing a transition to democracy, but there was, in most parts of the region,
a widely shared assumption that it was the hoped-for direction of travel. This is,
after all, one of the things which differentiate postcommunist regimes from those
which simply wish to maintain a capitalist status quo. (Lukashenka's Belarus,
which has preserved much of the *communist* status quo, including the name of the
KGB, is the exception which proves the rule.)

Theories of path dependence were, as we have seen, in part a reaction against
simplistic economic analyses and prescriptions on the one hand, and pessimistic political and sociological diagnoses on the other – what Helmut Wiesenthal
(2001: 22) calls the 'paradigm of the impossibility of holistic reforms'. With time,
models of this kind have been put into a broader comparative context, just as
analyses of the 'varieties of capitalism' have finally stretched beyond what was
the 'West'. The relative simultaneity of the postcommunist transitions (Holmes,
1993: 26; 1997: 127–130), although it makes this exceptional period of social
change an exceptional resource for social theory, tends to obscure the more fundamental geographical and social differences explored in the next chapters.

Jørgen Møller (2009: 2–4) describes

> . . . a fairly systematic partition between democracies and autocracies; the
> former cluster situated on the western fringes of the old empire, the latter
> cluster mostly inhabiting the eastern territories. Second, quite a number of
> post-communist states – very conveniently situated between the two others
> geographically – drifted towards a third alternative. Rather than closing ranks
> with either their democratic or their authoritarian neighbours, these 'hybrid
> regimes' came to be caught mid-stream.
>
> Which factors account for the systematic combination of intra-subregional
> similarities and inter-subregional differences in post-communist regime
> forms that has locked in since the early 1990s?
>
> [T]he actors, with a few notable and very interesting exceptions, have not
> been able to break out of what might seem to equal 'a geographical iron law
> of political change'.

Møller's approach substantially endorses that of Herbert Kitschelt and his collaborators, who have meticulously documented the interaction of structure and agency
and 'deep' and 'shallow' explanations of the diversity of postcommunist regimes.
Kitschelt et al (1999: 23–26) distinguish between 'national-accommodative'
and 'bureaucratic-authoritarian' communism. *All* communist regimes were, of
course, bureaucratic and authoritarian, but in Poland and Hungary, and also in
Slovenia and Croatia (and possibly the rest of Yugoslavia), these features were
moderated by elements of compromise with local social groups or civil society
organisations (independent peasants and the Catholic Church in Poland, small-
scale private enterprise and intellectuals in both Poland and Hungary, as well as
the Yugoslav republics). They identify a third variant, 'patrimonial communism',
which 'relies on vertical chains of personal dependence between leaders in the

state and party apparatus and their entourage, buttressed by extensive patronage and clientelist networks'. This type is represented in their study by Bulgaria, but also includes Romania, Albania, and the rest of Yugoslavia and the Soviet Union. In this type there may be greater scope for the role of actors in modifying the developmental path. As Kitschelt (2003: 75) suggests, there may be 'structural reasons for randomness'.

Before moving on to explore these differences in more detail, I should say something about the context of the transitions of the 1990s. Perhaps the biggest counterfactual question of all is how things might have been different if 1989 had happened ten years earlier or ten years later. Ten years earlier, the neoliberal model was less firmly entrenched, though Thatcher was already in power, followed two years later by Reagan; there might have been more interest in third-way solutions and a less brutal approach to shock therapy. Ten years later, by the end of the century, there was also more of an alternative to neoliberalism and a search for 'third ways'. We can only guess what difference this would have made in the long term; the comparison between states which embraced shock therapy in its strongest form and those which adopted a more gradualist strategy suggests that in the end the differences might not have been so great. A lot of people might have kept their jobs and, especially in the former Soviet Union, escaped premature deaths from suicide or alcoholism, or as a result of general social dislocation (Haerpfer, Wallace and Abbott, 2013), but in the longer term the jobs would probably have gone either way. The Soviet Union itself might have taken a path more like China's, though probably not once communism had collapsed in the satellites.

Notes

1 See, however, the critique by Michel Dobry (2000), discussed later, of the 'heroic illusion' and the alternative emphasis on the cumulative effects of what Bernhard Ebbinghaus (2009: 191) calls 'the unplanned "trodden trail"'.

2 See Elster (1978, chapter 6); also Elster (1979). In a major book to which he contributed (Elster et al, 1998), the term hardly appears, though he refers, for example, in the bibliography to an article by David Stark (1992), whose use of this term and of the related notion of 'recombinant property', discussed later, remains one of the main reference points of the literature. In a later book (Elster, 2007: 92 and 386) the term appears only in passing. See footnote 7 for another passing mention. Some economists suggest a more remote origin of the concept of path dependence in the work of historically oriented economists such as Schumpeter or economic sociologists like Veblen (see Hodgson, 2002). Another ancestor would be Gunnar Myrdal and his model of circular causation in his book on economic backwardness (see Tarkowski, 1988, for an application to late communist Poland and Bohutskyy, 2010, for its broader relevance).

3 As well as the examples mentioned in the previous chapter, see Ferguson (1997, esp. Chapter 7 by Mark Almond). Discussions of counterfactual history include Rosenfeld (2002) and Kaye (2010).

4 Lest an Irish joke be thought too slender a reference basis, here is Robert Putnam (1993; 179; cited in Ekiert, 2003: 93): '[W]here you can get to depends on where you're coming from, and some destinations you simply cannot get to from here. Path

dependence can produce durable differences in performance between two societies, even when the formal institutions, resources, relative prices, and individual preferences in [the] two are similar'.

5 'The Leninist extinction' was, of course, not accompanied by the extinction of the Leninists (not that that is a particularly good description of the disillusioned careerists and technocrats who filled the ruling communist parties in the 1980s). Jowitt (1992: 262–268) also described the postcommunist condition as a 'Genesis environment'.

6 There was a variant in political science and sociology, often known as 'transitology' or, more pejoratively, 'transitionology' (Cohen, 1999, 2000), which applied, or was thought to apply, a similarly standardised model of democratic transition derived from the earlier experiences of Latin America and Southern Europe. As usual with such -isms or -ologies, few people explicitly identify themselves with them. For a judicious and sceptical review, see Gans-Morse (2004).

7 See also Elster et al (1998: 295): '[S]ocial historians are likely to focus upon structures as they path-dependently assert themselves over the *longue durée*, (institutionalist) sociologists and political economists attribute explanatory weight to agents and the rules adopted to govern their interaction, while economists and political scientists focus on actor-specific variables such as choices and decisions, rationality, and power'.

8 Burawoy and Krotov's paper was specifically on the post-Soviet case, though Burawoy, basing his analysis on a series of superb ethnographic studies, characterised the post-communist region as a whole in similar terms.

9 Or in an alternative metaphor, 'turning a Trabant into a Mercedes while driving it' (Hankiss, 2004: 179).

10 An important book which *does* treat path dependence as primarily pathological is that by Stefan Hedlund (2005), whose magisterial survey of Russian history traces repeated failures to break out of a historical pattern of personalistic and irregular rule (Hedlund, 2005: 264).

11 The titles of two books discussed later bring out this theme: *Strategic Choice and Path-Dependency* (Hausner, Jessop and Nielsen, 1995) and *Opportunity and Decision* (Wiesenthal, 2001).

12 On ethnic cleavages, see also Chapter 7, drafted by Offe (Elster, Offe, and Preuss, 1998), on 'Consolidation and the cleavages of ideology and identity'. Elster (1993) had earlier written more drastically of 'The necessity and impossibility of simultaneous economic and political reform'.

13 Andrew Arato (2000: 263 n. 53) suggested that the transitions in Poland, Hungary, Romania, and Bulgaria (like the earlier one in Spain) were double rather than triple. This may be true, but, of course, Hungary and Romania have territorial concerns over Transylvania; Spain is also hardly an uncontested territorial state. More to the point is perhaps the question whether triple transitions are necessarily more problematic than double or single ones. See also Arato's comments (p. 40) on Preuss's view of double transition.

14 See also the editors' earlier volume (Hausner, Jessop, and Nielsen, 1993).

15 On this, see in particular the work of Wade Jacoby and, in relation to the EU, Vachudová (2005) and Schimmelfennig and Scholtz (2010).

16 Dobry (2000: 67); see also Greskovitz (2000).

17 Wiesenthal (2001). This contains a long chapter by Wielgohs on privatisation and chapters by Beyer on the importance of the *sequencing* of reforms and on foreign direct investment. More useful, Wielgohs (2001: 162) suggests, is the approach by Lorene Allio et al (1997) which stresses the power resources of the various groups of actors.

18 For a robust defence of path dependence in the context of Europeanisation, see Bafoil (2010).
19 See also Wydra (2007: 272–277).

References

Allio, Lorene, Mariusz M. Dobek, Nikolai Mikhailov, and David Weimer (1997) 'Post-communist Privatization as a Test of Theories of Institutional Change', in David L. Weimer (ed.), *The Political Economy of Property Rights*. Cambridge: Cambridge University Press, pp. 319–348.

Arato, Andrew (2000) *Civil Society, Constitution, and Legitimacy*. Lanham: Rowman and Littlefield.

Bafoil, François (2010) 'Europeanisation: Complying to or Domesticating EU Rules – Some Thoughts on a Comparative Approach to Europeanisation', in Sven Eliason and Nadezhda Georgieva (eds.), *New Europe. Growth to Limits?* Oxford: Bardwell Press, pp. 157–176.

Beyer, Jürgen and Jan Wielgohs (2001) 'Postsozialistische Unternehmungsprivatisierung und die Anwendungsgrenzen für Pfadabhängigkeitstheorien', in Dittrich, Eckhard (ed.) *Wandel, Wende, Wiederkehr. Transformation as Epochal Change in Central and Eastern Europe: Theoretical Concepts and Their Empirical Applicability*. Würzburg: Ergon, pp. 79–107.

Bohutskyy, Vilhelm (2010) 'Gunnar Myrdal's Brand of Institutionalism and the Prospects of Its Application in the Analysis of Modern Developmental Problems and Post-Socialist Socio-Economic Transformation', in Sven Eliason and Nadezhda Georgieva (eds.), *New Europe. Growth to Limits?* Oxford: Bardwell Press, pp. 221–235.

Bruszt, László (1995) 'Reforming Alliances: Labour, Management and State Bureaucracy in Hungary's Economic Transformation', in Hausner, Jerzy, Bob Jessop and Klaus Nielsen (eds) (1995) *Strategic Choice and Path-Dependency in Post-Socialism. Institutional Dynamics in the Transformation Process*. Aldershot: Edward Elgar, pp. 261–286.

Bruszt, László and David Stark (1991) 'Remaking the Political Field in Hungary: From the Politics of Confrontation to the Politics of Competition', *Journal of International Affairs* 45: 201–245.

Bunce, Valerie and Maria Csanadi (1992) 'A Systemic Analysis of a Non-System: Post-Communism in Eastern Europe.' *Cornell Working Papers on Transitions from State Socialism*. No. 92–5.

Burawoy, Michael (2001) 'Neoclassical Sociology: From the End of Communism to the End of Classes', *American Journal of Sociology* 106, January: 1099–1120.

Burawoy, Michael and Pavel Krotov (1992) 'The Soviet Transition from Socialism to Capitalism', *American Sociological Review* 57: 16–38.

Chavance, Bernard and Eric Magnin (1997) 'Emergence of Path-Dependent Economies in Central Europe', in Ash Amin and Jerzy Hausner (eds.), *Beyond Market and Hierarchy: Interactive Governance and Social Complexity*. Cheltenham: Edward Elgar, pp. 196–232. Reprinted in Geoffrey M. Hodgson (ed.) (2002) *A Modern Reader in Institutional and Evolutionary Economics*. Cheltenham: Edward Elgar, pp. 168–197. (Page references here are to the reprint.)

Cohen, Stephen (1999) 'Russian Studies Without Russia', *Post-Soviet Affairs* 15(1): 37–55.

Cohen, Stephen (2000) *Failed Crusade: America and the Tragedy of Post-Communist Russia*. New York: Norton.

Dobry, Michel (ed.) (2000) *Democratic and Capitalist Transitions in Eastern Europe: Lessons for the Social Sciences*. Dordrecht: Kluver.

Ebbinghaus, Bernhard (2009) 'Europe Through the Looking-Glass: Comparative and Multi-Level Perspectives', *Acta Sociologica* 41: 301–313.

Ebbinghaus, Bernhard (2009) 'Can Path Dependence Explain Institutional Change? Two Approaches Applied to Welfare State Reform', in Magnusson, Lars and Jan Ottosson (eds.) (2009) *The Evolution of Path Dependence*. Cheltenham: Edward Elgar, pp. 191–218.

Ekiert, Grzegorz (2003) 'Patterns of Postcommunist Transformation in Central and Eastern Europe', in Grzegorz Ekiert and Stephen E. Hanson (eds.), *Capitalism and Democracy in Central and Eastern Europe. Assessing the Legacy of Communist Rule*. New York: Cambridge University Press, pp. 89–119.

Elster, Jon (1978) *Logic and Society. Contradictions and Possible Worlds*. Chichester, John Wiley & Sons.

Elster, J. (1979) *Ulysses and the Sirens. Studies in Rationality and Irrationality*, Cambridge: Cambridge University Press and Paris: Editions de la Maison des Sciences de l'Homme.

Elster, J. (1993) 'The Necessity and Impossibility of Simultaneous Economic and Political Reform', in Douglas Greenberg, Stanley Katz, Melanie Beth Oliviero, and Steven C. Wheatley (eds.), *Constitutionalism and Democracy: Transition in the Contemporary World*. New York: Oxford University Press, pp. 267–274.

Elster, J. (2007) *Explaining Social Behavior. More Nuts and Bolts for the Social Sciences*. Cambridge, Cambridge University Press.

Elster, J., Offe, C. and Preuss, U., with Frank Boenker, Ulrike Goetting, and Friedbert W. Rueb (1998) *Institutional Design in Post-Communist Societies: Rebuilding the Ship at Sea*. Cambridge: Cambridge University Press.

Eyal, G., Szelényi, I. and Townsley, E. (1998) *Making Capitalism Without Capitalists: Class Formation and Elite Struggles in Post-Communist Central Europe*. London: Verso.

Ferguson, Niall (ed) 1997. *Virtual History. Alternatives and Counterfactuals*. London: Picador.

Gans-Morse, Jordan (2004) 'Searching for Transitologists: Contemporary Theories of Post-Communist Transitions and the Myth of a Dominant Paradigm', *Post-Soviet Affairs* 20(4): 320–349.

Greskovitz, Béla (2000) 'Rival Views of Market Society. The Path Dependence of Transitology', in Michel Dobry (ed.) (2000) *Democratic and Capitalist Transitions in Eastern Europe: Lessons for the Social Sciences*. Dordrecht: Kluver, pp. 19–48.

Haerpfer, C., C Wallace and P Abbott (2013). 'Health Problems and the Transition from Communism in the Former Soviet Union: Towards an Explanation'. *Perspectives on European Politics and Society* 14(4): 460–479.

Hankiss, Elemér (2004) 'De brillantes idées ou de brilliantes erreurs? Douze ans de recherche en sciences sociales en Europe de l'Est', in Maxime Forest and Georges Mink (eds.) *Post-communisme: les sciences sociales à l'épreuve*. Paris: L'Harmattan, pp. 175–189.

Hausner, Jerzy, Bob Jessop, and Klaus Nielsen (eds.) (1993) *Institutional Frameworks of Market Economies. Scandinavian and Eastern European Perspectives*. Aldershot: Edward Elgar.

Hausner, Jerzy, Bob Jessop, and Klaus Nielsen (eds.) (1995) *Strategic Choice and Path-Dependency in Post-Socialism. Institutional Dynamics in the Transformation Process*. Aldershot: Edward Elgar.

Hedlund, Stefan (2005) *Russian Path Dependence*. Abingdon: Routledge.

Hodgson, Geoffrey (2002) 'Varieties of Capitalism and Varieties of Economic Theory', in Geoffrey M. Hodgson (ed.), *A Modern Reader in Institutional and Evolutionary Economics*. Cheltenham: Edward Elgar, pp. 201–230.

Holmes, Leslie (1993) 'On Communism, Post-Communism, Modernity and Post-Modernity', in Janina Frentzel-Zagórska, *From a One-Party State to Democracy: Transition in Eastern Europe*. Amsterdam: Rodopi, 21–43.

Holmes, Leslie (1997) *Post-Communism. An Introduction*. Cambridge: Polity.

Horváth, Agnes and Árpád Szakolczai (1992) *The Dissolution of Communist Power. The Case of Hungary*. London: Routledge.

Jowitt, Ken (1992) *New World Disorder. The Leninist Extinction*. Berkeley: University of California Press.

Kaye, Simon (2010) 'Challenging Certainty: The Utility and History of Counterfactualism', *History and Theory* 49(February): 38–57.

Kitschelt, Herbert (2003) 'Accounting for Postcommunist Regime Diversity. What Counts as a Good Cause?', in Grzegorz Ekert and Stephen E. Hanson (eds.), *Capitalism and Democracy in Central and Eastern Europe. Assessing the Legacy of Communist Rule*. New York: Cambridge University Press, pp. 49–83.

Kitschelt, Herbert et al (eds.) (1999) *Post-Communist Party Systems. Competition, Representation, and Inter-Party Cooperation*. Cambridge: Cambridge University Press.

Koselleck, Reinhart (2000) *Zeitschichten. Studien zur Historik*. Frankfurt: Suhrkamp.

Møller, Jørgen (2009) *Post-communist Regime Change*. London: Routledge.

North, Douglass (1990) *Institutions, Institutional Change and Economic Performance*. Cambridge: Cambridge University Press.

Öberg, PerOla and Kajsa Hallberg Adu (2009) 'The Deceptive Juncture: The Temptation of Attractive Explanations and the Reality of Political Life', in Lars Magnusson and Jan Ottosson (eds.), *The Evolution of Path Dependence*. Cheltenham: Edward Elgar, pp. 108–138.

Offe, Claus (1996) *Varieties of Transition. The East European and East German Experience*. Cambridge: Polity.

Pierson, Paul (2000) 'Increasing Returns, Path Dependence, and the Study of Politics', *American Political Science Review* 94(2) June: 251–267. Incorporated in Pierson 2004.

Pierson, Paul (2004) *Politics in Time. History, Institutions, and Social Analysis*. Princeton and Oxford: Princeton University Press.

Putnam, Robert, et al. (1993) *Making Democracy Work*. Princeton: Princeton University Press.

Rosenfeld, Gavriel (2002) 'Why Do We Ask "What If?". Reflections on the Function of Alternate History', *History and Theory* 41(December): 90–103.

Schimmelfennig, Frank and Hanno Scholtz (2010) 'Legacies and Leverage: EU Political Conditionality and Democracy Promotion in Historical Perspective', *Europe-Asia Studies* 62(3): 443–460.

Scott, James (1998) *Seeing Like a State. How Certain Schemes to Improve the Human Condition Have Failed*. New Haven: Yale University Press.

Srubar, Ilja (1996) 'Neoliberalism, Transformation and Civil Society', *Thesis Eleven* 47(November): 33–47.

Stark, D (1992) 'From System Identity to Organizational Diversity: Analyzing Social Change in Eastern Europe', *Contemporary Sociology* 21(3) May: 299–304.

Stark, D (1995) 'Not by Design: The Myth of Designer Capitalism in Eastern Europe' in Jerzy Hausner, Bob Jessop and Klaus Nielsen (eds.), *Strategic Choice and Path-Dependency in Post-Socialism. Institutional Dynamics in the Transformation Process*. Aldershot: Edward Elgar, pp. 67–83.

Stark, D and Bruszt, L (1998) *Postsocialist Pathways: Transforming Politics and Property in East Central Europe*. Cambridge: Cambridge University Press.

Stark, D and Bruszt, L (2001) 'One Way or Multiple Paths: For a Comparative Sociology of East European Capitalism', *American Journal of Sociology* 106(4) January: 1121–1137.

Tarkowski, Jacek (1988) 'The Polish Crisis and Myrdal's Model of Circular Causation', *Political Studies* 36(3): 463–474.

Vachudová, Milada Anna (2005) *Europe Undivided. Democracy, Leverage, and Integration After Communism*. New York: Oxford University Press.

Wielgohs, Jan (2001) 'Varianten erfolgreicher Privatisierungspolitik – Die Konditionierung und Steuerung der Unternehmensprivatisierung in Estland, Polen und der Tschechischen Republik', in Wiesenthal 2001, pp. 93–168.

Wiesenthal, Helmut (ed.) (2001) *Gelegenheit und Entscheidung. Policies und Politics erfolgreicher Transformationsforschung*. Wiesbaden: Westdeutscher Verlag.

Wydra, Harald (2000) *Continuities in Poland's Permanent Transition*. Basingstoke: Macmillan.

Wydra, Harald (2007) *Communism and the Emergence of Democracy*. Cambridge: Cambridge University Press.

4   East–West divergences and convergences

> It is a perplexing irony of post-cold-war Europe that we have all been forced to rediscover issues of territory and boundaries, that the melting of that stark division between east and west should have revealed so many other disconcerting and difficult borders.
>
> (Wallace 1999: 287)

The previous chapter outlined the concept of path dependence, and this chapter addresses more empirical issues of the divergent paths taken by postcommunist states, which have puzzled Helen Wallace and all of us. Nick Manning (2004: 227–228) concluded his review of postcommunist developments in East Central Europe with the following image: 'Rather like a stream swirling over rocks, we can observe a complex picture of movement, sometimes slow, sometimes rapid, in which the currents at play converge, diverge, circulate and reverse.'

Before we look more closely at the determinants of the various postcommunist pathways, the continuing relevance of the terms postcommunist or postsocialist may require some justification. We no longer speak of postfascist Italy or post-Nazi Germany except perhaps to refer to the immediate postwar years, and some people have argued that it is time to pension off 'postcommunism' as well. I shall suggest here that this would be a mistake, both because the legacies of communism can be shown to persist and because the parts of Europe which experienced communism continue to be subject to differential dynamics in the development of Europe since 1989.[1] The sharpest expression of this is captured in Iván Berend's description of Eastern and Central Europe's 'Detour from the Periphery to the Periphery' (Berend, 1996), and the development of Europe, and of the European Union in particular, has done little to defuse the provocative phrase.[2]

It is no accident that it is in the more Western parts of the postcommunist region that one most often encounters the claim that the term postcommunist is passé. As we saw in the previous chapter, most particularly in the discussion of Møller (2009), the differentiation of the postcommunist world has most often taken a geographical form. What I called in an earlier version of this chapter 'cutting the postcommunist cake' was intended to refer to the way in which parts of the postcommunist world are distinguished in both academic analysis and public discussion.[3]

The first cut is that just mentioned, between the postcommunist world and the rest of Europe and Eurasia. As everyone recognizes, though, the postcommunist world, or even postcommunist Europe and the former Soviet Union, do not form a homogeneous entity. As Joseph Rothschild wrote of the difference between Western historians in the 1950s and those more recently,

> To our predecessors and teachers, the Stalinist imposition of monopolistic communist rule appeared – quite understandably – to be a profoundly revolutionary rupture with earlier patterns, traditions, and histories. Today, we are more impressed with the survival and resurgence of political continuities from the interwar period in such dimensions as the styles and degrees of political participation, the operational codes and cultures of political elites, the process of recruiting new political elites, their definitions of economic priorities, and so forth.
>
> (Rothschild and Wingfield, 2000: 223)

There is less agreement, however, on where the most important dividing lines are to be drawn.

Even a basic regional division, such as the tripartite one used for some time by the European Bank for Reconstruction and Development (EBRD) between Central Europe (including Slovenia) and the Baltic States (CEB), South-Eastern Europe (SEE), and Commonwealth of Independent States and Mongolia (CIS+M) is loaded with political and economic baggage, such as European Union (EU) membership, as discussed later. The EBRD now divides the third category into two: Eastern Europe and the Caucasus (Armenia, Azerbaijan, Belarus, Georgia, Moldova, Ukraine) and Central Asia (Kazakhstan, Kyrgyz Republic, Mongolia, Tajikistan, Turkmenistan, Uzbekistan). Russia and Turkey are listed under 'Other', and there is a further category of Southern and Eastern Mediterranean (Egypt, Jordan, Morocco, Tunisia).[4]

The simplest and most arbitrary division, though of course politically consequential, is that between the states which are currently or are likely to become members of the EU and those which are not. Although the location of the dividing line at a given moment may be contingent, there is a good deal of interest in following the processes by which potential members, such as postcommunist Slovakia in the 1990s, become acceptable, *salonfähig*, or remain excluded. (See Chapter 5 for a fuller discussion.)

Thinking still of institutional membership, there is an important difference in the postcommunist world between Eastern Germany and the rest. The German Democratic Republic (GDR), in the form of its newly created five federal states, was wholly absorbed into the Federal Republic. This had an upside (massive transfers of resources) and a downside (the virtual destruction of the East German economy).[5] Three other questions of national boundaries might be mentioned here. The early and relatively painless secession of Slovenia after its 'ten-day war') reinforced the special economic position which it had always occupied within Yugoslavia and was reflected in its accession to the European Union in 2004. The breakup of the Soviet Union created a line between regions remaining within Russia (including the Kaliningrad area as an exclave) and the republics which became independent, including, of course, the Baltic States now in the EU. Third, the velvet divorce between the Czech and Slovak republics made the former appear somewhat more attractive as an accession candidate and the latter much less so, even before the Mečiar dictatorship ruled it out for several years.

A more informal membership cluster is what became known as the Visegrád group, established at Havel's instigation at a meeting in Bratislava between Czechoslovakia, Poland, and Hungary and foreshadowed by transborder contacts between dissidents (Havel, 2008: 154–156; see also Kenney, 2011). As Havel notes, it served as an example to other postcommunist states – its members formed the core of the 2004 EU enlargement – as well as the primary focus of academic studies of postcommunism.

Havel and others in the Visegrád group were, of course, conscious of the historical links between its three, later four, members. The discussion of Central Europe had been revived in the 1980s by critical intellectuals in the region, notably Jenö Szücs (1983) in Hungary and the Czech Milan Kundera (1983) in Paris (see also Schöpflin and Wood, 1988). Kundera's notion of the 'captured West' was the dominant motif: this was framed as a centre closer to the West than the East (Prague is, of course, farther west than Vienna) and separated from it only by historical misfortune.

Another historical legacy which has served some commentators as an important dividing line is the Habsburg Empire, which included Slovenia and Croatia in the west, Transylvania in the east, and parts of modern Poland and Ukraine. As Ksenija Vidmar-Horvath and Gerard Delanty (2008) have pointed out, this entailed a stretched notion of Central Europe in the Slovene discussion. Kundera himself was quick to include it as Slovenia was threatened in 1991 by the Yugoslav National Army. 'I hear voices who in relation to the Slovenes speak of the "danger of Balkanization". But what does Slovenia have to do with the Balkans? This is a Western country' (Kundera, 1991, cited by Vidmar-Horvath and Delanty, 2008: 210).

Others point more to the dividing line between 'Western' Christianity and Greek and Russian Orthodoxy. Sven Eliaeson (2010: 4) stresses the historical importance of the line between Western and Eastern Christianity. Although the cause of the split in 1054, the doctrine of the holy trinity,[6]

> . . . is a minor issue today . . . It seems that this border line crossing through western Ukraine has a huge steering effect upon political culture and economic performance as well as the architecture of cities. Europe stretches as far as we have Gothic cathedrals and city halls in the middle of towns. Market culture and civic virtues are correlating phenomena, and cities are here the natural realm, despite some historical cases of peasant 'republican' civic societies.

This is what Samuel Huntington (1993: 30) called 'the Velvet Curtain of culture [which] has replaced the Iron Curtain of ideology as the most significant dividing line in Europe'.

The peoples to the east and south of this line are Orthodox or Muslim; they historically belonged to the Ottoman or Tsarist empires and were only lightly touched by the shaping effects in the rest of Europe; they are generally less advanced economically; they seem much less likely to develop stable democratic political systems.

Yet Bernhard Weßels, in the book edited by Eliaeson, shows on the basis of substantial survey evidence from the 1990s that these differences have little salience in observable attitudes and values in the economic sphere. 'Huntington . . . may be right in cultural terms – although some doubts are in place in this regard as well. But he is certainly wrong with regard to the relationship between religion, economic virtues and behaviour' (Weßels, 2010: 146).

The question of a line of division between the former Soviet Union (perhaps excluding the Baltic States) and Eastern and Central Europe also arises in relation to political attitudes. The Pew (2009) survey asked respondents in eight postcommunist countries (plus East Germany) whether they agreed that 'Most people are better off in a free market economy, even though some people are rich and some are poor'. Support for markets was higher in Poland (70%) than in West Germany (65%), Britain (67%), France (61%), and Spain (59%). These Western figures are comparable with those in much of the East (63% in the Czech Republic, 56% in Slovakia, 52% in Russia, and 50% in Lithuania. Opinion in Ukraine was evenly balanced, with 46% agreeing and 43% disagreeing, and only in Bulgaria and, interestingly, Hungary, was there majority disagreement (58% in Bulgaria and 65% in Hungary) (Pew, 2009: 41).

This compares strikingly with support for democracy. In all the postcommunist countries surveyed except Ukraine there was a majority in favour of the *change* to multi-party democracy, but with a range from 85% in East Germany and 80% in the Czech Republic to figures in the fifties in Hungary, Lithuania, Russia, and Bulgaria, which all recorded substantial declines since 1991 (Pew, 2009: 1).[7] Most dramatically, perhaps, a 2009 poll found a majority of East Germans saying that life in the GDR had 'more good sides than bad sides' and 8% saying it was better than in the reunified Germany.

A Polish survey cited by Stefan Garsztecki (2010: 9), though less upbeat about Polish opinion, strikingly illustrates the anomalous state of that in Hungary. Asked whether democratisation since 1989 should be considered 'a success or a defeat', Poles, Czechs, and Slovaks recorded more or less clear majorities for 'success', whereas two thirds of Hungarians opted for 'defeat'. On the other hand, when asked how important it was to them to live in a democratically ruled country, only half of Poles found it 'very important', as compared to over three quarters in Germany, France and Britain (Garsztecki, 2010: 12). The figures for Ukraine and Russia were 36% and 16%, respectively, though with a clear majority in both countries when those replying 'rather important' are added.

The best comparative survey evidence for East Central Europe and the former Soviet Union is probably that provided by Richard Rose and his associates, who have run the New Europe Barometer and New Russia Barometer series for nearly twenty years. Rose (2009) concludes that the division between the two regions *is* significant. Although one of his comparative tables, in which respondents were asked where they would like their political system to be, on a scale from dictatorship to democracy, and where they put it at present, does not show striking differences between the former Soviet states of Russia, Ukraine, and Belarus and the new EU states (Rose, 2009: 165), he points out that 'in new EU member states an average of 57 per cent say that democracy is always preferable; in Russia only 25 per cent are so strongly committed to democracy' (Rose, 2009: 188). And although there is no significant difference in opinion on these issues between Russia and central Asian states such as Kazakhstan and Kyrgyzstan, or between Russian Orthodox and Muslims in those states, 'the divergence of institutional development between CEE [Central and Eastern Europe] and post-Soviet countries means that both Russians and Muslims have learned to adapt to very different types of political regimes' (Rose, 2009: 190).[8]

Huntington, as we saw, more or less runs together the division between Western and Eastern Christianity with that between predominantly Christian and Muslim parts of Europe; orthogonal to the Western/Orthodox line is the boundary of the Ottoman Empire, separating the south from the north of Eastern Europe. Even the internal 'Western' division between Catholic and Protestant has played a part in post-1989 politics – for example, in Germany, where the East increased the proportion of Protestants and atheists, or on the East German–West German border between protestant Hesse in the west and Catholic Eichsfeld in the east (Berdahl, 1999). To these long-standing historical divisions one should add the economic one from the eighteenth and nineteenth centuries and separating regions like Bohemia, plugged into Western European circuits, from the 'rest of the east', providing essentially raw materials and agricultural products (Stokes, 1997: 21–26).

Then there is the division between pacted or negotiated and revolutionary transitions, which arguably separates Poland and Hungary from Czechoslovakia, with Germany, as always, a special case.[9] This division in turn may be argued to reflect the difference noted earlier between what Kitschelt et al (1999: 23–26) call 'national-accommodative' and 'bureaucratic-authoritarian' communism. Without going into the details of this analysis, one can see that differences of this kind cannot but affect the type of transition and its outcome.[10]

In Romania, Bulgaria, and Albania, the diagnosis and dating of transition itself becomes contentious. Many Romanians, for example, would see the crucial date not as 1989, despite the dramatic execution of the Ceauşescus, but 1996, when Iliescu's reform communist regime finally gave way to a more genuinely post-communist one, though one whose progress was faltering. In 1998 a European Commission official commented that Romania's economic performance was the worst of any applicant state (Gallagher, 2005: 179). In a survey in 2000, a majority said that the Ceauşescu period was the one when 'things went best for Romania'; only 8.5% chose the years after 1989 (Gallagher, 2004: 245). The National Salvation Front's (FSN's) programme of December 22, 1989, could not be faulted, specifying the introduction of democracy and the abolition of the leading role of the Communist Party, free elections, separation of powers, abolition of central economic planning, restructuring of agriculture, and so on (Gallagher, 2004: 74). The problem was one of implementation: as one reformer complained to Iliescu in 1991, 'Unfortunately Mr. President you believe that Stalinism and Ceauşescuism were errors made in applying Marxism-Leninism' (Gallagher, 2004: 99).

In July 2000 Iliescu's successor, President Constantinescu, dramatically announced that he would not run for a second term. 'When I launched myself in the fight against corruption, I discovered in Romania a mafia system in which a web of front organizations was backed by the highest state institutions . . . We live in a world where everything is for sale – principles, ideologies, parliamentary secrets. My place is not in this world' (Gallagher, 2004: 240–241). Iliescu returned as president after a close contest with the demagogue Vadim Tudor, now leader of the Greater Romania Party and a former Member of the European Parliament (MEP). (Gallagher, 2004: 267–307). Prime Minister Victor Ponta, narrowly defeated in the presidential election in November 2014, was widely perceived as an old-style communist, although he was only forty-two and therefore only just reaching adulthood in 1989.

Bulgaria began with a transition similar to (though less violent than) that in Romania, but rapidly moved to peaceful alternation of governments. As one analyst commented towards the end of the nineties, 'In institutional terms the Bulgarian political system seems to be over-performing . . . On the other hand, the Bulgarian economy and even Bulgarian society itself are visibly degrading due to ineffective governance' (Kolarova, 2002: 150). The immobilism of Romania in the early 1990s contrasts with a rather frenzied political style in Bulgaria (Elster et al, 1998: 263). Albania's fragile situation in the 1990s was not improved by what amounted to a civil war in 1997, following the collapse of a pyramid investment scheme, and the influx of refugees from Kosovo in 1999. It did not apply for EU membership until 2009, following a Stabilisation and Association Agreement in 2006.

Elster et al (1998) compared Bulgaria, Czechoslovakia, and Hungary, arguing that these countries more or less stood in for others with a similar past and trajectory: Romania, East Germany, and Poland, respectively. In their closing analysis, the political situation in Slovakia and Bulgaria led them to a contrast with the relative success of Hungary and the Czech Republic, though they noted that economically 'they performed better than one would expect in view of their problematic politico-institutional state of affairs' (Elster et al, 1998: 307). By the time their book was in print, of course, the Mečiar dictatorship was over and Slovakia was heading back on track for the EU membership which it achieved in 2004. As noted earlier, the authors defended their decision to include a Balkan country.

> This is not to deny the existence of different cultural traditions in the region. Nor is it to neglect the role of geography which clearly favors the Visegrád countries as against the Balkan states. Due to their geographical location, they are in a better position to benefit from West European economic growth and to attract Western financial support. Yet the distinction captures only a small part of the relevant initial conditions of societal transformation.
>
> (Elster et al, 1998: 47)

Mary Kaldor and Ivan Vejvoda (1999/2002) took a similarly even-handed position in their survey of democracy (discussed in more detail in Chapter 7) in the then ten EU candidate countries. All met (more or less) the formal conditions, yet all, in different ways, had 'deficiencies' (Kaldor and Vejvoda, 2002: ix) in democratic political culture. Moreover,

> ... some of the difficulties faced by transitional countries are also experienced elsewhere in greater or lesser degrees. The tendency for political parties to become instruments of patronage rather than vehicles for political ideas, the disillusion with and growing apathy towards formal politics, the distrust of politicians, and growing tendencies towards populism, can be observed in many parts of the world.
>
> (p. x)

The 'fission products', as Herbert Kitschelt called them, of the breakup of the Soviet Union produced several surprises. First, the Baltic States had an unexpectedly fast trajectory in the early 1990s, leading into the first EU eastern enlargement in 2004. Second, at the other political extreme, though geographically contiguous, Belarus under Lukashenka reverted from 1994 onwards to an essentially patrimonial or sultanistic communist system. Third, after the democratic transitions in Croatia and Serbia in 2000, first Georgia in 2003 and Ukraine in 2004, followed by Kyrgyzstan in 2005, launched a pattern of 'colour revolutions' which continues to the present (Lane and White, 2010).[11] Whether these should be seen as aftershocks of 1989, clearing up unfinished business, or whether, conversely, 1989 should be seen as exceptional, is a question addressed more fully in the next chapter. For the moment, I want to stress that the emerging pattern of postcommunist diversity was already becoming clear in the early 1990s. Leaving aside the anomaly of Slovakia under Mečiar and the complexities of a Yugoslav region emerging from a devastating set of civil wars, the postcommunist watershed appeared to be set. On the one hand, there was Central and Eastern Europe, making a triple return to 'Europe', democracy, and capitalism; on the other, a set of parts of the former Soviet Union (including Russia itself), in none of which (apart from the Baltics) could the democratic transition be seen as secure, if it had even begun.

The US historian of the Balkans, Gale Stokes, in a short article in 1993 entitled 'Is it Possible to Be Optimistic about Eastern Europe?' concluded that, with the exception of Albania and former Yugoslavia (apart from Slovenia):

> Eastern Europe is not in transition. To one degree or another, every East European political system is already pluralist. What we are seeing now is what we are going to get in the future – bitter political struggles, nasty elections, corruption, and fights over the media. This is what it means to have a normal political life . . . Each of these countries in its own way has committed itself to the pluralist adventure and has embarked on it. If we compare this commitment and the progress made in what is, historically speaking,

a very short time with the situation these societies faced in 1983, or 1953, or 1933, is it not possible to be at least a little bit optimistic about Eastern Europe?

(Stokes, 1997: 202–203)

This assessment was perhaps a little bold for 1993, but more secure by 1997 after the developments in Romania and Bulgaria, to be followed by the democratic (electoral) return to democracy in Slovakia at the 1998 election. Before the end of the decade, these problem cases could be confidently assigned to the democratic category, as measured by the Freedom House indicators.[12]

These cases show, however, that the image of the watershed, with the implication that it can only be altered by moving or at least blasting mountains, is too crude. We need an intermediate category, as described by Jørgen Møller (2009: 2–4) in the book mentioned earlier, which is one of the most creative discussions of these issues. First, as we saw, he notes

> . . . a fairly systematic partition between democracies and autocracies; the former cluster situated on the western fringes of the old empire, the latter cluster mostly inhabiting the eastern territories. Second, quite a number of post-communist states – very conveniently situated between the two others geographically – drifted towards a third alternative. Rather than closing ranks with either their democratic or their authoritarian neighbours, these 'hybrid regimes' came to be caught mid-stream.

Møller (2009: 3) takes four snapshots of the region, in 1992, 1997, 2002, and 2007. By 2007, what had been in 1992 a very large hybrid category, flanked by only four clear democracies (Czechoslovakia, Hungary, Poland, and Slovenia) and three clear autocracies (Tadjikistan, Turkmenistan, and Uzbekistan), has shrunk to just seven: Albania, Armenia, Georgia, Kyrgyzstan, Macedonia, Moldova, and Ukraine. The autocracies have gained Azerbaijan, Belarus, Kazakhstan, and Russia; the democracies (all European except for Mongolia) have the rest.[13]

How can one explain this polarisation? Møller offers essentially two kinds of explanations. The first, which he mentions in passing (pp. 139–410), is the long-standing argument (Eckstein, 1973; Gurr, 1974) recently made more substantial by Gates et al (2006): that pure democracies and pure autocracies are more stable than mixed regimes because they enable and encourage rulers (by different means) to preserve them. Autocrats can prevent opposition: democratic rulers are ideologically and institutionally discouraged from violating the rules of the game, and they may hope to return to power again. Møller's interest, however, is in explaining what determines the trajectories of postcommunist states and specifically the clear geographical pattern:

> [N]o East-Central European country has failed to reach the destination of democracy since the breakdown of communism. Conversely, no Central Asian country has consistently withstood the pull of autocracy.

His explanation involves a combination of three structural factors: communist political legacies, proximity to the West, and the degree of modernisation. The first of these essentially follows Kitschelt et al (1999: 23–26) in distinguishing between 'national-accommodative', 'bureaucratic-authoritarian', and 'patrimonial' communism. The first two are both conducive to democracy: despite the authoritarianism of the Czechoslovak late communist regime, the bureaucratic and legal structure could rapidly be taken over by the democratic opposition.

> Patrimonial communist regimes yielding less favourable conditions for democracy prevailed in Southeastern Europe and the core areas of the former Soviet Union, Albania, Belarus, Bulgaria, Georgia, Macedonia, Romania, Russia, and the Ukraine . . . The remaining fission products of the Soviet Union belonged to a colonial periphery with next to no articulation of civil society before the advent of communism and fully patrimonial administrative relations that jointly produced the dimmest opportunities for democratic regime entrenchment.
>
> (Kitschelt et al 1999: 32)

Second, Møller takes proximity to the West in the literal sense in which it is used by Kopstein and Reilly (2000), rather than including broader notions of Western ideological hegemony or more active forms of leverage and linkage such as those examined by Levitsky and Way (2006) or, in the specific case of the EU, which becomes increasingly important as time goes on Vachudová (2005). Again, he takes a simple measure of modernisation: per-capita gross domestic product (GDP). The assumption that the presence of all three attributes – positive legacies, proximity to the West, and modernisation (GDP>\$6236 in 2000) – ensures democracy and that the absence of all three predicts autocracies is broadly confirmed, except that Armenia, Georgia, and Kyrgyzstan (and Mongolia) were more democratic than expected. Of the mixed types, modern Russia and 'Western' Belarus are less democratic than the norm; the hybrid types, Møller concludes (pp. 139–140), require more detailed study.

Møller has, I think, convincingly demonstrated that these structural factors trump explanations in terms of independent agency (which has a role more or less confined to the hybrid types) or diffusion (which, he argues, should be seen 'as a causal mechanism through which the structural logic comes to the fore') (Møller, 2009, 131). 'The surprising merits of Bulgaria and Romania can probably, at least in part, be explained by . . . the causal importance of EU enlargement' (Møller, 2009: 137). Whereas the EU deliberately constrains variation, in a process which Larry Ray and I (Outhwaite and Ray, 2005) called heteronomous convergence, the 'colour revolutions' can be seen as an attempt to buck the regional trend or, more pessimistically, as essentially coups by counter-elites, with the crowds having merely a walk-on part.

Mongolia's democracy remains a puzzle: Steven Fish (1998, 2001) suggests some elements whose presence or absence may have helped. He discounts nomadic individualism as a factor (1998: 128) and stresses the absence of violence in the transition of 1990 and the fact that the Communist Party initiated privatisation and respected its defeat at the 1996 elections. Conversely, the lack of major natural resources, foreign interest, and a charismatic ruler may have benefited Mongolian democracy (2001). Belarus's authoritarian *Sonderweg* remains an anomaly which, however, may vanish overnight. We usually worry about excessive nationalism, but in Belarus, its peculiarly weak presence may have removed a possible source of democratic mobilisation (Ioffe, 2007). Ukraine is a particularly interesting case, since it is in Møller's terms Western and modern and, despite its relative isolation from perestroika, prominent in the 1989 process in which Rukh identified with Solidarity.[14] As we shall see later, the Orange Revolution had a long incubatory phase; Nemyria (2005; 53) traces its genesis back to 1991. Finally, Ukraine borders on four EU states and, though large, is not so large as to rule itself out as a potential member; the EU could undoubtedly have been more welcoming, and this might have transformed a very unsatisfactory political and economic situation (van Zon, 2001). Finally, Serbia in 2000 is often located at the beginning of the colour revolutions, although it did not actually use the imagery of colour and the dynamics, in particular its emergence from the Yugoslav wars, seem different from the others. Serbia is in some ways a miniature version of Russia, with residual imperial dreams complicating its withdrawal to a position as one Balkan state among others (Vujačić, 1996). Again, as Fish (2001) points out, Mongolia, though geographically large, has too small a population to aspire, like Kazakhstan and Uzbekistan, to regional power status.

1989 in Eastern and Central Europe was, or turned out to be, essentially a triple return to 'Europe', democracy, and capitalism. Everyone had had enough of qualifying adjectives for democracy such as the pleonastic 'people's democracy' (*'mensonge par pléonasme'*, as Raymond Aron aptly described it. It seemed inappropriate to go on speaking of *Eastern* Europe now the curtain was down, and even *Central* raised uncomfortable memories and seemed to drive a wedge through the Visegrád cluster or what were to become the 2004 accession states. Capitalism had not been at the top of the menu in 1989, even where the idea of markets had been, but it rapidly became a fait accompli. Vaclav Klaus brushed aside the 'social market economy', saying he preferred to drop the adjective. And yet it would be odd if nearly forty years of state socialism (and nearly seventy in the former USSR) had not left important traces. Even where Western forms were adopted wholesale, it remains the case, as Claus Offe (1996) pointed out, that they were introduced in a radically different context.

Both the political and economic transitions, then, were both easier and more difficult than expected. The German case is particularly striking. Chancellor Kohl's '10-point programme' with which he startled the Bundestag on November 28, 1989, envisaged a gradual approach to unity via a 'treaty community' (Vertragsgemeinschaft). Just over ten months later, however, unification was complete, and in between these two dates, on July 1, 1990, the president of the Bundesbank congratulated himself on the smoothness of the GDR's switch to the deutsche mark (D-Mark). Looking at the wave-like motion of federal election statistics, the only sign of unification (apart from a larger electorate) is the appearance of two new minority parties: the *PDS* and *Bündnis 90*. The devil was in the detail: monetary union decimated the East German economy, and the 'rush to unification' (Jarausch, 1994) left many East Germans feeling the victims of an Anschluss, or a colonial takeover (Christ and Neubauer, 1991). This is one of the issues on which there remains a really significant difference of opinion between East and West Germans: the former agreeing two to one that East Germany was 'overwhelmed and taken over by West Germany in the process of unification', whereas in the West the proportions are almost inversed (59% to 38%) (Pew, 2009: 47).

The German situation was particularly extreme, despite massive transfers from West to East, because of Kohl's encouragement of unrealistic expectations ('blooming landscapes') on the one hand and the shock of monetary union on the other. The whole region, however, experienced a 'transition shock' which was partly inevitable and partly due to the excesses of neoliberalism. Ernest Gellner described the pre-industrial European state in terms of dentistry, operating by means of 'extraction', but the metaphor fits even better the strategy adopted in postcommunist transitions, whose protagonists argued that 'of course, if you haven't been to the dentist for forty or, in the worst case, seventy years, the necessary treatment will be extensive and expensive'. To shift the image from one orifice to another, postcommunist capitalism had a difficult birth, as the appalling waste of the communist-planned economies was followed by a similar waste of economic and human resources in often chaotic and ill-conceived (and often criminal) privatisations.

And yet, somehow or other, there emerged in the more favoured parts of the bloc, and the more favoured sectors, something recognisably like Western capitalist economies, showing the same sort of variation between neoliberal and more corporatist styles of economic governance that can be found in the West. An important alternative approach which deserves fuller treatment is that by Andreas Nölke and Arjan Vliegenhart (2009), following the approach of Dorothee Bohle and Béla Greskovits, most recently in Bohle and Greskovitz (2012). Nölke and Vliegenhart argue that East Central Europe, and *a fortiori* other postcommunist states, should be assigned to a third category of 'dependent market economies', dependent on foreign investment, ownership, and export markets. This leaves them in a subordinate position in the world economy, but one which has enabled substantial relative progress. The Baltic States, by contrast, with their more neoliberal approach, 'might still be caught in a "postsocialist developmental trap" that hinders structural economic development' (pp. 692–693). Bohle and Greskovits (2012: 36) also argue for a triadic model contrasting the Baltic States, the Visegrád states, and Slovenia.

> [T]he Baltic states have been the least and Slovenia the most willing to compensate for the transformation costs of economic actors and members of society. The Visegrád countries fell in between these extremes, and also differed among themselves in terms of prioritizing compensation through industrial or social policies. The first preference is expressed by the Czech Republic and the second by Poland. Finally, Bulgaria and Romania tried to compensate

economic actors more, while in terms of the GDP share and generosity of welfare state benefits they lagged behind the Visegrád group.

Lucian Cernat (2006: 18), following David Lane and others, also offers a third category of 'developmental capitalism', where 'state and business collaborate positively'. He suggests (p. 29): 'There is at present a lack of consensus as to whether the processes of institution building in post-socialist Europe reflect the development of a well-defined European capitalist model or contribute to the creation of a "cocktail capitalism" '. This is substantially determined by the broader political context, both domestic and international. Timothy Frye (2010), for example, has made a substantial and powerful argument that political polarisation in postcommunist democracies is inimical to sustained and coherent reform programmes. This explains, he argues, why reform was more successful in Poland, where there was a greater degree of consensus cutting across the political oppositions, than in Bulgaria, where this consensus was absent. Autocracies isolated from democratic pressure (his case studies here are Russia and Uzbekistan) also tend towards incoherent and contradictory reform strategies.

Debates of this kind will, of course, continue on a country, regional, and sectoral basis (see, for example, Crouch, Schröder, and Voelzkow, 2009). What is crucial in all this, I think, is to attend to both dimensions: domestic variation as analysed in the 'variety of capitalism' literature, and global position. It is time to ask whether Berend's image of the detour of Eastern Europe from the periphery to the periphery is too pessimistic. One Škoda doesn't make a summer, but the prospect of a gradual catch-up, at least for parts of the former bloc and for favoured sectors in them, began to seem realistic. At the same time, as Bohle and Greskovitz (2012: 269) note, the more peripheral parts of Western 'old Europe' may converge with the 'new' Eastern periphery, both in their economic position and politically: 'a new round of open-ended struggles against capitalism's propensity to weaken its own social and political foundations'.

Notes

1 See Stenning and Hörschelmann (2008); also the volume discussed later, edited by David Lane and Martin Myant, in which 'The contributors were asked to consider how far the societies in transition from state socialism carry a common footprint from their communist pasts' (Lane and Myant, 2007: 1).
2 For an impressive attempt to isolate these dynamics using a broadened notion of 'civilizational competence', see Adam et al (2005, 2009).
3 The pejorative use of the adjective 'Balkan' both inside and outside the region would be one example. There are, of course, echoes in my analysis of what is called 'constructivism' in international relations, though I shall not pursue these connections here. See also Eder (2006).
4 http://2013.ar-ebrd.com/overview/.
  Elster et al (1998: 46–47) write: 'In the literature an "invisible map" drawing a distinction between East Central and South East Europe plays a prominent part . . . [but] . . . this distinction with its familiar discriminatory connotations is a rather shaky basis for

comparative research on East European transitions'. The authors recall in a footnote that they were rebuked by Czechs and Hungarians for also including Bulgaria in their four-country study.

5 For a comparative discussion, see Offe (1996).

6 More precisely, whether the Holy Spirit derives only from God the Father or also from the Son ('filioque' in the Latin version of the Nicene Creed). Papal authority was, of course, also an issue.

7 Sometimes the relation is the other way round. Bohle (2011: 135–136) cites the 1997 Eurobarometer figures for Hungary and Latvia: the market economy seemed 'right' to no Latvians and only 6% of Hungarians, whereas democracy satisfied 30% in Hungary and 24% in Latvia.

8 These differences tend not to show up in comparative value surveys, such as that by Miller, White, and Heywood (1998), which found little difference on socialist, nationalist, liberal, and democratic values, except that what they call 'external nationalism', or support for power politics, was stronger in the formerly imperial states (Russia and Hungary) than in the Czech or Slovak Republics or Ukraine. See also Magun and Rudnev (2010).

9 An early comparative analysis which remains useful is that by Judy Batt (1991). More recently, a Bulgarian commentator, Boyko Vasiliev (2010), has provided an ironical gloss on these differentiations. On the Polish–Hungarian comparison, see Renwick (2006).

10 As, for instance, in the early development in Hungary of a multi-party system.

11 Vitali Silitski (2005) suggested that there might be no more, as autocratic rulers like Lukashenka became more skilled at averting them. As Freedom House (Puddington 2011: 6) noted, however, the removal of Bakiyev in Kyrgyzstan suggested continuing movement; more recently, the 'Arab Spring', which has clearly shaken the Chinese dictatorship, is a further promising sign.

12 In a suggestive comparison of Poland and Romania, Alina Mungiu-Pippidi (2005: 234) later suggested that in postcommunist democracies '. . . the main indicator of . . . success became the distance between the formal institutions adopted – which were the same everywhere – and the informal practices in politics and society . . . The greater the difference between the past and the present formal institutions, the larger the distance between current formal and informal institutions'. She concludes (p. 235) that '. . . there is an "unbearable lightness" to democracy: Only after you have it do you realise how many other things are needed for a government to be able to provide quality of life to its citizens'.

13 Freedom House (Puddington, 2011) has essentially the same picture, with minor additions of new (and in some cases disputed) Balkan and Caucasian states. Møller (p. 7) excluded Bosnia-Herzegovina, Serbia, and Montenegro for technical reasons. Ukraine, which Freedom House had categorised as free after the Orange Revolution, has now reverted to 'semi-free' status.

14 See Solohubenko (2009). In Mongolia, too, transition began with a demonstration on Human Rights Day (December 10, 1989).

References

Adam, Frane, Matej Makarovič, Borut Rončević, and Matevž Tomšič (2005) *The Challenges of Sustained Development. The Role of Sociocultural Factors in East-Central Europe*. Budapest and New York: Central European University Press.

Adam, Frane, Kristan Primož and Matevž Tomšič (2009) 'Varieties of Capitalism in Eastern Europe (with Special Emphasis on Estonia and Slovenia)', *Communist and Post-Communist Studies* 42: 65–81.

Batt, Judy (1991) 'The End of Communist Rule in East-Central Europe: A Four-Country Comparison', *Government and Opposition* 26(3): 368–390.

Berdahl, Daphne (1999) *Where the World Ended. Reunification and Identity in the German Borderland.* Berkeley and London: University of California Press.

Berend, Iván (1996) *Central and Eastern Europe 1944–1993: Detour from the Periphery to the Periphery.* Cambridge: Cambridge University Press.

Bohle, Dorothee (2011) 'East European Transformations and the Paradoxes of Transnationalization', in Joan Debardeleben and Achim Hurrelmann (eds.), *Transnational Europe: Promise, Paradox, Limits.* Basingstoke: Palgrave Macmillan, pp. 130–150.

Bohle, Dorothee and Béla Greskovits (2012) *Capitalist Diversity in Europe's Periphery.* Ithaca and London: Cornell University Press.

Cernat, Lucian (2006) *Europeanization, Varieties of Capitalism and Economic Performance in Central and Eastern Europe.* Basingstoke: Palgrave Macmillan.

Christ, Peter and Ralf Neubauer (1991) *Kolonie im eigenen Land. Die Treuhand, Bonn und die Wirtschaftskatastrophe der fünf neuen Länder.* Berlin: Rowohlt.

Crouch, Colin, Martin Schröder, Helmut Voelzkow (2009) 'Regional and Sectoral Varieties of Capitalisms', *Economy and Society* 38(4): 654–678.

Eckstein, Harry (1973) 'Authority Patterns: A Structural Pattern for Inquiry', *American Political Science Review* 47 (December): 1142–61.

Eder, Klaus (2006) 'Europe's Borders: The Narrative Construction of the Boundaries of Europe', *European Journal of Social Theory*, 9(2): 255–271.

Eliaeson, Sven (2010) 'Introduction', in Sven Eliaeson and Nadezhda Georgieva (eds.), *New Europe. Growth to Limits?* Oxford: Bardwell Press, pp. 1–29.

Elster, Jon, Claus Offe, and Ulrich Preuss, with Frank Boenker, Ulrike Goetting, and Friedbert W. Rueb (1998) *Institutional Design in Post-Communist Societies: Rebuilding the Ship at Sea.* Cambridge: Cambridge University Press.

Fish, M. Steven (1998) 'Mongolia: Democracy Without Prerequisities', *Journal of Democracy* 9(3): 127–141.

Fish, M. Steven (2001) 'The Inner Asian Anomaly: Mongolia's: Democratization in Comparative Perspective', *Communist and Post-Communist Studies* 34: 323–338.

Frye, Timothy (2010) *Building States and Markets after Communism. The Perils of Polarized Democracy.* Cambridge: Cambridge University Press.

Gallagher, Tom (2005) *Theft of a Nation. Romania since Communism.* London: C. Hurst.

Garsztecki, Stefan (2010) 'Demokratie in Polen – Auf dem Weg zu *Good Governance*?', *Polen-Analysen* Nr. 68, 20.04.

Gates, Scott, Håvard Hegre, Mark P. Jones, and Håvard Strand (2006) 'Institutional Inconsistency and Political Instability: Policy Duration, 1800–2000', *American Journal of Political Science* 50(4) October: 893–908.

Gurr, Ted Robert (1974) 'Persistence and Change in Political Systems, 1800–1971', *American Political Science Review* 68 (December): 1482–1504.

Havel, Václav (2008) *To the Castle and Back.* London: Portobello Books. First published 2006.

Huntington, Samuel P. (1993) 'The Clash of Civilizations?', *Foreign Affairs.* See online reprint on www.foreignaffairs.com/articles/united-states/1993-06-01/clash-civilizations. Accessed 13 July 2015.

Ioffe, Grigory (2007) 'Culture Wars, Soul-Searching, and Belarusian Identity', *East European Politics and Societies* 21(2): 348–381.

Jarausch, Konrad (1994) *The Rush to German Unity*. New York: Oxford University Press.

Kaldor, Mary and Ivan Vejvoda (eds.) (1999/2002) *Democratization in Central and Eastern Europe*. London: Pinter; paperback edition (2002) London and New York: Continuum.

Kenney, Padraic (2011) 'Borders Breached: The Transnational in Eastern Europe since Solidarity', *Journal of Modern European History* 9(1): 179–195.

Kitschelt, Herbert et al (eds.) (1999) *Post-Communist Party Systems. Competition, Representation, and Inter-Party Cooperation*. Cambridge: Cambridge University Press.

Kolarova, Rumyana (2002) 'Democratization in Bulgaria: Recent Trends', in Kaldor and Vejvoda (eds.), pp. 150–161.

Kopstein, Jeffrey S. and David A. Reilly (2000) 'Geographic Diffusion and the Transformation of the Postcommunst World', *World Politics* 53(1) October: pp. 1–37.

Kundera, Milan (1983) 'L'Occident kidnappé ou la tragédie de l'Europe centrale', *Le Débat* 27: 3–22.

Kundera, Milan (1991) 'Point de vue: Il faut sauver la Slovénie', *Le Monde*, 4 (July).

Lane, David and Myant, Martin (eds.) (2007) *Varieties of Capitalism in Post-Communist Countries*. Basingstoke: Palgrave.

Lane, David and Stephen White (eds.) (2010) *Rethinking the 'Coloured Revolutions'*. Abingdon: Routledge.

Levitsky, Steven and Lucan A. Way (2006) 'Linkage and Leverage. How Do International Factors Change Domestic Balances of Power?', in Andreas Schedler (ed.), *Electoral Authoritarianism. The Dynamics of Unfree Competition*. Boulder: Rienner, pp. 199–216.

Magun, Vladimir and Maksim Rudnev (2010) 'The Life Values of the Russian Population. Similarities and Differences in Comparison with Other European Countries', *Sociological Research* 49(4) July-August: 3–57.

Manning, Nick (2004) 'Diversity and Change in Pre-accession Central and Eastern Europe since 1989', *Journal of European Social Policy* 14(3): 211–232.

Miller, William, Stephen White and Paul Heywood (1998) *Values and Political Change in Postcommunist Europe*. Basingstoke: Macmillan.

Møller, Jørgen (2009) *Post-communist Regime Change*. London: Routledge.

Mungiu-Pippidi, Alina (2005) 'Poland and Romania', in Larry Diamond and Leornardo Molino (eds), *Assessing the Quality of Democracy*. Baltimore: Johns Hopkins University Press, pp. 213–223.

Nemyria, Hryhoriy (2005) 'The Orange Revolution: Explaining the Unexpected', in Michael Emerson (ed.), *Democratisation in the European Neighbourhood*. Brussels: Centre for European Policy Studies, pp. 53–62.

Nölke, Andreas and Arjan Vliegenthart (2009) 'Enlarging the Varieties of Capitalism. The Emergence of Dependent Market Economies in East Central Europe', *World Politics* 61(4) October: 670–702.

Offe, Claus Offe (1996) *Varieties of Transition. The East European and East German Experience*. Cambridge: Polity.

Outhwaite, William, and Larry Ray (2005) *Social Theory and Postcommunism*. Oxford: Blackwell.

Pew Global Attitudes Project (2009) 'Two Decades After the Wall's Fall', www.pewresearch.org. Accessed July 27, 2015.

Puddington, Arch (2011) *Freedom in the World 2011: The Authoritarian Challenge to Democracy*, Washington, DC: Freedom House.

Renwick, Alan (2006) 'Why Hungary and Poland Differed in 1989: The Role of Medium-Term Frames in Explaining the Outcomes of Democratic Transition', *Democratization* 13(1): 36–57.

Rose, Richard (2009) *Understanding Post-Communist Transformation: A Bottom Up Approach.* London: Routledge.

Rothschild, Joseph and Nancy M. Wingfield (2000) *Return to Diversity. A Political History of East Central Europe Since World War II* (3rd edn.) New York: Oxford University Press.

Schöpflin, George and Nancy Wood (eds.) (1988) *In Search of Central Europe.* Cambridge: Polity.

Silitski, Vitali (2005) 'Is the Age of Post-Soviet Electoral revolutions Over?', *Democracy at Large*, 1(4): 8–10.

Solohubenko, Olexiy (2009) 'How 1989 fanned flames in Ukraine', BBC News 10.6.09. http://news.bbc.co.uk/go/pr/fr/-/1/hi/world/europe/8091737.stm. Accessed January 5, 2011.

Stenning, Alison and Kathrin Hörschelman (2008) 'History, Geography and Difference in the Post-Socialist World: Or, Do We Still Need Post-Socialism?', *Antipode* 40(2): 312–335.

Stokes, Gale (1997) *Three Eras of Political Change in Eastern Europe.* New York: Oxford University Press.

Szücs, Jenö (1983) 'Three Historical Regions of Europe', *Acta Historicae Academia Scientiarum Hungaricae* 29(23): 131–184. Reprinted in John Keane (ed.) (1988) *Civil Society and the State.* London: Verso, pp. 291–332.

Vachudová, Milada Anna (2005) *Europe Undivided. Democracy, Leverage, and Integration After Communism.* Oxford: Oxford University Press.

van Zon, Hans (2001) 'Neo-Patrimonialism as an Impediment to Economic Development: The Case of Ukraine', *Journal of Communist Studies and Transition Politics* 17(3) September: 71–95.

Vassiliev, Boyko (2010) 'The Region No One Could Name', *Transitions Online*, 22.4.10.

Vidmar-Horvath, Ksenija and Gerard Delanty (2008) '*Mitteleuropa* and the European Heritage', *European Journal of Social Theory* 11(2): 203–218.

Vujačić, Veljko (1996) 'Historical Legacies, Nationalist Motivation, and Political Outcomes in Russia and Serbia: A Weberian View', *Theory and Society* 25(6): 763–801.

Wallace, Helen (1999) 'Whose Europe Is It Anyway? The 1998 Stein Rokkan Lecture', *European Journal of Political Research* 35(3): 287–306.

Weßels, Bernhard (2010) 'Religion and Economic Virtues' in Sven Eliaeson and Nadezhda Georgieva (eds.), *New Europe. Growth to Limits?* Oxford: Bardwell Press, pp. 131–147.

5 Convergence and catching up
EU enlargement and colour revolutions

The EU's response to 1989, like that of the West as a whole, will surely be judged by history as slow and mean spirited. East Germany's incorporation without accession, however, demanded an immediate response. As Mary Sarotte (2009: 8) notes, Kohl, with impeccable pro-European credentials as a German, a Rhinelander, and in his personal orientation, had presented German reunification as 'an extension of European integration. Just as West and East would unify within existing German structures, so too would West and East join under the existing EU institutions'. This "prefab model', as Sarotte calls it, had the disadvantage that they were 'creating a common European home of many rooms – just without one for Russia' (Sarotte 2009: 214). After reunification, Kohl presented the 1991 Maastricht Treaty at the Christian Democratic Union conference as 'a European answer to the collapse of the Communist dictatorships in Central, Eastern and South-Eastern Europe. With it we take up our responsibility for the whole of the European continent' (Tewes, 1998: 125). As Tewes points out, however, although Germany was in the forefront of the EU's opening to the East, this conflicted with its attachment to deepening Western integration, articulated, for example, in the Schäuble–Lamers paper of 1994 which urged that a core–periphery model for the EU was necessary if it was to be able to absorb the Visegrád countries and Slovenia in the early 2000s. Joschka Fischer (2011), who had taken up this suggestion in a speech in 2000 when he was foreign minister, reiterated this theme, arguing that it has become a fact 'since the first rounds of enlargement'.

For the rest of postcommunist Europe, however, there were just the PHARE and TACIS programmes;[1] some loan aid from the European Investment Bank; and a gradual move by the end of 1991 to association agreements with Czechoslovakia, Hungary, and Poland, providing for free trade within five years. The region's interest in accession is illustrated by the facts that Civic Forum's foreign policy agenda, drafted less than ten days into the Velvet Revolution, called for Czechoslovakia to be included in the integration process (Vachudová, 2005: 83) and that Poland had a Government Office for European Integration from the beginning of 1991 (Mayhew, 2000: 5).

The EU's position that these countries had first to sort out their economic problems before envisaging closer integration amounted, as Delpeuch (1994: 283) complained in the Czechoslovak case, to offering them 'a ladder without rungs'.[2]

Vachudová (2005: 92–93) suggests that 'by 1990 the divergent approaches to enlargement of the EU's key member states were already on display'. The line-up was France (with BeNeLux) against, for a mix of federalist ('deepening' of integration) and agrarian motives; the United Kingdom in favour, for anti-federalist ('widening' versus deepening) and free trade reasons; and with Germany tipping the balance in favour, for the sake of security and economic opportunities. The north of Europe (including Austria) broadly sided with Germany and the south (including Ireland) with France – the poorer members wanting to avoid competition from others even poorer and to retain the transfers they got for being poor.

Jackie Gower (1993: 289) wrote that until the coup attempt in Russia in August 1991

> . . . the prevailing view in Brussels was that none of the former Comecon states could realistically be regarded as candidate members of the Community until well into the next century. Indeed, it is arguable that the EU's overriding objective at this time was to avoid the question of membership.

If, as she suggests, it was the coup that concentrated minds in Brussels, it would not, of course, be the first time that European integration had been speeded up by a perceived Soviet threat. As Baldwin et al wrote (1997: 168, quoted in Ingham and Ingham, 2002: 15): 'Imagine how eager western Europe would have been in 1980 to pay ECU 8 billion a year in order to free central Europe from communism and remove Soviet troops from the region'.[3] Mattli and Plümper (2002: 551) also quote a European Commission official saying 'in the mid-1990s that "the level of seriousness about enlargement is not minimal, it simply does not exist"'. The Union took a step forward at the Copenhagen summit of 1993, with the declaration that 'the associated countries in Central and Eastern Europe that so desire shall become members of the European Union', and Klaus Kinkel announced an EU Ostpolitik as a goal for the German presidency in the second half of 1994. This, however, rather ran into the sand in the middle 1990s, perhaps because the EU was preoccupied with the European Free Trade Association (EFTA) countries' enlargement (Austria, Finland, and Sweden) as well as the economic crisis. In 1996 the European Commission produced a white paper which received the equivalent of a C grade from a Sussex European Institute working paper: 'Signs that there is a risk of the pre-accession strategy losing its focus have been evident from the start' (Smith et al, 1996: 7). The authors went on to point to 'the need to push the process forward in a way that generates a reciprocal response from the EU side to actions taken by the CEECs' (Smith et al, 1996: 22).

The EU's remarkably slow response to 1989 provoked considerable resentment in Poland (Blazyca, 2002: 206–207, 212) and elsewhere in the region. Melinda Kovács (2001) neatly describes this response, even in the late 1990s, as 'putting down and putting off'. A more cosmopolitan Union, one must conclude, would have been more responsive and understanding – not least since it had just emerged from a potentially lethal cold war.[4] Beck and Grande (2004: 172) rightly point to a certain 'western European racism'. Even when the process heated up in the late

1990s, the review of the state of research by Frank Schimmelfennig and Ulrich Sedelmeier (2002) concluded that it was rather undeveloped. The European Commission's *Agenda 2000* (1997)

> ... divided the candidates between those deemed ready to start negotiations – Estonia, Hungary, Poland, the Czech Republic, and Slovenia – and those evaluated as not yet ready for negotiations – Bulgaria, Latvia, Lithuania, Slovakia, and Romania . . . The first five states started membership negotiations with the EU in 1998 . . . the next five . . . in 2000.
>
> (Dimitrova, 2005: 73)

Breaking with its previous enlargement practice of negotiating with groups of states, the Union adopted the 'regatta' model of evaluating the progress of each state separately. An open-ended list of potential member states, Dimitrova suggests, 'appears to have been adopted with credibility in mind'.

From 1997, Dimitrova (2005: 76) argues, the EU began in earnest the process of evaluation which had been articulated in 1995 and which continues to the present, as can be seen from the Enlargement website (http://ec.europa.eu/enlargement). From 1995 Poland and Hungary checked all legislation for its conformity with EU law (Vachudová, 2005: 91) and by 1999, over 80% of laws passed in Hungary in June were not debated in parliament because they were part of the *acquis communautaire* (Schimmelfennig and Sedelmeier, 2005: 2). As Vachudová has shown, this 'active leverage' by the EU, building on the 'passive leverage' exercised by the prospect of membership, has had a transforming effect in the region. Moreover, the EU's initial indifference and hesitation may have strengthened the effect in due course of its active leverage over accession candidates (Vachudová, 2005: 109).[5]

The effect of passive leverage on 'illiberal' states is perhaps the most striking in the long run:

> Meeting EU requirements threatened to undermine the domestic power of ruling elites in Romania, Bulgaria, and Slovakia, by strengthening opposition forces, limiting rent-seeking opportunities for political cronies, and precluding ethnic scapegoating as an easy ploy for rallying support . . . [however] . . . It turned out that they could not abandon the project of building closer ties with the EU because this project was so popular with the electorate . . . and because it offered immediate economic rewards including greater market access and international development aid. So Bulgaria, Romania, and Slovakia signed Europe Agreements and put in their applications for EU membership in step with Poland, Hungary, and the Czech Republic.
>
> (Vachudová 2005: 73)

The liberalising effects were not immediate, but following the opening of negotiations in 2000 (as against 1998 for the Visegrád states, Slovenia, and Estonia), Slovakia caught up in time for the 2004 accession round.

This was, of course, a contentious process. It was one thing for Slovaks to ditch Mečiar for the sake of prospective EU membership and another for the EU to demand total compliance with microscopic elements of the *acquis* as a precondition for accession. Wade Jacoby (2002: 135) aptly compares the process to the Catholic rites of confession and (conditional) absolution: '[T]he priestly authority has the right, indeed the obligation, to impose responsibilities upon the penitent to remedy the weakness, lest forgivable lapses give way to a pattern of recidivism'.[6] As Smith et al (1996: 7) pointed out, existing member states had enjoyed much greater flexibility in relation to environmental regulations, and the United Kingdom had even been allowed to opt out of the Social Chapter. Some of these states had blocked free trade measures, and in general 'EU negotiators of the "Europe Agreements" acted decisively to protect the interests of powerful producer groups within the member states' (Vachudová, 2005: 86).[7]

More ominously still, the requirement of unanimity for accession gave each member state an ultimate veto power, in a context where 'member states are always tempted to put short-term national interest before medium-term European strategic interest' (Mayhew, 2000: 12). Even if the Union had wanted to commit itself to an accession date, as it refused for a long time to do (Mayhew, 2000: 64), it could not commit its member states. The 'European dynamic', as Georg Vobruba (2005) has called it, in which states on the border of the Union have an interest in supporting their neighbours' accession (Germany for Poland and Czechoslovakia, Poland for Ukraine, and so on), was operating very undynamically.[8] On the other hand, Vachudová (2005: 77–78) stresses that the EU did not discriminate against Romania and Bulgaria[9] and 'that it was the meritocracy of the EU's pre-accession process that helped make the EU's leverage so powerful in the late 1990s'. These 'borderline countries', as Pop-Eliches (2007) describes them (he includes mid-1990s Slovakia and Moldova) are where democracy promotion has worked best. Elsewhere, however, leverage seems to have been relatively ineffective, as, for example, in Albania (Vurmo, 2008). Coricelli (2007) suggests that states which are authoritarian or only partly free tend to stick in a partial reform trap; he and Schimmelfennig (2007: 134) concur that only domestic revolutions of the Serbian or Ukrainian kind can break this impasse (Schimmelfennig and Scholtz, 2008, 2010). The Union's relatively generous treatment of Bulgaria and Romania, like that afforded earlier to Greece, substantially reflects a perceived political imperative to preserve them from something worse.

The constitutional convention of 2002–2003 is an interesting episode to observe in this connection. It was contingently related to the impending enlargement in that it could (and perhaps should) have taken place well before 1989, but it was intrinsically linked, in that its mission, to make a larger Union viable, implied that the new members be fully represented in its deliberations. Although the convention failed to produce an acceptable constitution, initiating a whole series of subsequent failures and fudges, in other respects, it was quite an impressive deliberative assembly which may be remembered when more immediately successful ventures are forgotten (Norman, 2005). It was also one in which Old and New Europe met on relatively egalitarian and open terms; as Fraser Cameron

(2004: 152) notes, 'it was difficult to distinguish speakers coming from existing or future member states'.[10] For all this, however, the dominant impression of the enlargements of 2004 and 2007 remains that of a bureaucratic process managed in a bureaucratic manner and tinged with arrogance on the part of the existing members.

The impact on democracy is at best ambiguous. Kristi Raik (2004: 591) concluded from a study of Estonia in the pre-accession years that

> . . . the underlying logic of enlargement integration promoted bureaucratic, executive-dominated policy making and left little room for democratic politics in applicant countries. The keywords of the office discourse of enlargement/integration – inevitability, speed, efficiency, and expertise – formed a set of mutually reinforcing principles that all constrained democratic politics and tended to limit enlargement to a narrow sphere of elites and experts.

From the viewpoint of democracy, the choice between joining and staying outside is one between bad and worse (Raik 2004: 592–593).

As a number of contemporaries in the region pointed out, compliance with EU impositions in many ways replicated earlier forms of overt compliance with and quiet resistance to Soviet power. Raik (2004: 586) quotes a poignant Estonian response:

> Now, being close, that Europe of a dream rather appears as a boring administrative machinery that produces restrictions and bureaucracy. We must close many more countryside shops and pubs, install thousands of steel washbasins in school refectories, in order to pass the strict sanitary tests. It's like the army! First delouse in the sauna, and only after that you get to wear the gold-starred uniform. First tidiness, then – administrative capacity.[11]

After accession, the EU's leverage over new member states is drastically reduced. Geoffrey Pridham (2008a, 2008b) concludes from studies of Slovakia and Latvia that, despite some loss of momentum, there have been few reversals of democratic and other reforms imposed before accession by the EU. This is just as well, since apart from the 'nuclear option' of suspending membership, sanctions are more or less confined to the symbolic. The Austrian government was frozen out for a time in 2000 on the basis of Article 6 (1) of the EU Treaty, when it included the extreme-right Freiheitspartei Österreichs (Austrian Freedom Party) (FPÖ), and the European Parliament passed a resolution in 2006 condemning racist and homophobic intolerance in Poland (Zielonka, 2007: 175–176). The restrictions on press freedom and other repressive measures by the Hungarian government since 2011 have so far met no substantial response. On the broader issue of the impact of EU membership on national democracy, discussed in more detail in Chapter 7, Zielonka (2007: 173–174) suggests that the new member states are particularly affected by three more general implications. The increased complexity of governance tends to make citizens feel that they have less influence on political decisions, and this feeling may be especially strong in postcommunist states. The weakening of parliaments is particularly salient in a region where they were only recently established as genuine parliaments and where they remain weak. Third, the widespread sentiment of isolation from the centre of EU governance in Brussels may be particularly strong in a part of Europe which has been treated as marginal for so long.

What has been called, somewhat oddly, the 'Europeanisation' of Central and Eastern Europe can be seen overall as a process of convergence, though it is still not clear whether the convergence is towards an EU mean or towards a persisting condition of marginality (Rowlands, 2010).[12] In the case of the authoritarian states farther south and east in Europe, Habermas' slogan of 'rectifying' or 'catching-up' revolutions seems more appropriate to these later 'colour revolutions' than it did when he originally coined it in 1990.

The electoral victory over Mečiar's regime in Slovakia in 1998 can be seen either as a return to normalcy in a region of East Central Europe which had gone off track or (or also) as prefiguring a set of successful or unsuccessful attempts to remove authoritarian regimes in the following years. Whereas the 1989 transitions were marked by months in the various countries of East Central Europe, these 'colour revolutions' were in successive years: Serbia in 2000 (the Bulldozer Revolution), Georgia in 2003 (Rose), Ukraine in 2004 (Orange), Kyrgyzstan in 2005 (Tulip) and again in 2010, and the unsuccessful 'Jeans Revolution' in Belarus in 2006.[13] Unlike the 1989 revolutions, there was no pattern of acceleration and no visible domino effect, though there was a process of teaching and learning in which activists from one country played a role in others. Here, the chain goes back as far as Bulgaria and Romania in 1996–1997; the flow of informal advice moved to Croatia – where a democratic regime followed the death of Tuđman and the defeat of his party in 2000 – Serbia, and Ukraine. The movements' names and slogans had a common pattern, from 'IZLAZ (exit) 2000' and 'gotov je' ('he [Milošević] is finished') in Serbia to 'pora' ('it's time') in Ukraine (and less successfully in Russia) and 'kmara' and 'mjaft' ('enough') in Georgia and Albania, respectively.[14] Mark Beissinger (2007) sees the colour revolutions as 'modular' phenomena, in which one serves as an example for others. There was also, however, a learning process on the other side, in which ruling elites learned to pre-empt threats of this kind. Shevardnadze, after losing power in Georgia, is reported to have said: 'I did not think I should pay serious attention to these young people running around waving flags and painting graffiti on the streets. I was wrong' (Kandelaki and Meladze, 2007: 105). Beissinger (2007: 259) describes this as an 'elite learning' process, 'limiting the likelihood of further revolutionary successes'.

Whereas 1989 yielded a democratising region, with just a few laggards in the Balkans and back-sliding for a time in Slovakia, the revolutions in the following decade have produced so far only one now solidly democratic outcome: in Serbia. It is still too early to say whether the cycle is over, as Silitski suggested as early as 2006, but the paucity of recent examples and their highly ambiguous outcomes suggest scepticism. Yet these are slow-falling dominos – necessarily so because colour revolutions have been linked to elections and typically follow results rigged by the incumbents.[15] Beissinger (2007: 263) points out that where opposition movements have acted outside an electoral cycle, as in Belarus in 2005, they have not enjoyed much support; in the election year 2006 they achieved a good deal more, though not, of course, enough to change the regime. Both sides have raised their game: Beissinger (2007: 266) cites Pora activists joking about setting up a new democratic Comintern, but, as Silitski (2007: 170) points out, the Shanghai Cooperation Organisation, linking the dictatorships in China, Kazakhstan, Kyrgyzstan, Russia, Tadjikistan, and Uzbekistan, and with Belarus as a 'conversation partner', provides a more convincing 'Authoritarian Internationale'.[16] Henryk Szadziewski (2011: 1) writes that 'the SCO member states established a definition of "terror" that lent itself to the targeting and quelling of routine, non-violent domestic political opposition'.

The colour revolutions were indeed colourful, and those in Serbia and Ukraine have been celebrated by the film maker Steve York (2002, 2007); his film of the events in Kyiv was made even more dramatic by footage of Yushchenko's face ravaged by the poison administered by what we continue for some reason to call 'security' forces. The unsuccessful attempt in 2006 in Belarus was filmed by Yury Khaschchavatsky (2007). Others have taken a more jaundiced view of the colour revolutions. Francis Fukuyama (2006: 67), the prophet of 1989 and of the end of history, wrote that:

> . . . the democratization of Central Europe was a miracle. And, one can react to a miracle either by dramatically raising expectations for a repeat-effect or by being grateful, pocketing one's luck, and reflecting on the uniqueness of circumstance. Unfortunately, the democracy promotion community shared the first reaction, and tried to turn the miracle into a natural law.[17]

David Lane, who would not I think use the word miracle for 1989, and not just for secularist reasons or for the sake of sociological rigour, points out that the 'carnation revolution' in Portugal in 1974, in which soldiers decorated their gun barrels with carnations and which is one of the sources of all this floral and florid imagery, was 'more like a military coup . . . This coup-like character continued . . . in the later coloured revolutions' (Lane, 2009: 114). For Lane (2009: 116–117),

> While the masses may be captivated by euphoric revolutionary ideology, they are in political terms instruments of indigenous counter-elites, often encouraged by foreigners with their own agendas.[18] If successful, rather than such revolutions leading to significant socio-political change, a circulation of elites follows the ousting of former rulers or their co-option into another elite structure.

This analysis is perhaps a little harsh. Even if the only manifestly successful democratic outcomes were in Serbia and perhaps Georgia, most observers agree that Ukraine, for example, became freer after the Orange Revolution, with better prospects for a still weak civil society to flourish (Stepanenko, 2006; Gromadzki et al,

2010) and despite the prosecutions of former prime minister Yulia Timoshenko and former interior minister Yuri Lutsenko (Solomko, 2011). Taras Kuzio (2011), in an interesting comparison with Italy and Georgia, suggested that Ukraine was likely to remain 'an immobile state' for the foreseeable future. As things turned out, of course, the immobility has given way to something a good deal more dramatic and, in part, tragic.[19]

A survey in 2007 listed freedom of speech as the greatest gain, along with the quality of public information and improved relations with the United States and the EU; the greatest losses were seen to be in relations with Russia, corruption, and economic and standard of living issues, along with interethnic relations. Among responses to the Orange Revolution (which were highly polarised, both in 2007 and in an earlier survey of 2005), ethnic Russians and/or Russian speakers were predominantly negative, with around half seeing it as a Western coup, as against less than a third of ethnic Ukrainians and Ukrainian speakers. (White and McAllister, 2009: 233, 246). In the EU survey of 2012, Ukraine had the lowest score in the Eastern European Partnership Region for satisfaction with democracy and 'the way things are going' (www.enpi-info.eu/files/publications/ANSA_ENPI_EAST_Infographic_April%2013.jpg).

Ten years after the Orange Revolution, a similar situation emerged in an even more dramatic form. The February 2014 Euromaidan Revolution against President Yanukovich led to an ongoing civil war between the new pro-EU government and Russian (and Russian-backed) insurgents in the east of the country; in March 2014 Russia annexed Crimea.

Although the short-term effects of unsuccessful protests, as in Belarus or Armenia, may be negative, as was the defeat of anticommunist opposition movements in 1953, 1956, or 1968, the longer-term weakening of authoritarian regimes may be the more important consequence. As we saw in East Central Europe, what has been called 'competitive authoritarianism' (Levitsky and Way, 2002), in which opposition is tolerated at the margin while systematically undermined,[20] still allows more open possibilities than regimes where it is simply outlawed.[21] Even within the sequence discussed here, from Slovakia in 1998 through Croatia and Serbia in 2000, the opportunities for political opposition and the relative openness of elections were a crucial part of the context.

Way (2008: 60) stresses two elements: the strength of a regime's ties to the West (see also Levitsky and Way, 2006, and the discussion of his article, and his response in Way, 2009) and the strength of the ruling party and/or state. On the second element, he writes:

> Postcommunist autocrats in Belarus, Tajikistan, and Uzbekistan have maintained state economic control by refraining from large-scale privatization . . . In countries where there had been extensive privatization, however – Georgia, Kyrgyzstan, and Ukraine, for example – the opposition was able either to draw on domestic business support or to benefit from the business community's neutrality.

(Way, 2008: 65)

If this plausible analysis looks a little neat, in retrodicting precisely the outcomes we saw in the mid-2000s, Way (2008: 66) also predicted other countries where he expected further developments: 'Regimes in Belarus and Armenia are particularly vulnerable. In both cases, autocrats are especially susceptible to defection by allies due to the weakness of ruling parties'.

A rather stronger version of the sceptical position on 'colour revolutions', drawing on Kitschelt's model of patrimonial communism and postcommunism, is provided by Henry Hale (2006). For Hale, they are simply part of the 'normal dynamics' of what he calls 'presidential patrimonialism', in which powerful rulers can play off rivals as long as they are perceived to be firmly entrenched.[22] Autocratic presidents, if they do not simply declare themselves permanent, as in Belarus, Tadjikistan, Turkmenistan, and Uzbekistan (and, of course, Haiti . . .), have to organise the election of a successor, 'opening up a Pandora's box of political struggle' (Hale, 2006: 309). Colour revolutions are therefore one form of succession, usually leaving the presidential system intact. 'Among the revolutionary countries, only Ukraine appears to have bucked the cyclical dynamic, transferring significant presidential power to its parliament in the wake of the Orange Revolution's stalemate' (Hale, 2006: 326). Petra Stykow (2010: 148–149) points out that from this point of view democratisation is irrelevant to the question of the success or failure of a revolution, 'since its function is merely to resolve the reproduction crisis of the regime'.

Stykow concludes from her wide-ranging and balanced survey of the literature in English, German, Russian, and Ukrainian, that this perspective fits the facts best, 'at least for the present and for the post-soviet region' (2010: 156). The alternative approach, couched in terms of democratising processes under conditions of globalisation, begs the question of whether these regimes are in any sense on the way to democracy or whether they should more appropriately be analysed in terms of an emerging comparative approach to autocracies. This latter approach is indeed a powerful alternative to the more teleological approach of democratic transition, but in a context where so much changes from one year to the next, I suggest what one might pretentiously call a more dialectical reading of the situation.

As analysts of the colour revolutions have pointed out, there is a tension between a logic of democratic institutionalism and one of informal elite accommodations (Stykow, 2010: 148). Howard and Roessler (2006: 369) write:

> Competitive authoritarianism is inherently contradictory. Legitimate procedures (i.e., regular, competitive elections) are undermined by illegitimate practices such as vote rigging, violent disenfranchisement, and media bias. These inherent tensions simultaneously raise and frustrate the expectations of the population (and even moderates and reformers within the incumbent regimes) that a more liberal order is possible . . . And in fact, electoral 'upsets' do sometimes take place, where the dominant party (or candidate) sometimes loses despite the considerable advantages it had enjoyed . . . In other cases . . . the dominant party may still win, but the elections are considerably

more free and fair than in the past, and the country moves in a liberalizing direction following the elections. Either scenario fits into our conception of a liberalizing electoral outcome.

Taking fifty cases between 1990 and 2002, they identify fifteen liberalizing outcomes, including, in postcommunist Europe, Armenia (1998), Croatia (2000), Romania (1996), and Yugoslavia (2000) (Howard and Roessler, 2006: 370).

The tension they identify parallels in some ways the old contrast between communist regimes' and dissidents' understanding of democracy. The communists followed the doctrine enunciated by Walter Ulbricht as he took power in East Germany after World War Two, that 'it must look democratic but we must control everything' (Leonhard, 1957). The dissidents in the 1980s often took the regimes' democratic and legal pretensions literally, addressing appeals to parliaments, presidents, and judges as though they enjoyed in practice the independent capacity to act which they had on paper. In a context where almost everyone at least pays lip service to democracy and human rights, this tension between form and content remains a source of instability in postcommunist authoritarian regimes, however well established they may seem at present. As Vicken Cheterian (2009: 157) wrote, 'Coloured revolutions are the dominant form in which "change" is imagined today in the heart of Eurasia'.

This suggests a final observation. The small number of full-blown colour revolutions, and the continuing controversy over questions of diffusion and whether or not they constitute a 'wave', might suggest that too much is being made of a limited range of cases, all affected by specific and local contingencies. In fact, however, as Way (2009: 91) points out,

> Postcommunist autocrats have been falling almost continuously since the collapse of communism in 1989–91 . . . the end of communism led to the emergence of a number of relatively weak autocrats who faltered from the get-go.

The colour revolutions narrowly defined are, of course, of considerable interest to the comparative study of revolutions, where they fit into a longer-term pattern from the last decades of the twentieth century of largely nonviolent, media-oriented popular revolutions. In the study of postcommunism, however, it is probably more helpful to think in terms of a broader spectrum, including transformative elections or electoral revolutions. Stykow (2010: 140–141) warns against this, on the grounds that it blurs the distinction between revolution and the electoral defeat of a government. It may, however, be what we need in a context where the lines between stasis and significant change are themselves so often blurred. And it is certainly a good idea, as Way does in the quotation earlier, to consider South–East Europe along with the former Soviet Union, while not overlooking the significant differences between the two.[23] After all, Ukraine was involved in the 1989 movements; three former Soviet republics (the Baltic States) are now in the EU, and Moldova might have been. It therefore makes sense to see the colour revolutions as, at least in part, an attempt to continue in the spirit of 1989, as well as a response to what Lane (2009: 131) calls a 'disappointment with the consequences of the transformation' which 'is common to all the Central and East European countries outside the European Union'.[24]

Notes

1 Political correctness may have determined the balance between languages. PHARE (the French for lighthouse) stands for Pologne, Hongrie: Activité pour la Restructuration Économique; TACIS for Technical Assistance to the Commonwealth of Independent States. The Latin *TACETE* ('shut up and be grateful for what you're given') might also have been appropriate to the context. In their analysis of leverage exercised by the EU, known as 'conditionality' and discussed in more detail later, Hughes, Sasse, and Gordon (2004: 12) note that in early association agreements and later accession negotiations, 'Conditionality towards the CEECs was strongly shaped by the transfer of development aid models'.

2 The value of Central and Eastern European (CEE) exports actually fell substantially between 1992 and 1993 (Gowan, 1996).

3 This figure (the European Currency Unit was the ancestor of the euro) was the authors' upper estimate of the likely budget cost of an eastern enlargement including the Visegrád states plus Slovenia. Revisiting the issue now, those who question the wisdom of the eastern enlargement, at least in the form it actually took, tend to say the same about Greece, Portugal, and Spain (see, for example, Scharpf, 2011, 2014; Streeck, 2013).

4 I discussed the limits of the EU's cosmopolitanism in Outhwaite (2006). See also Holmes (2003), Lane (2007), and Gudžinskas (2010).

5 See, however, the more sceptical analysis of Hughes, Sasse, and Gordon (2004). Their study is based on the example of regional policy, but their critique (Chapter 1) of the undifferentiated way in which conditionality has often been approached is of more general relevance.

6 See also Jacoby (1999). It is also true, of course, that issues such as corruption needed to be addressed. As Mungiu-Pippidi (2002–2003) wrote, 'If the European Union and other donors continue to believe that governments alone can solve their ills, the plague of Eastern Europe will simply be transplanted into the EU, as a kind of contamination'.

7 A 1994 study by the European Bank for Reconstruction and Development described the EU's trade policy as 'the main threat to eastern European exports and investment' (Vachudová, 2005: 88).

8 The other side of the European expansionary dynamic is what Richard Baldwin (1995) has called the domino effect, in which, as Vachudová (2005: 71) puts it, 'the EU market from which a non-member is excluded will continue to expand'.

9 See also Noutcheva and Bechev (2008).

10 The research of Ruth Wodak and her colleagues suggests, however, a rather more pessimistic assessment of the convention: see Krzyzanowski (2005) and Oberhuber (2005). See also Dobson and Follesdal (2004) and Tsebelis (2008). For a vigorous critique of the abortive constitution itself, see Brunkhorst (2006). Laure Delcour (2010: 143) notes that 'the adjectives "old" and "new" were never used before 2004 to distinguish among member states. They suggest deeply rooted differences'.

11 Another Estonian, cited by Hughes, Sasse, and Gordon (2004: 78), said that they were like 'mice in laboratories . . . anything could be asked of them'.

12 As Jan Palmowski (2011: 647–650) notes, the impact of the EU and 'Europeanisation' has been particularly strong in Central and Eastern Europe.
13 For a detailed account of the events in Georgia, Ukraine, and Kyrgyzstan, as well as an explanation discussed later, see Hale (2006).
14 Forbrig and Demeš (2007) provides a good account of the role of activist groups and more sceptical analyses of their significance by Ivan Krastev and Vitali Silitski.
15 As Way (2008: 57) points out, 'the departure of autocrats in Georgia, Kyrgyzstan, and Ukraine occurred in accord with each country's regular and domestically prescribed election cycle'. As he notes, this limits the usefulness of diffusion models.
16 He suggests (p.171 n.41) that China may have helped Belarus with technology to curb Internet use. For the Russian regime's response, see Horvath (2011).
17 See Krastev (2007: 236).
18 Lane (2009: 120) notes that the US agencies and global nongovernmental organisations (NGOs) concerned with democracy promotion 'have said very little about social security or rights to work or welfare, and made no criticisms of economic fraud, which occurred on a massive scale in the process of privatization'.
19 See Chapter 6.
20 'In competitive authoritarian regimes, formal democratic institutions are widely viewed as the principal means of obtaining and exercising political authority. Incumbents violate these rules so often and to such an extent, however, that the regime fails to meet conventional minimum standards for democracy' (Levitsky and Way, 2002: 52). They cite as examples in the postcommunist region Croatia, Serbia, Russia, Ukraine, Albania, and Armenia. See also Schedler (2006).
21 Maksym Zherebkin (2009) stresses the theme of collective agency and the formation of political identities.
22 Hale (2006: 308). This is what Norbert Elias (1939) called the 'royal mechanism' (*Königsmechanismus*), but it works equally well for presidents. Their children are, of course, not automatically entitled to succeed them, though this did happen in Azerbaijan, where Heidar Aliyev was succeeded by his son, Ilham. The Box and Cox succession of Putin and Medvedev in Russia is a nongenetic and reversible alternative.
23 Way gives a very prominent place in his analysis to Western links, which are facilitated by, though not reducible to, geographical proximity.
24 See also Lane (2007, 2008). The ambiguity of revolutions and the difference between intentions and outcomes is, of course, nothing new; Christopher Hill once said of the English revolution of the mid-seventeenth century that it was certainly a bourgeois revolution but that the bourgeoisie were on both sides.

References

Baldwin, Richard E. (1995) 'A Domino Theory of Regionalism', in Richard Baldwin, Pertti Haaparanta and Jaakko Kiander (eds.), *Expanding Membership of the European Union*. Cambridge: Cambridge University Press, pp. 25–48.
Baldwin, Richard E., Joseph F. Francois, and Richard Portes (1997) 'The Costs and Benefits of Eastern Enlargement: The Impact on the EU and Central Europe', *Economic Policy*, April: 126–176.
Beck, Ulrich and Edgar Grande (2004) *Das kosmopolitische Europa*. Frankfurt: Suhrkamp. Tr. in 2007 as *Cosmopolitan Europe*. Cambridge: Polity.
Beck, Ulrich and Edgar Grande (2007) 'Cosmopolitanism: Europe's Way Out of Crisis', *European Journal of Social Theory*, 10(1): 67–85.

Beissinger, Mark R. (2007) 'Structure and Example in Modular Political Phenomena: The Diffusion of Bulldozer/Rose/Orange/Tulip Revolutions', *Perspectives on Politics*, 5(2) June, 259–276.

Blazyca, George (2002) 'EU Accession: The Polish Case', in Hilary and Mike Ingham (eds.), *EU Expansion to the East. Prospects and Problems*. Cheltenham: Edward Elgar, pp. 205–221.

Brunkhorst, Hauke (2006) 'The Legitimation Crisis of the European Union', *Constellations* 13(2): 165–180.

Cameron, Fraser (ed.) (2004) *The Future of Europe. Integration and Enlargement*. London: Routledge.

Cheterian, Vicken (2009) 'From Reform and Transition to "Coloured Revolutions"', *Journal of Communist Studies and Transition Politics* 25(2–3) June–September, 136–160.

Coricelli, Fabrizio (2007) 'Democracy in the Post-Communist World: Unfinished Business', *East European Politics and Societies*, 21(1): 82–90.

Delcour, Laure (2010) 'Towards a Global Europe?' in George Lawson, Chris Armbruster, and Michael Cox (eds.), *The Global 1989: Continuity and Change in World Politics 1989–2009*. Cambridge: Cambridge University Press, pp. 135–156.

Delpeuch, Jean-Luc (1994) *Post-communisme: L'Europe au défi. Chronique pragoise de la réforme économique au coeur d'une Europe en crise*. Paris: L'Harmattan.

Dimitrova, Antoaneta (2005) 'Europeanization and Civil Service Reform in Central and Eastern Europe', in Schimmelfennig and Sedelmeier (eds.), Chapter 4, pp. 71–90.

Dobson, Lynn and Andreas Follesdal (eds.) (2004) *Political Theory and the European Constitution*. Abingdon: Routledge.

Elias, Norbert (1939) *Über den Prozeß der Zivilisation*. Basel: Verlag Haus zum Falken. Published in English in 2000 as *The Civilizing Process*. Oxford: Blackwell.

Fischer, Joschka (2011) 'Europe's Sovereignty Crisis', /www.social.europe.eu. August 4. Accessed July 27, 2015.

Forbrig, Joerg and Pavol Demeš (eds.) (2007) *Reclaiming Democracy. Civil Society and Electoral Change in Central and Eastern Europe*. Washington, DC: The German Marshall Fund of the United States.

Fukuyama, Francis (2006) *America at the Crossroads: Democracy, Power, and the Neoconservative Legacy*. New Haven: Yale University Press.

Gowan, Peter (1996) 'Eastern Europe, Western Power and Neo-Liberalism', *New Left Review* 216 (March–April): 129–140.

Gower, Jackie (1993) 'EC Relations with Central and Eastern Europe', in Juliet Lodge (ed.), *The European Community and the Challenge of the Future* (2nd edn). New York: St Martin's Press, pp. 289–290.

Gromadzki, Grzegorz et al (2010) *Beyond Colours: Assets and Liabilities of 'Post-Orange' Ukraine*. Kyiv: International Renaissance Foundation and Warsaw: Stefan Batory Foundation.

Gudžinskas, Liutauras (2010) 'European Integration of Postcommunist States: Safe Future or Evolutionary Trap?', *World Political Science Review* 6(1): Article 4.

Hale, Henry E. (2006) 'Democracy or Autocracy on the March? The Colored Revolutions as Normal Dynamics of Patronal Presidentialism', *Communist and Post-Communist Studies* 39: 305–329.

Holmes, Stephen (2003) 'A European Doppelstaat?', *East European Politics and Societies*, 17(1): 107–118.

Horvath, Robert (2011) 'Putin's "Preventive Counter-Revolution": Post-Soviet Authoritarianism and the Spectre of Velvet Revolution', *Europe-Asia Studies* 63(1) January: pp. 1–25.

Howard, Marc Morjé and Philip G. Roessler (2006) 'Liberalizing Electoral Outcomes in Competitive Authoritarian Regimes, *American Journal of Political Science* 50(2) April: pp. 365–381.

Hughes, James, Gwendolyn Sasse, and Claire E Gordon (2004) *Europeanization and Regionalization in the EU's Enlargement to Central and Eastern Europe: The Myth of Conditionality*. Basingstoke: Palgrave.

Ingham, Hilary and Mike Ingham (eds.) (2002) *EU Expansion to the East. Prospects and Problems*. Cheltenham: Edward Edgar.

Jacoby, Wade (1999) 'Priest and Penitent: The European Union as a Force in the Domestic Politics of Eastern Europe', *East European Constitutional Review* 8(1–2): 62–67.

Jacoby, Wade (2002) 'Talking the Talk and Walking the Walk: The Cultural and Institutional Effects of Western Models', in Frank Bönker, Klaus Müller and Andreas Pickel (eds.), *Postcommunist Transformation and the Social Sciences*. Boulder: Rowman & Littlefield, pp. 129–152.

Kandelaki, Giorgi and Giorgi Meladze (2007) 'Enough! Kmara and the Rose Revolution in Georgia', in Forbrig and Demeš (eds.), pp. 101–125.

Khaschchavatsky, Yury (2007) *Kalinovski Square* (Плошча) Baltic Film Production DVD.

Kovács, Melinda (2001) 'Putting Down and Putting Off: The EU's Discursive Strategies in the 1998 and 1999 Follow-Up Reports', in József Böröcz and Melinda Kovács (eds.) *Europe's New Clothes. Unveiling EU Enlargement*. Telford: Central European Review, pp. 196–234.

Krastev, Ivan (2007) 'Where Next or What Next?, in Forbrig and Demeš (eds.), pp. 235–244.

Krzyzanowski, M. (2005) '"European Identity Wanted": On Discursive and Communicative Dimensions of the European Convention', in R. Wodak and P. Chilton (eds.), *A New Agenda for Critical Discourse Analysis: Theory, Methodology, and Interdisciplinarity*. Amsterdam: J. Benjamins, pp. 137–163.

Kuzio, Taras (2008) 'Democratic Breakthroughs and Revolutions in Five Postcommmunist Countries: Comparative Perspectives on the Fourth Wave', *Demokratizatsia* Winter: 97–109.

Kuzio, Taras (2011) 'Political Culture and Democracy: Ukraine as an Immobile State' *East European Politics and Societies* 25(1) February: 88–113.

Lane, David (2007) 'Post-Communist States and the European Union', *Journal of Communist Studies and Transition Politics* 23(4): 461–477.

Lane, David (2008) 'From Chaotic to State-led Capitalism', *New Political Economy* 13(2) June: 177–184.

Lane, David (2009) '"Coloured Revolution as a Political Phenomenon"', *Journal of Communist Studies and Transition Politics* 25(2): 113–135.

Leonhard, Wolfgang (1957) *Child of the Revolution*. London: Collins.

Levitsky, Steven and Lucan A. Way (2002) 'The Rise of Competitive Authoritarianism', *Journal of Democracy* 13(2): 51–65.

Levitsky, Steven and Lucan A. Way (2006) 'Linkage and Leverage. How Do International Factors Change Domestic Balances of Power?', in Andreas Schedler (ed.), *Electoral Authoritarianism. The Dynamics of Unfree Competition*. Boulder: Rienner, pp. 199–216.

Mattli, Walter and Thomas Plümper (2002) 'The Demand-Side Politics of EU Enlargement: Democracy and the Application for EU Membership', *Journal of European Public Policy* 9(4) August: 550–574.

Mayhew, Alan (2000) 'Enlargement of the European Union: An Analysis of the Negotiations with the Central and Eastern European Countries' SEI Working Paper 39.

Mungiu-Pippidi, Alina (2003) 'Culture of Corruption or Accountability Deficit?', *East European Constitutional Review*, 11/12(4/1).

Norman, Peter (2005) *The Accidental Constitution: The Story of the European Convention.* Brussels: EuroComment.

Noutcheva, Gergana and Dimitar Bechev (2008) 'The Successful Laggards: Bulgaria and Romania's Accession to the EU', *East European Politics and Societies* 22(1): pp. 114–144.

Oberhuber, F. (2005) 'Deliberation or "Mainstreaming"? Empirically Researching the European Convention', in R. Wodak and P. Chilton (eds.), *A New Agenda for Critical Discourse Analysis: Theory, Methodology, and Interdisciplinarity.* Amsterdam: J. Benjamins, pp. 165–187.

Outhwaite, William (2006) 'Europe after the EU Enlargement: Cosmopolitanism by Small Steps' in Gerard Delanty (ed.) *Europe and Asia: Beyond East and West,* London: Routledge, pp. 193–202.

Palmowski, Jan (2011) 'The Europeanization of the Nation-State', *Journal of Contemporary History* 46(3): 31–657.

Pop-Eleches, Grigore (2007) 'Between Historical Legacies and the Promise of Western Integration: Democratic Conditionality after Communism', *East European Politics and Societies,* 21, 1, pp. 142–161.

Pridham, Geoffrey (2008a) 'The EU's Political Conditionality and Post-Accession Tendencies: Comparisons from Slovakia and Latvia', *Journal of Common Market Studies,* 46 ( ): 365–387.

Pridham, Geoffrey (2008b) 'Status Quo Bias or Institutionalisation for Reversibility?: The EU's Political Conditionality, Post-Accession Tendencies and Democratic Consolidation in Slovakia', *Europe-Asia Studies,* 60(3): 423–454.

Raik, Kristi (2004) 'EU Accession of Central and Eastern European Countries: Democracy and Integration as Conflicting Logics', *East European Politics and Societies* 18(4): 567–594.

Raik, Kristi (2010) 'Is the EU (Still) Attractive for Ukraine, Belarus and Moldova?', in Andres Kasekamp (ed.), *Estonian Foreign Policy Yearbook 2010,*: Tallinn: Estonian Foreign Policy Institute, pp. 21–42.

Rowlands, Carl (2010) 'Europe's Periphery', *Soundings* 46, pp. 112–123.

Sarotte, Mary (2009) *1989. The Struggle to Create Post-Cold-War Europe.* Princeton: Princeton University Press.

Scharpf, Fritz (2011) 'Monetary Union, Fiscal Crisis and the Preemption of Democracy', London School of Economics: LEQS Annual Lecture Paper, May: 1–56.

Scharpf, Fritz (2014) 'Political Legitimacy in a Non-Optimal Currency Area', in Olaf Cramme and Sara B. Hobolt (eds.), *Democratic Politics in a European Union under Stress.* Oxford: Oxford University Press, pp. 19–47.

Schedler, Andreas (ed.) (2006) *Electoral Authoritarianism: The Dynamics of Unfree Competition.* Boulder: Lynne Rienner.

Schimmelfennig, Frank (2007) 'European Regional Organizations, Political Conditionality and Democratic Transformation in Eastern Europe', *East European Politics and Societies,* 21(1): 126–141.

Schimmelfennig, Frank and Ulrich Sedelmeier (2002) 'Theorizing EU Enlargement: Research Focus, Hypotheses, and the State of Research', *Journal of European Public Policy* 9(4) August: 500–528.

Schimmelfennig, Frank and Ulrich Sedelmeier (eds.) (2005) *The Europeanization of Central and Eastern Europe.* Ithaca: Cornell University Press.

Schimmelfennig, Frank and Hanno Scholtz (2010) 'Legacies and Leverage: EU Political Conditionality and Democracy Promotion in Historical Perspective', *Europe-Asia Studies* 62(3): 443–460.

Silitski, Vitali (2005) 'Is the Age of Post-Soviet Electoral revolutions Over?', *Democracy at Large* 1(4): 8–10.

Silitski, Vitali (2007) 'Different Authoritarianisms, Distinct Patterns of Electoral Change', in Forbrig and Demeš (eds.), pp. 155–173.

Smith, Alasdair, Peter Holmes, Ulrich Sedelmeier, Edward Smith, Helen Wallace, and Alasdair Young (1996) 'The European Union and Central and Eastern Europe: Pre-Accession Strategies'. University of Sussex, Brighton: SEI Working Paper 15.

Solomko, Iryna (2011) 'Yuri Lutsenko: Views from a Prison Cell', *openDemocracy* 15.7.11.

Stepanenko, Victor (2006) 'Civil Society in Post-Soviet Ukraine: Civic Ethos in the Framework of Corrupted Sociality?, *East European Politics and Societies*, 20(4): 571–597.

Streeck, Wolfgang (2013) *Gekaufte Zeit. Die vertagte Krise des demokratischen Kapitalismus*. Berlin: Suhrkamp.

Stykow, Petra (2010) '"Bunte Revolutionen" – Durchbruch zur Demokratie oder Modus der autoritären Systemreproduktion?', *Politische Vierteljahresschrift* 51: 137–162.

Szadziewski, Henryk (2011) 'The Uyghurs, China and Central Asia', *openDemocracy* 26 July.

Tewes, Henning (1998) 'Between Deepening and Widening: Role Conflict in Germany's Enlargement Policy', *West European Politics* 21(2): 117–133.

Tsebelis, George (2008) 'Thinking about the Recent Past and the Future of the EU', *Journal of Common Market Studies* 46(2): 265–292.

Vachudová, Milada Anna (2005) *Europe Undivided. Democracy, Leverage, and Integration After Communism*. Oxford: Oxford University Press.

Vobruba, Georg (2005) *Die Dynamik Europas*. Wiesbaden: VS Verlag für die Sozialwissenschaften.

Vurmo, Gjergji (2008) 'Relations of Albania with the EU.' Budapest: Center for EU Enlargement Studies.

Way, Lucan (2008) 'The Real Causes of the Color Revolutions', *Journal of Democracy* 19(3): 55–69.

Way, Lucan (2009) 'A Reply to My Critics', *Journal of Democracy* 20(1): 90–97.

White, Stephen and Ian McAllister (2009) 'Rethinking the "Orange Revolution"', *Journal of Communist Studies and Transition Politics*, 25(2–3): 227–254.

York, Steve (2002) *Bringing Down a Dictator*. DVD.

York, Steve (2007) *Orange Revolution*. DVD.

Zherebkin, Maksym (2009) 'In Search of a Theoretical Approach to the Analysis of the 'Colour Revolutions': Transition Studies and Discourse theory', *Communist and Post-Communist Studies* 42(2): 199–216.

Zielonka, Jan (2007a) *Europe as Empire. The Nature of the Enlarged European Union*. Oxford: Oxford University Press.

Zielonka, Jan (2007b) 'The Quality of Democracy after Joining the European Union', *East European Politics and Societies*, 21(1): 162–180.

6   The Russian enigma

I cannot forecast to you the action of Russia. It is a riddle wrapped in a mystery inside an enigma. (Winston Churchill, broadcast of October 1, 1939)

The cliché is an old one, but no less relevant today. As a leading US Sovietologist, Raymond Bauer (1952: ix), used to say, 'it is axiomatic in the field of Soviet Studies that one is never right . . . only wrong with varying degrees of vulnerability'.[1] Russia, like the United States, can never be just a 'normal country' because of its vast size. And like the United States, though in a rather different way, it has historically been pulled between European and continental attachments. Its relationship to its past tsarist and communist empires remains deeply problematic. Dualistic in a way which recalls Latin America or even India, it served as a source of raw materials to the more advanced countries which it dominated politically in the second half of the twentieth century, and is now doing so also, on a more equal basis, with China. For the European Union, it is too big to include, but also too big to treat as just another bit of the eastern periphery.

Russia, in the form of the Soviet Union, was the key factor behind the transition process with which this book is concerned. If Gorbachev had not been selected as general secretary in 1985, or if he had become incapacitated, '1989' might well have taken place a decade or more later, and in a very different form. For a time it looked as if Russia might have responded to the 1989 process in Central and Eastern Europe in a more cautious manner appropriate to a much larger and less easily manageable state. To put it crudely, it might have looked more like China or Belarus today. Alternatively, in the more attractive counterfactual scenario sketched out by David Lane (1996: 196),

> Had the political leadership of Gorbachev supported reformist elements within the political class (including the military), and relied on support from the working class and those with positions in the public sector (such as teachers and health workers), there would have been an alliance which would have backed within-system reform and would have opposed a radical (and uncontrollable) move to the market and the privatization of assets.

Peter Rutland (2013: 349) seems to concur:

> All the usual preconditions for social democracy seemed to be in place: a
> large organized working class; an urban, educated workforce with high levels
> of female participation; low levels of social inequality; full employment; uni-
> versal welfare state institutions . . . There was a large army of bureaucrats and
> managers accustomed to working within a state-owned economy. There was
> a broad consensus on the importance of social rights, with polls indicating a
> preference for Swedish-style social democracy as an ideal form of political
> regime.

In the event, Russia probably got the worst of the alternative postcommunist
worlds of fast-track transition and gradualism. (As Rutland (2013: 345) points
out, there is rarely a simple choice between these alternatives, which are politically constrained.) In most of its economic and political structures, Russia can
be located at one extreme of the continuum sketched out in the previous chapter;
in its geopolitical situation, both internally and externally, and its national self-
perception, it is *sui generis*. (Dawisha and Parrott, 1997; Shevtsova 2010)

Valerie Bunce (1999: 25) uses an image developed by Maria Csánadi (1997)
of Soviet-type party-states as 'fractal' structures, in which 'each unit within the
system reproduced the overall structure of the system'. In the case of the Soviet
Union, which she examines along with two rather different federations, Czechoslovakia and Yugoslavia, the imperial structure was both inside (the Soviet Union)
and outside (the Soviet bloc). Both, while projecting the power of the Russian
centre, imposed massive economic costs on it and 'tie[d] the fate of the state
and the bloc to the fate of the regime' (Bunce, 1999: 39). Under Gorbachev, the
Soviet Union destabilised the satellite dictatorships by its own example of reform[2]
and by withdrawing the guarantee of the 'Brezhnev doctrine' that the fraternal
states would come to the aid wherever socialism was threatened in the bloc. The
1989 revolutions, in turn, destabilised the Soviet Union, whose breakup in 1991
resulted from both secessionist moves by states and regions in the periphery and
by Russia itself under Yeltsin's leadership.

> Thus, while neither Boris Yeltsin of Russia nor Václav Klaus of the Czech
> lands favored an end to the state, this outcome nonetheless met their most
> cherished concerns: to leave socialism, to build a new order, to defeat their
> main rivals, and to maintain at the least their regional bases of political power.
>
> (Bunce 1999: 136)

Putin is not alone in bemoaning, as he did in a speech in 2005, the breakup
of the Soviet Union as a 'geopolitical catastrophe': in a recent survey (Levada,
November 2014), over half of respondents said they regretted it and that it could
have been avoided, against just over a quarter saying they did not regret it. An
even larger proportion (61%) disapproved of the agreement between Russia,
Belarus, and Ukraine which sealed the dissolution. Whereas only 13% favoured

the 'restoration of the USSR in its previous form', two thirds supported closer union of the former republics or at least the continuation of the Commonwealth of Independent States in its present form, as opposed to complete independence, supported by only 11%. An earlier survey (Levada, January 2011) had over three quarters 'definitely' or 'probably' in support of 'the opinion that Russia should restore its status of "Great Empire"'.[3]

Postimperial issues have shaped the subsequent history of Russia at least as much as domestic political and economic concerns. As Stephen Kotkin (2008: 6) wrote, 'Russia has inherited everything that had caused the Soviet collapse, as well as the collapse itself'. The broad outlines of political and economic developments in postcommunist Russia, as well as in the rest of the bloc, have been discussed in earlier chapters, and this chapter therefore concentrates on geopolitical issues.

It is tempting to present Russian postcommunism as Hegel's revenge on Marx and Lenin, in the sense that many of the developments seem to produce their opposites. Gorbachev's programme of acceleration (uskorenie) led to economic dislocation and stagnation. An apparently egalitarian privatisation programme based on the distribution of vouchers to employees led to the concentration of economic ownership in a new class of merchant capitalist oligarchs[4] and obscene extremes of wealth and poverty redolent of the precommunist period. A crash programme of economic transformation produced stagnation in production and an economy massively dependent on the sale of natural resources and on speculation. The abolition of the Communist Party's monopoly and of the party itself led to a super-presidential system, in which 'democrat' was often a term of abuse and a facade coexisting with authoritarian rule. Some observers have suggested that, beyond the 'Box and Cox' exchanges of office between Putin and Medvedev, there is a longer-term prospect of an endless oscillation between Putinian stability or stagnation and Yeltsinian chaos (Prozorov, 2009: 82).

The economic malaise is illustrated by the simple contrast between the loss of gross domestic product (GDP) in the Soviet Union/Russia in the early 1990s and that in the rest of the bloc. By 1995 Poland, which had also been subjected to a crash programme, was back to the level of 1989, and most of the bloc to three quarters of that level or, in some cases, such as Czecho-Slovakia and Hungary, much better. In Russia the figure is 60%, and more like 50% if one assumes that the growth of the 1980s had continued (Dunford, 1998: 92, 94–95) By then, the intensity of the programme had declined, with Yegor Gaidar (1995), who had presided over it as acting prime minister, providing a good description of

> ... the main problem of present-day capitalism ... the utmost intertwining of property and power ... the closest intertwining of business and bureaucracy. In the majority of cases the success of an enterprise depends not on the ability of the director or the owner to organize normal production, but on his ability to correctly give bribes, on whether he has sufficiently high patrons ... his ability to get cheap money out of the budget, and so on.

After the 1998 economic crisis and Yeltsin's anointing of Putin as his successor at the end of the century, the economic upturn was comparably dramatic, with Putin taking firm control of many of the private oligarchs (by means up to and including state terrorism) as well as those in the public sector. Setting a kleptocrat to catch other kleptocrats (Dawisha, 2014) looked like a promising path, though the economy remained seriously imbalanced and dependent on raw material exports, as recently demonstrated by the fall in oil prices. Oil and gas themselves account for less than 20% of GDP but over 70% of exports, which are heavily dominated by raw materials rather than manufactured goods. Already in the 1990s, commentators were writing of the 'Kuwaitization' of Russia. As Hanson and Teague (2007: 152) argue, Russia does not really fit the 'varieties of capitalism' model: Max Weber's model of 'political capitalism' is a better guide. In Russia, 'Big business is both subdued by the state and unpopular with the people' (Hanson and Teague, 2007: 162).

As for democracy, there is a certain parallel between Putin's Russia and models of postdemocracy focused on the West. In both cases, the democratic forms of elections and so on remain, but hollowed out and undermined by media control and electoral manipulation. Steven Fish's model focuses rather more narrowly on domestic economic and political factors. 'In this book's story, three variables explain Russia's failure to democratize. They are too much oil, too little economic liberalization, and too weak a national legislature' (Fish, 2005: 247). Russia is, however, probably best understood, as Richard Sakwa (2010) has argued, in terms of Ernst Fraenkel's model of a dual state as he applied it to Nazi Germany, in which the formal institutions of democracy and the rule of law coexist with practices of authoritarian rule which, at worst, are neatly captured in the state socialist euphemism of 'administrative measures' or what used to be called 'terror'. Sakwa (2010b: 41) points to the differences:

> In Germany the regime openly proclaimed the priority of non-constitutional imperatives as the guiding principles of the state . . . whereas in Russia the fundamental legitimacy of the regime is derived from it being embedded in a constitutional order that it is sworn to defend. On the other side, Germany had a long history of robust constitutionalism, whereas Russia lacks a strong constitutional culture, and thus the rule of law and the independence of the judiciary are at best tenuous . . . the tension between the two systems defines the political order in Russia.

In a depressing paradox, the presidency becomes *more* respected than the parliament (Sakwa, 2010a: 200; 2010b). The year 2013 was the first in which 'yes' responses to the rather loaded question 'Do you think that V. Putin concentrating practically all the power in the country is going to be beneficial for Russia?' dipped below 50%, to 49% (Levada, 2013: 110). Whether this is a lasting feature of the system remains to be seen. Where Prozorov foresees a continuing oscillation between stagnation and 'messianic' and disorderly innovation, Sakwa (2010: 203) points to the possibility of a happier outcome. 'Genuine constitutionalism and the rule of law may well develop in Russia without necessarily having to change the letter of the constitution'.[5]

Historians, especially in Germany, have traditionally argued about the relative explanatory primacy of domestic versus foreign policy. Russia is unusual in the degree of their imbrication in both elite and public opinion. Iver Neumann (2008: 128–129), in a survey covering nearly two centuries, notes 'the tacit assumption that a small-power Russia is an impossibility. Russia has to be a great power, or it will be nothing'. He quotes the tsarist foreign minister Izvolsky's assertion that 'decline to the level of a second class power . . . [and] . . . an Asiatic state . . . would be a major catastrophe for Russia'.

The term 'state' refers, in all the languages I know, both to a territorial entity and to the governmental apparatus within that entity. In Britain, the historian Linda Colley (1992) has shown how the development of the state in the eighteenth century was crucially shaped by the interstate and military context. In the Russian case, too,

> The creation of centralised autocracy from the sixteenth century was a response to security threats and memories of centuries of Mongol domination. Despite the profundity of Russia's post-communist transition, this causal link remains between relatively autonomous state power at home and geopolitical challenges abroad.
>
> (Sakwa 2011: 209)

State power in Russia in its relation to society has always been imperial, both domestically, in the empire itself, and in the wider world. Moshe Lewin, the author of a brilliant book with the modest title *Political Undercurrents in Soviet Economic Debates* (1974), drew more general conclusions in his later book (1988) on Gorbachev. In the Soviet debates on economic reform which began in the 1960s, critics focused on 'the clash . . . between "interests of social groups" or of "society", as they saw it, and state policy and its plans' (Lewin, 1974: 159).

> To replace or reshape the bureaucratic centralized agencies, now obviously inadequate for their tasks, to unleash more initiative of producers and of social forces in general were the big aims. Obviously, such goals could be reached only through a redefinition of roles and relations between state and society, limiting and reorganizing the former, diminishing its prerogatives and immense power, and redistributing it in new ways over different social groups.
>
> (Lewin 1974: 215–216)

The obstacles in the 1960s, the 1980s, and, in a different way, the 1990s were political, with the closing down by a nervous Soviet state of earlier reforms of Stalinist central planning (Lewin, 1988; Neumann, 2008: 143), later paralleled by Putin's restoration of state control over the oligarchs.

Imperial rule, whether in eighteenth-century Prussia, colonial Africa (Spittler, 1981), or Russia, is necessarily distanced, with instructions emitted from the centre, reports submitted to it, and occasional demonstrative interventions and displays to reinforce the power and prestige of the local or metropolitan centre. It can be contrasted, as in Neumann's analysis, with Foucault's model of 'governmentality' as it emerged from as early as the sixteenth century in parts of Western Europe, which 'has as its discursive prerequisite a move away from thinking about subjects as part of a household headed by the sovereign, towards thinking of them as a partially self-organized productive group (Neumann, 2008: 133). There are elements of this shift in Russian policy in the reign of Catherine the Great, but reform programmes were limited by concerns for domestic and national security (Lincoln, 1982; Neumann, 2008). Running through late tsarism and the Soviet period to the present, the idea of the strong state (both internally and internationally) remains a constant.

We should not perhaps be surprised to see this way of thinking among political and intellectual elites. What is more surprising is for it to be replicated in public opinion. In the Levada (2013) survey cited earlier, nearly a quarter of respondents said they would like Russia to become 'a socialist state like the USSR', with a third each for the two alternatives offered: 'a state like Western states with a democratic government system and market economy' and 'a state with a special system and a unique course of development'. Surveys in 2002 and 2012 registered stable levels of support for the following statements:

> To ensure a successful development, Russia should become an open country, join the world community; otherwise we are doomed to fall behind other countries (58% and 59%, respectively).
>
> To ensure a successful development, Russia should not open to the world – otherwise openness will destroy our unique culture, whereas we should not be afraid of lagging behind others, as we have enough resources to be successful (42%).

The same survey had a substantial minority wanting Russia to be

> A powerful military country, where the interests of the state and country's prestige and the position in the world is of paramount importance (30% in 2002; 22% in 2012),

as against

> A comfortable and liveable country, where human wellbeing, interests and opportunities is the prime concern (70% in 2002; 78% in 2012).

In 2012, those who thought Russia needed democracy (nearly two thirds, as against a quarter who saw it as 'unsuitable') wanted this to be

> Like in developed countries of Europe and America (27%)
>
> Like in the former Soviet Union (20%)

A special kind, which suits national traditions and the specific Russian character (38%)

Of those who regretted the breakup of the USSR, equal numbers cited as the reason that

'People no longer feel they belong to a great power', and 'A single economic system is destroyed'.

(Other reasons were more practical concerns about travel and so on.)

Attitudes of this kind to Russia's position in the world, rather than his personal charisma, such as it is, may explain the continuing popularity of Putin's rule.[6] They are, of course, partly sustained by state propaganda in a country where the vast majority of citizens rely on state-controlled media, but they are also shaped by more substantial deep structures of a postimperial consciousness captured in the quotation earlier from Izvolsky. Another much-cited remark in 2004 by a nationalist politician and publicist, Natalia Narochnitskaya, currently director of the Paris office of a Russian think tank, illustrates this, claiming that

The dilemma of 'Russia and Europe' does not haunt Russia and the Russians: on the contrary, it haunts Europe, which, having built its 'paradise on earth', remains apprehensive of our magnitude and our capacity to withstand all challenges.

(Prozorov 2006: 42; 2007: 316)

Four words or phrases, two Russian and the other two more familiar internationally, encapsulate this set of attitudes. First, *derzhava*, or power (in the sense in which it is used in English in 'great powers', or in the first line of the current Russian national anthem, rather than the more general term '*vlast*'). Derzhava is also, as it happens, the name of a small nationalist party founded by Alexander Rutskoi in 1994 and to which Narochnitskaya briefly belonged. Used by Catherine the Great in her decree (nakaz) of 1767, which asserted that 'Russia is a European power' (Ram, 1998: 41), it came into use in the 1990s in the nationalist opposition to what was perceived as a sell-out to the West by Gorbachev and Yeltsin. Second, *imperia*, or empire, which has moved from the discourse of extremist politics to the centre and is increasingly used by Putin and others (Ryazanova-Clarke, 2008, 2013). Dmitry Trenin (2012: 14) has written that 'It was in a fit of self-renewal, which also included an element of self-denial, that Russia in 1990–1991 simply shook off its empire – a move with few parallels in history'. He goes on:

Russia . . . is a rare case of a former imperial polity having neither disappeared nor reinvented itself as a nation-state, but seeking to reconstitute itself as a great power, with a regional base and global interests . . . While no longer a pretender to world hegemony and staying within its new, shrunken borders, Russia has been trying hard to establish itself in the top league of the world's major players and as the dominant power in its neighborhood. Even more strikingly, as it promoted its bid on the world stage, it has been striving, simultaneously, to keep itself in one piece. This is a dual adventure almost unparalleled in modern history.

(Trenin 2012: 30)

For Trenin (2012: 244) 'Russia will never again be an empire. To be seen as a great power in the twenty-first century, however, it has to become a great country, above all for its own people'. For the moment, the empire functions mainly as an object of confused nostalgia for a gradually shrinking number of Russians and as a slogan legitimating a set of rather dangerous orientations in foreign policy. These are encapsulated in the other two themes: the 'near abroad' (blizhneye zarubezhye) and 'Eurasia'. The first is a relatively recent coinage from the early 1990s to refer to the former Soviet republics, with echoes of the Monroe Doctrine in the United States. 'Eurasia', by contrast, is a long-standing conception, going back at least to the late nineteenth century, which links a geographical region to an idea of Russia's special position, often as a bridge between Europe and Asia. Nurtured by Soviet émigrés, it returned as a trope of right-wing discourse and echoes through some of the survey responses cited earlier. Although, as Andrei Tsygankov (2003) has argued, Eurasianist geopolitical thinking is quite diverse, the liberal segment of Eurasianist opinion which he characterizes as 'Westerniz-ers' is very much a minority current.

Trenin, who had written off the concept in 2002, has more recently canvassed the idea of a larger conception of Eurasia, taking account of flows of tourists and migrants between Russia and South and East Asia. A Russia orienting itself, as the United States has done, more strongly towards the Pacific might, on this account, be more cosmopolitan and less paranoid. On the other hand, as Abbott Gleason (2010: 31) points out,

> In the east and south, the Indian and Chinese economies are already crowd-ing Russia. Despite Russia's energy resources and all their political uses, the booming economies and expanding populations of China and India too contrast almost grotesquely with Russia's looming demographic crises and dwindling Slavic population.

The current Russian regime, and perhaps any future one, will expect to play some sort of hegemonic role in the region, while suffering from a legacy of suspicion which undercuts its cultural resources of soft power and a variety of connections which have been sustained over the post-Soviet decades. The alternative of isola-tionism, which was an option for the United States, is probably not for a Russia with a host of unstable states around its borders. As Peter Rutland (2012: 345) points out,

> Russia's real security concerns are battling Islamist terrorism emanating from the Caucasus, Central Asia, and the Middle East, and preventing the further consolidation of a US military presence around Russia's periphery – again, in

the Caucasus and Central Asia. The US military 'encirclement' of Russia is more a diffuse strategic or economic challenge than a direct military threat.

In surveys such as those cited earlier, suspicion of the United States is particularly strong.[7] The 2014 Levada survey recorded only 1% of 'very positive' or 'likely positive' attitudes to President Obama, as against 16% neutral and 76% negative or likely negative. The United States was listed as the fourth country 'most unfriendly and hostile to Russia', sandwiched between Georgia, the Baltic States, and Ukraine (with which Russia was already in a covert war). Six months later, 13% of respondents felt 'good' about the United States, as against 81% 'bad'. Attitudes to the EU, which had earlier been generally favourable, with 62% positive as against 20% negative in 2012, had by now caught up with the United States, with 20% feeling 'good' and 71% 'bad' – probably in the wake of the economic sanctions introduced following the annexation of Crimea and the incursions into Ukraine. Russians, like Belorussians and Ukrainians, had been feeling themselves 'less European' over the early years of this century (Korosteleva and White, 2006), with rather little difference between 'European' Russia and the rest of the country. Maria Chepurina (2011) writes that, whereas a 1999 poll

> . . . revealed that 79% of Russians consider Russia to be a European country, while 21% identify themselves with Asia . . . less than 10 years later, in 2007, the Levada center together with the EU-Russia Center poll revealed a completely opposite tendency. Only 20% of the 1600 people polled considered themselves European, while 71% did not. Moreover, 45% considered the EU a potential threat to Russia, either financially, politically or culturally.[8]

All this makes relations with Russia a particularly sensitive issue for the EU, widely perceived in Russia and also in much of Europe to be too subservient to the United States and the North Atlantic Treaty Organization (NATO). This should not be exaggerated: even if the United States did not exist or embraced an isolationist foreign policy, there is a substantial body of opinion in the European Union which is highly suspicious of Russia. What can be said is that, as Mary Sarotte (2009) argued, chances were missed in 1989–1990 to establish a more cooperative relation between the West and the Soviet Union which would no doubt have shaped relations with Russia in the following decades.[9] The size of the country is, of course, a constant; imagine if North America were attached to Scotland, as it was a geological age ago, and Europe were heavily dependent on its mineral resources. One does not need to be an old-fashioned geopolitical determinist to attach some importance to space and size.

Notes

1 Martin Malia (1999) documents the largely unsuccessful attempts by foreign observers to understand Russia.
2 In the German Democratic Republic (GDR), as noted earlier, the slogan that 'learning from the Soviet Union means learning how to win' became an embarrassment.

3 The theme of empire across the end of the Soviet Union was brilliantly theorised by Alexander Filippov; see, for example, Filippov (1992). See also Ryazanova-Clarke (2013: 109–114) on the imagery of space in state propaganda.
4 Michael Burawoy (1995: 82–85) stressed the parallel between postfeudal merchant capital in Western Europe and the postcommunist form.
5 See also Fish (2005), esp. Chapter 8.
6 See, for instance, March (2012). Opposition is weak and divided, though displaying impressive bravery in the face of repression and state terrorism. Mischa Gabowitsch (2013) provides a thorough and optimistic survey.
7 This may, however, be more a product of current state propaganda than more fundamental attitudes (Shlapentokh, 2011: 878; see also Fekylyunina, 2014: 105).
8 See also Dutkiewicz and Sakwa (2014).
9 For some alternative scenarios up to 2030, see Hett, Kellner, and Martin (2014). For a recent overview of Russia in the context of postsocialist transformation as a whole, see Lane (2014: Chapter 18).

References

Bauer, Raymond (1952) *The New Man in Soviet Psychology*. Cambridge: Harvard University Press.

Bunce, Valerie (1999) *Subversive Institutions. The Design and the Destruction of Socialism and the State*. Cambridge: Cambridge University Press.

Burawoy, Michael (1995) 'From Sovietology to Comparative Political Economy', in Daniel Orlovsky (ed.), *Beyond Soviet Studies*. Washington, D.C.: Woodrow Wilson Center Press, pp. 72–102.

Chepurina, Maria (2011) 'Is Russian Identity European Identity?' *In Focus*: http://infocusre vue.com/2011/04/21/is-russian-identity-european-identity/#_edn13. Accessed July 27, 2015.

Colley, Linda (1992) *Britons. Forging the Nation 1707–1837*. New Haven: Yale University Press.

Csanádi, Mária (1997) *Party-States and Their Legacies in Post-Communist Transformation*. Cheltenham: Edward Elgar.

Dawisha, Karen (2014) *Putin's Kleptocracy: Who Owns Russia?* New York: Simon and Schuster.

Dawisha, Karen and Bruce Parrott (eds.) (1997) *The End of Empire? The Transformation of the USSR in Comparative Perspective*. New York: M. E. Sharpe.

Dunford, Michael (1998) 'Differential Development, Institutions, Modes of Regulation and Comparative Transitions to Capitalism', in John Pickles and Adrian Smith (eds.), *Theorising Transition. The Political Economy of Post-Communist Transformations*. London: Routledge, pp. 76–111.

Dutkiewicz, Piotr and Richard Sakwa (eds.) (2014) *Eurasian Integration: The View from Within*. Abingdon: Routledge.

Fekylyunina, Valentina (2014) 'Constructing Russophobia', in Ray Taras (ed.), *Russia's Identity in International Relations: Images, Perceptions, Misperceptions*. Basingstoke: Palgrave, pp. 91–109.

Filippov, Alexander (1992) 'Eliten im postimperialen Reichsraum', *Berliner Debatte – Initial* 6: 45–49.

Fish, M. Steven (2005) *Democracy Derailed in Russia. The Failure of Open Politics*. Cambridge: Cambridge University Press.

Gabowitsch, Mischa (2013) *Putin kaput!? Russlands neue Protestkultur*. Berlin: Suhrkamp.

Gaidar, Yegor (1995) Press conference, cited in James Leitzel, 'Rule Evasion in Transitional Russia', in Joan Nelson, Charles Tilly, and Lee Walker (eds.) (1997) *Transforming Post-Communist Political Economies*. Washington, D.C.: National Academy Press, p. 127.

Gleason, Abbott (2010) 'Eurasia: What Is it? Is it?', *Journal of Eurasian Studies* 1: 26–32.

Hanson, Philip and Elizabeth Teague (2007) 'Russian Political Capitalism and Its Environment', in David Lane and Martin Myant (eds.) *Varieties of Capitalism in Post-Communist Countries*. Basingstoke: Palgrave, pp. 149–164.

Hett, Felix, Anna Maria Kellner, and Beate Martin (2014) *The EU and the East in 2030 – Four Scenarios for Relations between the EU, The Russian Federation, and the Common Neighbourhood*. Berlin: Friedrich-Ebert-Stiftung.

Korosteleva, Julia and White, Stephen (2006) "Feeling European": The View from Belarus, Russia and Ukraine. *Contemporary Politics* 12(2): 193–205.

Kotkin, Stephen (2008) *Armageddon Averted: The Soviet Collapse, 1970–2000*. Oxford: Oxford University Press.

Lane, David (1996) *The Rise and Fall of State Socialism*. Cambridge: Polity.

Lane, David (2014) *The Capitalist Transformation of State Socialism*. Abingdon: Routledge.

Levada Center and CSSP, Strathclyde (n.d.) *Russia Votes*. www.russiavotes.org/#. Accessed July 27, 2015.

Levada Center (2013) *Russian Public Opinion 2012–2013*. www.levada.ru/books/obshchestvennoe-mnenie-2012-eng. Accessed July 27, 2015.

Lewin, Moshe (1974) *Political Undercurrents in Soviet Economic Debates*. London: Pluto.

Lewin, Moshe (1988) *The Gorbachev Phenomenon: A Historical Interpretation*. Berkeley and Los Angeles: University of California Press (2nd edn. 1991).

Lincoln, Bruce (1982) *In the Vanguard of Reform: Russia's Enlightened Bureaucrats, 1825–1861*. DeKalb: Northern Illinois University Press.

Malia, Martin (1999) *Russia Under Western Eyes*. Cambridge: Harvard University Press.

March, Luke (2012) 'Nationalism for Export? The Domestic and Foreign-Policy Implications of the New "Russian Idea" ', *Europe-Asia Studies* 64(3): 401–425.

Neumann, Iver (2008) 'Russia as a Great Power, 1815–2007', *Journal of International Relations and Development* 11: 128–151.

Prozorov, Sergei (2006) *Understanding Conflict Between Russia and the EU: The Limits of Integration*. Basingstoke: Palgrave.

Prozorov, Sergei (2007) 'The Narratives of Exclusion and Self-exclusion in the Russian Conflict Discourse on EU-Russian Relations', *Political Geography* 26: 309–329.

Prozorov, Sergei (2009) *The Ethics of Postcommunism. History and Social Praxis in Russia*. Basingstoke: Palgrave.

Ram, Harsha (1998) 'Russian Poetry and the Imperial Sublime', in Monika Greenleaf and Stephen Moeller-Sally (eds.), *Russian Subjects: Empire, Nation, and the Culture of the Golden Age*. Evanston: Northwestern University Press, pp. 21–49.

Rutland, Peter (2012) 'Still Out in the Cold? Russia's Place in a Globalizing world', *Communist and Post-Communist Studies* 45(3–4) September–December: 343–354.

Rutland, Peter (2013) 'Neoliberalism and the Russian Transition', *Review of International Political Economy* 20(2): 332–362.

Ryazanova-Clarke, Lara (2008) 'Identity and Masculinity at the Extremities of the Russian Mainstream', Paper given at the AAASS National Convention, Philadelphia.

Ryazanova-Clarke, Lara (2013) 'The Discourse of a Spectacle at the End of the Presidential Term', in Helena Goscilo (ed.), *Putin as Celebrity and Cultural Icon*. London: Routledge, pp. 104–132.

Sakwa, Richard (2010a) 'The Dual State in Russia', *Post-Soviet Affairs* 26(3): 185–206.

Sakwa, Richard (2010b) *The Crisis of Russian Democracy. The Dual State, Factionalism and the Medvedev Succession.* Cambridge: Cambridge University Press.

Sakwa, Richard (2011) 'Russia and Europe: Whose Society?', *Journal of European Integration* 33(2): 197–214.

Sarotte, Mary (2009) *1989. The Struggle to Create Post-Cold-War Europe.* Princeton: Princeton University Press.

Shevtsova, Lilia (2010) *Lonely Power: Why Russia Has Failed to Become the West and the West Is Weary of Russia.* Washington, D.C.: Carnegie Endowment for World Peace.

Shlapentokh, Vladimir (2011) 'The Puzzle of Russian Anti-Americanism: From Below or From Above', *Europe-Asia Studies* 63(5): 875–879.

Spittler, Gerd (1981) *Verwaltung in einem afrikanischen Bauernstaat: Das koloniale Französisch-Westafrika 1919–1939* (Beiträge zur Kolonial- und Überseegeschichte). Wiesbaden: Steiner.

Trenin, Dmitri (2002) *The End of Eurasia: Russia on the Border Between Geopolitics and Globalization.* Washington, D.C.: Carnegie Endowment for International Peace.

Trenin, Dmitri (2012) *Post-Imperium. A Eurasian Story.* Washington, D.C.: Carnegie Endowment for International Peace.

Tsygankov, Andre P. (2003) 'Mastering Space in Eurasia: Russia's Geopolitical Thinking after the Soviet Break-up', *Communist and Post-Communist Studies 36*: 101–127.

7   European democracy and civil society

The uniting of Europe was initiated as a Western European project in the 1950s, and since 1989 it has made sense to think of Europe as a whole, even if statistical resources, academic specialisms, and political arrangements have taken some time to catch up. As we saw in the previous chapters, the process is far from complete. More seriously, Laure Delcour (2010: 148) has argued that 'through making the EU more diverse and more fragmented, through shifting the integration project from its initial philosophy, 1989 has indirectly contributed to blockages in the European construction'. Although this chapter focuses quite substantially on the European Union, I am concerned with Europe in a broader sense which is not reducible to, though it is partially determined by, the Union. As I argue more fully in Chapter 9, if the Union ceased to exist or had never existed, Europe would still be a region of the world made up of states with considerable economic, political, and cultural commonalities and substantial transnational processes and structures. As we have seen, however, the centripetal force of the Union has been a crucial element in the conjuncture facing European states. Alan Milward (1992) wrote of the 'European rescue of the nation-state', and we might ask, twenty years on, if something like this process has continued (Stråth, 2011).

The alleged rescue of the nation-state was both political and economic, with the political rescue carried out essentially by economic means. Part of the motivation behind the formation of the Coal and Steel Community was to prevent political tension or worse between France and the recently created Federal Republic of Germany, but putting their mining and steel industries, along with those of four other states, under a common authority was certainly a roundabout route. If we accept Milward's assessment that economic integration 'was probably one of the primary causes of the increase in incomes and prosperity throughout most of the common market over the last twenty years' (Milward, 2004: 145), the political effects are less easy to assess. Economic prosperity was, of course, itself a substantial contributor to the political legitimacy of European governments, but one should also remember that France experienced governmental instability in the 1950s and a major political crisis in 1958, culminating in what was effectively a coup by De Gaulle, while Italy was also fraught with political conflict and right-wing and other criminal conspiracies – in particular the 'p2' (Propaganda Due) Masonic lodge which operated until 1981. With hindsight, West German democracy seems extremely robust, but it was not always seen that way, as documented by the heated character of various controversies, such as the 'Spiegel affair' in 1962, the emergency legislation of 1968, or the Guillaume espionage case of 1974.

Did the European Economic Community help democracy in its member states? Certainly not directly: when De Gaulle, under pressure in 1968, flew to Germany, it was to consult one of his own generals at a French military base. Overall, though, the existence of shared structures (European Community, North Atlantic Treaty Organization, Organisation for European Cooperation and Development [EC, NATO, OECD], and others) may have had a calming influence over the postwar period. The significance of this line of thinking becomes clearer when the Community took in Greece in 1981, newly emerged from a military dictatorship, and the formerly postfascist Spain (which had suffered two coup attempts, in 1981 and again in 1982) and Portugal in 1986. As we saw in the previous chapter, it seems to have been another coup attempt, in the Soviet Union in 1991, which persuaded the EU member states of the importance of an opening to the East. Bulgaria and Romania were later pressed to continue along their accession paths (albeit with a 'safeguard clause' imposed on Romania at the end of 2004 that might have delayed its accession until 2008 if it did not fulfil specified 'commitments and requirements'), because of fears that the political windows of opportunity might not remain open indefinitely. 'Romania (with Bulgaria) was placed under constant pressure to improve its level of implementation right up to the final decision over entry in September 2006' (Pridham, 2007: 239; see also Pridham, 2010).

The democratic credentials of the EU remain, of course, crucially dependent on the quality of democracy in its member states. The restoration of formal democratic structures after 1989 went extremely smoothly in most of the postcommunist region, despite ongoing controversies over constitutional issues, lustration, and so on. By 1997, Mary Kaldor and Ivan Vejvoda and the country specialists contributing to their volume, which had been commissioned by the EU in 1995, were able to record that formal procedures were in place in all ten accession candidate countries in the following areas:

> [I]inclusive citizenship, rule of law, separation of powers, election of power-holders ('members of the legislature and those who control the executive'), free and fair elections, freedom of expression and alternative sources of information, associational autonomy and civilian control of the armed forces and security services.
>
> (Kaldor and Vejvoda, 2002: 6)

With the exception of Slovakia, the only serious 'hindrances to implementation' concerned citizenship issues in Estonia and Latvia (as well as Slovakia). The rule of law, they noted, was not fully bedded in, leaving 'a continued sense of individual insecurity in a number of the countries under review' (Kaldor and Vejvoda, 2002: 6). Presidents (Wałęsa, Iliescu) and prime ministers (Mečiar) had on occasion done violence to the constitution and the separation of powers and 'in some countries, especially Romania and Slovakia, the so-called dark forces, remnants of the secret police, lurk in the shadows of politics and society' (Kaldor and Vejvoda, 2002: 7).

The editors went on, however, to examine elements of what they called 'substantive democracy':

> These features include the character of constitutions and the way in which human rights are perceived; the role of political parties and the extent to which they provide a vehicle for political participation; the role of the media and the extent to which they are capable of representing the broad political debate; whether and how far the former communist administration has been able to transform itself into a genuine public service which individuals trust; the degree to which local government is able to manage and respond to local concerns; and finally, the existence of an active civil society.
>
> (Kaldor and Vejvoda, 2001: 8)

On the first issue, while broadly welcoming the constitutional developments, they note that

> . . .[t]he problem of individual and collective (minority) rights is one of the stumbling-blocks of the CEES. Lacking a rights-based culture, slanted towards a communitarian outlook, with a scarcity of resources and the absence of any tradition of community policing, there are persistent problems in certain countries – particularly those in which there are important minorities. This relates to the Russians living in Estonia and Latvia, the Hungarians living in Slovakia and Romania, and the Roma living in the Czech Republic, Slovakia, Hungary, Romania and Bulgaria; as well as discrimination and abuse of foreigners, especially from developing countries.
>
> (Kaldor and Vejvoda, 2001: 9)[1]

As for political parties, they noted that '[b]oth the former communist and the new parties tend to be highly centralized and to have markedly hierarchical structures' (Kaldor and Vejvoda, 2002: 11). Ruling parties tend to control the media: 'In this part of the world, "independent" media usually means opposition media' (Kaldor and Vejvoda, 2002: 13). Administrative services 'are still experienced by people in the CEECs as clientelistic, dependent on ruling party allegiance, and not as neutral institutions working in the interest of the public'. Local government tends to be weak.[2] (Kaldor and Vejvoda, 2002: 15–16). Finally, their assessment of civil society and the rise of nongovernmental organisations (NGOs) was broadly positive, even in Slovakia, where the authoritarian regime had tried to control independent associations. The gravitational attraction of the EU is stressed in several of the country chapters. Marcin Król (2002: 76) wrote: 'Hope for membership of the EU and NATO is currently the most important factor in Polish politics. Without this hope we would already have had a lightly authoritarian system'. András Bozóki (2002: 120) wrote even more poignantly: 'Now, for many Hungarian citizens, the desire to join Europe in the foreseeable future serves as a substitute for rapid economic development'.

Two decades later, it is interesting to see how much of this diagnosis remains relevant. 'State capture' by political parties and/or corporations remains a serious concern in East Central Europe (Innes, 2014),[3] as it was earlier in the West in a less extreme form, where parties such as the Gaullists or the Italian Christian Democrats ruled uninterruptedly for long periods. On the issue of rogue politicians mentioned in the previous chapter, the EU seems to have produced two serious cases each in West and East: Haider and Berlusconi in the West, and the Kaczynskis and Orbán in the East. The last of these is probably the most serious, as well as the most recent, and the EU's response has been largely ineffective (Sedelmeier, 2014; Grabbe, 2014). As the former dissident Miklós Haraszti (2011) said,

> The liberal features that were put into the constitutions as a result of the handshake between fragile communists and fragile oppositions proved to be too weak against a tide of uncivilized, illiberal instincts that are themselves part of post-communism, even if they are played out in the name of a belated anti-communism.

In the Austrian case, it was clearly repellent to have a neo-Nazi sympathiser and his party in government, but there was little serious risk that the country would decline into authoritarianism, and the same goes for the xenophobic and homophobic behaviour of the Kaczynski duumvirate. Berlusconi's subversion of Italian democracy has left it in a state which is probably better described as postdemocratic (Crouch, 2004) than anything worse. In Hungary, there seems a reasonable prospect that the Orbán regime is running out of steam and that the country will return to a more normal state after the 2018 elections, if not before.

Within the EU, in both East and West, it is in fact postdemocracy, in 'societies where democratic institutions are strong, and . . . problems . . . occur for democracy within and despite that strength' (Crouch, 2008), that is the main cause for concern. In this analysis, extreme individualistic attitudes, addressed by populist politicians, inhibit any process of collective will formation. Crouch worked in the 1990s in Berlusconi's Italy; Berlusconi's model of practical postdemocracy was adopted by Sarkozy in France, as it was in some ways by Blair in Britain. Ingolfur Blühdorn (2009: 38) has developed this analysis, tying it more strongly than Crouch does to the eclipse of what he calls 'the modernist subject':

> Whilst the *participatory revolution* of the 1970s and 1980s as well as the *deliberative turn* which according to Dryzek (2000) occurred in the early 1990s had emphatically reasserted the centrality of the modernist autonomous subject, late-modern democracies are witnessing a desubjectification of legitimacy and a *post-democratic turn* (original emphasis).

Blühdorn (2009: 40) goes on to explicate this notion in more detail:

As the values and demands of late-modern individuals are becoming increasingly inconsistent and changeable, and critical and erratic citizens represent an unmanageable obstacle to efficient policy making, it was perhaps inevitable that the generation of legitimacy had to turn into a matter of science-oriented and supposedly issue-focussed professionals applying rule-based procedures in order to optimize policy performance.

The technocratic theme is not, of course, new, and the conjunction of bread and circuses older still. In the new version, one might say, the composition of bread is carefully tailored to the current demands of political consumers, as monitored by focus groups and legimated as 'evidence-based policy', while the political and media circus continues above it, with greater or less clownishness and, in Crouch's neat formulation, 'encouraging the maximum level of minimal participation' (Crouch, 2004: 112). In European Union politics it is the technocratic face of postdemocracy which predominates; where policy is publicly legitimated, it is largely in rituals performed by national politicians for whom European meetings are just one item on their busy agendas.

Figures such as those from the 2009 Pew survey quoted earlier (see Chapter 5, p. 50) raise once again the question of a line of division between the former Soviet Union (perhaps excluding the Baltic States) and Eastern and Central Europe. The best survey evidence is probably that provided by Richard Rose and his associates, who have run the New Europe Barometer and New Russia Barometer series for nearly twenty years. Rose (2009) concludes that this difference is significant. Although one of his comparative tables, in which respondents were asked where they would like their political system to be, on a scale from dictatorship to democracy, and where they put it at present, does not show striking differences between the former Soviet states of Russia, Ukraine, and Belarus and the new EU states (Rose, 2009: 165), he points out that 'in new EU member states an average of 57 per cent say that democracy is always preferable; in Russia only 25 per cent are so strongly committed to democracy' (Rose, 2009: 188). And although there is no significant difference in opinion on these issues between Russia and central Asian states such as Kazakhstan and Kyrgyzstan, or between Russian Orthodox and Muslims in those states, 'the divergence of institutional development between CEE [Central and Eastern Europe] and post-Soviet countries means that both Russians and Muslims have learned to adapt to very different types of political regimes' (Rose, 2009: 190).

In all the postcommunist countries except East Germany, where opinion was evenly divided, there was majority support in the Pew survey for the view that a strong economy is more important than a good democracy, with figures in the fifties in Poland and the Czech and Slovak Republics and in the mid-seventies in the others (Pew, 2009: 25). Satisfaction with the current working of democracy showed a similar pattern: massively negative except in the same three countries, with a substantial positive majority only in Poland (Pew, 2009: 32).[4] A recent issue of the *Journal of Democracy* records 'Deepening Dissatisfaction' (Krastev, 2010) and the need for 'a New Model' (Rupnik, 2010). A Freedom House report describes 2008 as 'Democracy's Dark Year' (Shkolnikov, 2009), and the Central European University in Budapest has a 'Center for the Study of Imperfections in Democracy'.

Germany is a good place to look for comparative data. A survey in 2000 asked whether the social market economy 'had proved itself' (sich bewährt). Two thirds overall said it had, but with a third of Eastern and a quarter of Western respondents disagreeing. Asked whether its future development should tend to more market and free competition or to more social security, around half chose the latter as against a quarter for the former. Eastern opinion was much more emphatic: 67% to 20% (Bürklin and Jung, 2001: 691–692). More recently, the Pew survey of 2009 shows rather more Eastern than Western Germans (39% as against 31%) disagreeing with the suggestion that 'Most people are better off in a free market economy, even though some people are rich and some are poor'; the East German figure is, however, equal to that in France (40%), whereas support for markets is higher in Poland than in West Germany (Pew, 2009: 41).

Here, then, there is not so much of an East/West divide, apart from a certain impatience with 'democracy' in a part of the world where 'democrats' has often come to mean kleptocratic oligarchs and their political stooges. The point is that it is *national* democracy which people are thinking of, even when they are responding to Eurobarometer polls with an increasingly EU-focused agenda. The EU's own 'democratic deficit' is of much less concern, except to disappointed federalists and what are euphemistically called 'Eurosceptics'.[5]

The term 'democratic deficit' has been current since the 1980s. Simon Hix (2008: 68–71) neatly summarised the 'standard claims' running through the diverse usages:

> The first claim is that European integration has led to an increase in executive power and a decrease in national parliamentary control.
>
> The second claim . . . is that the European Parliament is too weak.[6]
>
> The third claim is that, despite the growing power of the European Parliament, there is not a democratic electoral context for EU political office or over the direction of the EU policy agenda.
>
> The fourth claim is that the EU is simply 'too distant' from voters.
>
> The fifth claim is that there is a gap between the policies that citizens want and the policies they actually get, largely as a result of the other four factors . . . some scholars claim that EU policy outcomes are more skewed towards the interests of the owners of capital than is the case for policy compromises at the national level in Europe.

Hix rejected all but the third claim, arguing that even the strongest national parliaments are anyway dominated by governments, that the European Parliament's powers have significantly increased, and that EU policy making, despite the partly unjustified secrecy in the Council, is 'more transparent than most domestic systems of government'(Hix, 2008: 74). More contentiously, he claimed that checks and balances in the EU system means that outcomes are centrist rather than skewed to the right, and are as distasteful to many British Conservatives as to French Socialists.[7]

The claim which he considered justified is the absence of serious electoral politics at the European level, and his main proposed remedy, apart from making the voting system more majoritarian (and opening up more of the activities of the Council), was to make candidates for the position of president of the Commission, supported by transnational party groupings in the European Parliament, campaign in Parliament elections, rather like 'chancellor-candidates' in Germany. Just as the German president more or less automatically appoints as chancellor the leader of the largest party in the Bundestag, the European Council would hopefully rubber-stamp the leading candidate.

The second proposal was implemented in the 2014 election in quite an impressive manner,[8] but I doubt whether they would do much to resolve the underlying problem of the relationship between the Union and the decline of member state democracy. The two are related in the way convincingly analysed by Vivien Schmidt (2006: 10):

> Although it began as a regional trade association of nation-states, the EU has gone much further than any such association toward a formal governance system with jurisdiction over a wide range of issues and areas. Among regional trade associations, only the EU has developed a single currency, a single market, a single voice in international trade negotiation, a single anti-trust authority, common policies on environmental protection, worker safety and health, a common foreign and security policy, and even the beginnings of a common defense policy.
>
> [Thus] [w]hile the use of the term state may . . . be difficult for classically trained IR theorists, there is no other word that does justice to the growing power and developing sovereignty – however contingent – of the EU.
>
> (Schmidt, 2006: 14)

Schmidt's preference is for the term regional state; the focus of her book is on the impact of the EU on member-state polities (see also Katenhausen and Lamping, 2003; Jacquot and Wolf, 2003; Schimmelfennig and Sedelmeier, 2005a). Clearly one has to think of the EU polity or state as significantly constituted by its interrelations with national and subnational levels. This is not really the case with national states, whose internal structure, unified, decentralised, federal, or whatever, will only sometimes be of importance for analysis. It may be much more relevant to know whether or not they are EU members, though even here the variety of association agreements means that this difference, too, may not be so significant. For some purposes, it is true – the same is true of the EU. When it acts in trade negotiations, its interlocutors do not need to know the details of its membership or internal constitutional arrangements. More often, however, Union policies are ratified by national ministers and implemented, often in differently modulated ways, via the agency of national governments, local courts and public officials, and so on. In this sense, 'multi-level governance' is simply a fact. To invert Marx's phrase: 'Europe has changed; the point is to understand it'.

Joseph Weiler (2001: 70), in a classic discussion of Europe's *Sonderweg*, or special path, writes that 'Europe has charted its own brand of constitutional federalism. It works. Why fix it?' Weiler's argument echoes in a curious, and no doubt deliberate way, Ernest Renan's account of national sentiment, grounded in a common past and a constantly renewed affirmation of belonging together, 'a daily plebiscite'.

> Constitutional actors in the member states accept the European constitutional discipline not because as a matter of legal doctrine, as is the case in the federal state, they are subordinate to a higher sovereignty and authority attaching to norms validated by the federal principle, the constitutional *demos*. They accept it as an autonomous voluntary act; endlessly renewed on each occasion of subordination, in the discrete areas governed by Europe, which is the aggregate expression of other wills, other political identities, other political communities.
>
> (Weiler, 2001: 68)

Weiler's focus here is on constitutional law, but his view seems to be shaped by the relatively smooth operation of European legal integration as a whole. The primacy of European law has been largely unquestioned,[9] and Court decisions almost always accepted, despite the Court's lack of bailiffs or other means of enforcement.

It is at the democratic end of the European polity that matters become more problematic. The attention of European citizens is primarily focused on national or regional, rather than European politics, and the transfer of power to the European level has mostly not been stressed by member state governments, except when they are seeking an excuse for unpopular policies. Where the policies are popular, national governments tend, not surprisingly, to take the credit themselves. Vivien Schmidt (2006: 33), in her exceptionally innovative study of the interface between European and national politics, concludes that

> . . . while the EU has *policy without politics*, the member-states end up with *politics without policy* in EU-related areas. And this makes for major problems for national democracy (original emphasis).

The democratic deficit, in other words, is not only in the relatively unpolitical (though, of course, politically *relevant*) spheres of EU policy making,[10] with their confusing interplay of parliamentary, executive, and legislative entities, but back home in the member states themselves, and also in nonmembers like Norway, who participate in the European Economic Area, Schengen, etc., without even a formal place in EU nonpolitics.[11]

> National elections tend to be focussed on substantive policy issues that increasingly can only be fully addressed at the EU level, such as immigration,

food safety, environment, or economic growth, while European Parliamentary elections tend to focus more on general polity issues that can only be resolved by nationally based actors, such as how to reform EU institutions – where, that is, they are concerned with EU issues at all.

(Schmidt, 2006: 33)

This is not so much a 'joint decision trap' (Scharpf, 1984) as what, borrowing from Bachrach and Baratz (1962), one might call a 'non-decision trap' – at least from the citizen's point of view.

To speak of the European polity, then, is to address not just the EU and the individual member states (including close associates like Norway and Switzerland), but, crucially, the interplay between them. Schmidt shows how essentially unitary states like the United Kingdom[12] and France interact differently with the EU from more decentralised ones like Germany.

Europeanization . . . has been more disruptive to simple polities with unified structures like France and Britain, where the traditionally powerful executive has given up significant autonomy and control, as a result of the diffusion of decision-making upward to the EU, downward to more autonomous regional authorities, and sideways to more independent judicial authorities. Compound polities with federal structures like Germany, Belgium, and Austria, instead, have largely maintained an equilibrium between executive, legislature and judiciary as well as between centre and periphery – although not without some renegotiation of powers. The impact has been mixed with regard to regionalized states such as Italy and Spain, where the EU has served to reinforce executive power and regional autonomy at one and the same time – although not without a struggle between center and periphery.

(Schmidt, 2006: 54–55)[13]

The details of Schmidt's analysis of her four states are briefly summarised in her concluding recommendations (Schmidt, 2006):

The French need to rethink their vision of leadership in Europe . . . given that they know that France no longer leads Europe, are in crisis over national identity, and increasingly blame EU 'neoliberalism' for their economic problems. The British need to develop a vision of Britain in Europe, given that the discourse of economic interest does not respond to growing concerns about sovereignty and identity, while the idea of British separateness in Europe could very well lead to the reality of British separation from Europe . . . The Germans need to update their vision of 'German-as-European' in light of the changes related to unification and fading memories of World War II, especially since they increasingly question the benefits of membership and worry about the EU's impact on the social market economy. The Italians . . . need to concern themselves not so much with their vision of Italy in Europe as with their implementation of European rules in Italy, since their pride in being

European is likely to suffer as a result of the fact that the EU 'rescue of the nation-state' is no longer enough to rescue the nation-state.

Schmidt's diagnosis may seem worrying, but her conclusion is relatively optimistic. As long as we recognise that the EU should be seen as a regional state and do not try to democratise it according to the model of national democracies, we can live with something like its present arrangements. 'Its "federal" checks and balances, its voting rules ensuring supermajorities, its elaborate interest intermediation process *with* the people, and its consensus politics go very far toward guaranteeing good governance *for* the people' (Schmidt, 2006: 222–223). All that is needed is for the member states to recognise this and adapt their political discourse and practices accordingly.

In a related approach, Jan Zielonka and others have presented a vision of the EU as a kind of empire, more specifically a neomedieval one in which political authority is divided and multiple, not clearly nested as in idealised descriptions of feudalism, but a messier picture of competing sovereignties, statuses, and rights. This has a particularly compelling quality in relation to the status of citizens in the EU; if anything, the analogy is with the Roman Empire, in which being able to say 'civis romanus sum' conferred some immunity from local jurisdictions, just as being a European citizen now confers rights of movement and employment denied to those known in Italy as 'extracommunitari'. Rome also had, of course, a common currency, language, army, and legal system (Zielonka, 2006: 17). The crucial difference, of course, is that it was based on conquest and central rule rather than voluntary accession and democratic representation. Zielonka's book is substantially concerned with Eastern enlargement, since 'it is the European integration project that needs to be adjusted to enlargement, and not the other way around' (Zielonka, 2006: 89; see also Verdun and Croci, 2005).[14]

Claus Offe and Ulrich Preuss (2006) adopt a similar answer to 'The Problem of Legitimacy in the European Polity'. The start from a similar point to Schmidt: '[T]he problem is not primarily that the *EU* must become democratic; it is that *member states* must *remain* democratic' (original emphasis). Following Philippe Schmitter's model of a *condominio*, 'an entity which unites elements of a federal state (*Bundesstaat*) and of a confederation (*Staatenbund*) without strictly conforming to either of them',[15] they suggest the deliberately paradoxical image of a republican empire.

> The European Union is [the] first spatially extended union of a great number of highly distinctive peoples that is governed as a republican regime. It reconciles the main attribute of an empire – multinationality – with an essential quality of a republic, political freedom, the latter resulting from the voluntary character of the former.

The appeal of a model of this kind is, of course, its flexibility, which Ulrich Beck and others have linked to a cosmopolitan vision which transcends old-fashioned oppositions between inside and outside, us and them (Beck and Grande, 2004;

Lavenex, 2004). A cosmopolitan Europe is also reflexive not just in the sense of responding to humanly generated risks (the sense of reflexivity which Beck had stressed in his earlier work),[16] but also in that it relativizes conceptions of inside/outside, self/other, Europe *or* the nation-state: 'Europe is another word for variable geometry, variable national interests, variable concern (Betroffenheit), variable internal and external relations, variable statehood, variable identity'. As Beck and Grande argue at length, a reflective and cosmopolitan conception of Europe can, to some extent, escape the dilemmas of in/out, us/them, nation-state/federation.[17]

Against this happy vision, however, the negative votes on the European constitution in France and the Netherlands, two states involved from the beginning in the integration project and generally reckoned among the most favourably inclined to it, carry a powerful lesson. Kees van der Pijl (2006: 36) provides a damning indictment which puts an analysis like Vivien Schmidt's analysis in a broader context:

> There is a European Parliament, and there are various channels of interest articulation at the level of the EU, all institutions which one will not find at the Atlantic level, or NAFTA or ASEAN. Hence political mobilization and class struggle or compromise *could* always develop at the EU level, however unlikely this may now seem. But compared to the clear separation between national politics and transnational economy in the original homeland, which reserves the transnational space for capital whilst containing democratic aspirations within each separate state, a 'European politics' is best characterized as a contradiction that could go either way – that is, it could re-nationalize politics entirely, leaving only a regulatory infrastructure in place at the EU level . . . or else press forward to develop a full-fledged politics at the EU level. The 'only' problem here is that the populations of Europe have been *doubly disenfranchised*, both by the general restriction of democracy in the neoliberal reform drive, and by the specific displacement of key prerogatives of national parliaments to European structures in the economic domain.[18]

The problem, as many see it, is that it may be impossible to democratise the EU without undermining the democratic states which make it up.[19] Yet federal polities elsewhere manage this, with only occasional grumbles in Bavaria, Texas, or the Valais about goings-on in the national capitals. Klaus von Beyme (2005) has sketched out some ways in which federal structures accommodate differences in, for example, the size of their component states.)[20] But to speak like this, Euro-realists would say, is to fail to grasp the reality of the EU, where legitimating structures are inevitably embedded at a national level and the pursuit of a stronger European identity is a dangerous diversion (Weiler, 2001; Scharpf, 2004). Philippe Schmitter's ironically meant 'Why Bother?' (Schmitter, 2000) rings out over the subsequent debates, and the debacle of the Constitution keeps the echo going. Offe and Preuss suggest that the representation of European citizens in the

Parliament could become more genuinely 'direct' and less a reflection of national political formations, but this modest suggestion remains imprecise and very limited. Their basic message is one of caution:

> Democratizing Europe after the model of the nation-state will not increase but undermine the capacity of the Euro-polity to allocate rights and claims in a 'nation-blind' manner. Even the most robust national democracy (or, rather, precisely the most robust national democracy) does not help here, as it will function as an obstacle to, rather than a promoter of . . . an institutionalized form of solidarity.

If, then, the problem of the EU polity is essentially that of its decoupling from society, which reproduces in spades the alienation of the national political sphere diagnosed by Marx in the nineteenth century and by Régis Debray (1981) in the twentieth, we are returned to the neglected theme of European society and its global context. Delanty and Rumford (2005: 163) point to the similarities between European and global politics:

> In Europe, as in the world polity more generally, cultural control is exerted by those who are seen to work for the common good rather than self-interest, framing their calls for development, progress, standardization, and rational organization in terms of the potential benefits to everyone.

The European polity thus displays in microcosm the tension between the stylistic democratisation of modern politics, marked by the informal style of leaders like Blair and Bush, and the increasing alienation of marginalised and excluded populations, which in the European context tends to be expressed at best by hostility to the European project and at worst by a generalised xenophobia (Bale, 2003).

The pursuit of European integration was always, in a phrase also applied in a different way to fascism, an 'extremism of the centre'. In its well-meaning but arrogant elitism it has now generated an anti-European extremism which may be spreading from the extreme right to the mainstream.[21] As Cas Mudde (2006) wrote a decade ago, 'Europe is currently experiencing a populist *Zeitgeist*, in which populism is prevalent in politics as well as in many other aspects of life'. It is this populist *mouvance* at both the national and (anti-)EU level that is perhaps the most striking feature of contemporary European politics. The populist politicians of both West and East often resemble one another in style, though some elements play better in regionally differentiated audiences. In the East, homophobia is relatively acceptable: sympathetic remarks about Nazism less so.[22] The structural conditions in East and West are significantly different: in much of the East, parties are more volatile and they are necessarily new creations, with new members: some social democrats, monarchists, or whatever may have dropped out of politics in the late 1940s and come back in after 1989, but there cannot be many left. The East is different, too, in that anti-communism has a resonance which, for obvious reasons, it lacks in the West. Like Christianity for the US extreme right (except for its really extreme neopagan fringe), anti-communism provides a metapolitical vocabulary shared with a much broader constituency. It is not surprising that anti-communism is particularly strong in the Baltic States: more surprising to see it so strong in Hungary. Slavoj Žižek (2009) suggested that the recent upsurge in anti-communism has been driven by the economic crisis and a belief that the failures of capitalism can be blamed on the fact that former communists have retained power and denatured and distorted it: '[T]he newly-born anti-Communists don't get that what they are denouncing as perverted pseudo-capitalism simply is capitalism'. Like anti-Semitism, in the remark attributed to August Bebel, anti-communism may be the 'socialism of fools'.

Another East/West difference may be the greater salience of what the Slovak anthropologist Juraj Buzalka (2008: 767) has called 'post-peasant populism' in southeast Poland and eastern Slovakia, where he has worked, and elsewhere:

> [I]in the contemporary post-peasant setting of south-east Poland, a nascent anti-capitalist movement exists, but no organised political protest has yet come out of it. Instead, it is manifested in Catholics' increasing support for conservative and populist politics.
>
> The post-peasant populism that I believe has emerged in the post-peasant context of post-socialist Poland, but also other parts of Eastern Europe, is built upon the pre-modern myths and rural imagery that help to create an enemy in the form of a wealthy capitalist society or a godless socialist society.

As Buzalka (2008: 768) notes, there is a complex relation between local rural-ism and Europeanisation. This, like globalisation, is often seen as a purely homog-enising process, but in fact the EU, as well as eroding by its mere existence the national state's monopoly of identification, has deliberately strengthened regional governance and identities; development policies, including tourism, may take a strongly regional and local form. Tom Nairn (1998: 768) suggested, more suspi-ciously, that the EU 'remains deeply compromised by the very ruralist inheritance which has in the past so often nourished ethnic nationalism'. The rurality may become increasingly vestigial, imaginary, and nostalgic, but it can still motivate: a *Front National* election poster in the late 1990s featured a rural scene with a vil-lage church, white shepherdess, white sheep, and so on.

It may be, however, that we worry too much about populism and postdemoc-racy. Despite all the talk about political 'dealignment' in the West and volatility in the East, what is striking is the continuity of many party structures. Gilbert and Sullivan's comic opera *Iolanthe* (1882) declared that 'every boy and every gal that's born into the world alive is either a little liberal or else a little conserva-tive'. England still has Liberals and Conservatives, albeit now with Labour as well. Elsewhere, party labels may change, as those of the French right do almost annually, yet the personnel remains much the same. As noted earlier, if one exam-ines election results for the Bundestag, the only signs of when reunification took place are the arrival on the scene of a small new party, the Partei des demok-ratischen Sozialismus (PDS), a temporary boost to the Christlich-Demokratische

Union (CDU) vote, and, of course, a larger electorate. Further east, party families formed and split along more or less recognisable lines. Even in stable Western Europe, we have got used to seeing socialist parties with neoliberal economic policies; Zhirinovsky's 'Liberal Democratic' party label was no more misleading, though more dangerous, than that of the French Radicaux de Gauche, who would hardly count as radical leftists even in the United States. Parties may have seemed passé in 1968, but they outlived most of the new social movements, if these did not themselves mutate into parties like the German and other Greens or the Dutch D-66.

If, on the other hand, politics goes seriously sour in Europe, it seems unlikely that the EU has the resources to rescue it. Although capable of specific actions in relation to one or two states at a time, it would rapidly be overburdened by a substantial slide towards authoritarianism. And as Bo Stråth (2011: 2) points out, the system which Milward described, the division of labour 'between the European level, which was responsible for economic market integration, and the member state level responsible for social welfare' has become problematic.

> The European rescue of the nation state through the distribution of labour between the European market and national social legislation functioned rather well in the economically and socially much more homogeneous EEC of the six or the nine than in today's EU 27. The big enlargement in 2004 failed to address the problem of growing social differences within the Union in a way that convinced broad opinions and so did the proposed constitution which aimed at confirming and sealing the enlargement.
>
> (Stråth, 2011: 5)

The next chapter examines the EU and Europe as a whole in the context of the post-2007 crisis.

Notes

1 On minority rights in the Czech Republic, Slovakia, Hungary, and Romania, see Csergö and Deegan-Krause (2011).
2 For some interesting memoirs of local government officials in the early postcommunist period in Czecho-Slovakia and Poland, see Surazska (1996).
3 Innes (2014: 90) notes that the Czech Republic scores particularly highly on corrupt diversion of public funds. See also www.transparency.org/cpi2014/infographic/global.
4 Andrew Roberts (2010) uses objective rather than subjective indicators of 'accountability' and 'responsiveness', including detailed case studies of policy areas (pensions and housing) in the Czech Republic, Poland, and Hungary. Stein Ringen (2010: 33) used a mix of objective and subjective indicators to measure 'quality of democracy', resulting in an interesting index with the Netherlands coming top, followed by Canada, then by Belgium and Germany, then by France, the United Kingdom and the Czech Republic, then by Spain and the United States, then Poland and finally Italy. See also Ringen (2007).

5 A majority of respondents to Eurobarometer surveys seem reasonably content with the current division of labour on policy areas between Union and member states, giving primacy to the national state on (in increasing order of preference) issues of debt, unemployment, health, education, taxation, and pensions. Respondents in many countries also 'trust' the EU more than their domestic polities (Standard EB 74, 2010).

6 He notes that the Parliament's powers grew over time (as, of course, they tend to in all systems, in the absence of countervailing forces) and it became clear that this was not, after all, the main threat to national parliaments.

7 It could also be argued, on the basis of some European Court judgments in the recent past, giving primacy to the open market over local minimum wage and safety legislation, that the Court, in its application of EU law, is as much a threat to the social democratic *acquis* as explicit policies.

8 See generally favourable responses by myself (Outhwaite, 2014) and by Michael Shackleton (2014), who hosted the first substantial 'hustings' meeting in Maastricht, and a more sceptical view by Christian Joerges and Florian Rödl (2014).

9 The most substantial challenge came from the German Federal Constitutional Court, which had previously been the supreme legal authority and the guardian of the German Rechtsstaat – a role which, of course, it retains except where EU law has priority.

10 '[N]ational partisan politics has been marginalized. Ministers speak in the Council more in the name of the national interest than for governmental majorities. Members of the EP speak more in terms of the public interest than for electoral majorities. Citizens have more influence in Brussels when lobbying as organized interests than when voting or protesting in national capitals' (Schmidt, 2006: 2).

11 See, for example, the Norwegian Study of Power and Democracy, part of a larger series of Nordic studies, at www.sv.uio.no/mutr/english/index.html.

12 The United Kingdom, like Spain, has, of course, now substantial devolution to Scotland and to a lesser extent to Wales, and the Blair government reversed Thatcher's abolition of metropolitan institutions in London and elsewhere. Its political style, however, remains essentially unitary, reinforced by a strongly majoritarian voting system in which coalitions have historically been rare.

13 In a useful review symposium of Schmidt's book, Tanja Börzel and Carina Sprungk (2009) have questioned the importance she gives to the distinction between simple and compound polities, suggesting that the impact of the EU may have been more disruptive on a strong parliament like the German Bundestag than on a weak one like the French Assemblée Nationale. Without going into the details, I suggest that Schmidt (2009: 402) is right to insist on the greater flexibility of a federal state. More broadly, this is clearly one of the reasons why Germany, accustomed to federalism and all the messiness of 'Politikverflechtung' and 'joint decision traps', is more comfortable with the architecture of the EU than is the United Kingdom, which has not yet learned to handle the implications of its relatively recent devolution.

14 The book is also a superb guide through recent literature on the EU. For a critique of the imperial analogy, see Schulz-Forberg and Stråth (2010: 160–163).

15 As they note, the German Constitutional Court called the EU a *Staatenverbund*, in a somewhat desperate neologism.

16 See the collective volume by Beck, Giddens, and Lash (1994).

17 See, in particular, Chapter 2, Section 3. Among the divisions transcended, or at least relativized, is that between domestic social policy and European regional policy: 'regional policy becomes European social policy' (p. 271).

18 Schmidt's analysis, though less radical, is essentially complementary to this. She writes: 'Currently, there is no consensus to increase democratic legitimacy by shifting government *by* and *of* the people to the EU level through the direct election of EU leaders or EU-wide parliamentary elections – nor would this necessarily help democratize the EU, given the lack of a collective identity or will. But this means that democratic reforms of the EU still focus mainly on improving governance *for* the people, through greater accountability and transparency, and *with* the people, through more interest-based access and a greater opening to "civil society". But this does little to decrease the fragmentation of EU democracy as a whole'.

19 As David Bailey (2006) points out, studies of European integration might benefit from paying more attention to critical state theory, drawn from, among other sources, Marx and Foucault, which has consistently addressed contradictions generated by forms of governance themselves and what have been called 'crises of crisis management'.

20 On the related issue of division or interpenetration of powers, see, for example, Benz (2003).

21 On right-wing populism, see Boettcher (2011), Langenbacher and Schellenberg (2011), and other work published by Friedrich-Ebert-Stiftung, Berlin.

22 I am indebted here to remarks by Frances Millard, Paul Taggart, and other participants in a session on populism at the Europeanists' Conference in Barcelona, June 2011. I tend, however, to define populism more broadly than in the mainstream represented there: I would not hesitate, for example, to call Berlusconi a populist despite the majority position he enjoyed in Italian politics. For a useful recent overview of the concept, see Houwen (2011).

References

Bachrach, Peter and Morton S. Baratz (1962) 'Two Faces of Power', *American Political Science Review* 56(4) December: 947–952.

Bailey, David (2006) 'Governance or the Crisis of Governmentality? Applying Critical State Theory at the European Level', *Journal of European Public Policy* 13(1) January: 16–33.

Bale, Tim (2003) 'Cinderella and Her Ugly Sisters: The Mainstream and the Extreme Right in Europe's Bipolarising Party Systems', *West European Politics* 26(3): 67–90.

Beck, Ulrich, Anthony Giddens, and Scott Lash (1994) *Reflexive Modernization: Politics, Tradition and Aesthetics in the Modern Social Order*. Cambridge: Polity.

Blühdorn, Ingolfur (2009) 'Democracy Beyond the Modernist Subject', in Ingolfur Blühdorn (ed), *In Search of Legitimacy. Policy Making in Europe and the Challenge of Complexity*. Opladen and Farmington Hills: Barbara Budrich, pp. 17–50.

Boettcher, Alexander (2011) 'Rechtspopulismus in Europa. Fragen und Antworten', *Internationale Politikanalyse*, August: 1–7.

Bohle, Dorothee (2011) 'East European Transformations and the Paradoxes of Transnationalization', in Joan Debardeleben and Achim Hurrelmann (eds.), *Transnational Europe: Promise, Paradox, Limits*. Basingstoke: Palgrave Macmillan.

Börzel, Tanja and Carina Sprungk (2009) 'The Goodness of Fit and the Democratic Deficit in Europe', *Comparative European Politics* 7(3): 364–373.

Bozóki, András (2002) 'Democracy in Hungary: 1990–97', in Mary Kaldor and Ivan Vejvoda (eds.), pp. 105–120.

Bürklin, Wilhelm and Christian Jung (2001) *Germany in Change*. Berlin: Bundesverband deutscher Banken. GESIS Data Archive, Cologne.

Buzalka, Juraj (2008) 'Europeanization and Post-peasant Populism in Eastern Europe', *Europe-Asia Studies* 60(5) July: 757–771.

Crouch, Colin (2004) *Postdemocracy*. Cambridge: Polity.

Crouch, Colin (2008) 'British Professor: We Are Living in a "Postdemocracy"', *Deutsche Welle*, September 13. www.dw.de/british-professor-we-are-living-in-a-postdemocracy/a-3617727–1. Accessed July 27, 2015.

Csergő, Zsuzsa and Kevin Deegan-Krause (2011) 'Liberalism and Cultural Claims in Central and Eastern Europe: Toward a Pluralist Balance', *Nations and Nationalism* 17(1) January: 85–107.

Debray, Régis (1983) *Critique of Political Reason*. London: New Left Books.

Delanty, Gerard and Chris Rumford (2005) *Rethinking Europe: Social Theory and the Implications of Europeanization*. London: Routledge.

Delcour, Laure (2010) 'Towards a Global Europe?' in George Lawson, Chris Armbruster, and Michael Cox (eds), *The Global 1989: Continuity and Change in World Politics 1989–2009*. Cambridge: Cambridge University Press, pp. 135–156.

Dryzek, John (2000) *Deliberative Democracy and Beyond*. Oxford: Oxford University Press.

Garsztecki, Stefan (2010) 'Demokratie in Polen – Auf dem Weg zu *Good Governance*?, *Polen-Analysen* Nr. 68, 20.04: 2–14.

Grabbe, Heather (2014) 'Six Lessons of Enlargement Ten Years On: The EU's Transformative Power in Retrospect and Prospect', *Journal of Common Market Studies* 52 (Annual Review): 40–56.

Haraszti, Miklos (2011) 'A Little of Everything', in 'Is Europe's Democratic Revolution Over?', *Transitions Online*, 9 May.

Hix, Simon (2008) *What's Wrong with the European Union and How to Fix it*. Cambridge: Polity.

Houwen, Tim (2011) 'The Non-European roots of the Concept of Populism', Sussex: SEI Working Paper No. 120.

Innes, Abby (2014) 'The Political Economy of State Capture in Central Europe', *Journal of Common Market Studies* 52(1): 88–104.

Jacquot, Sophie and Cornelia Wolf (2003) 'Usage of European Integration – Europeanisation from a Sociological Perspective', *European Integration Online Papers (EIoP)* 7(12): http://eiop.or.at/eiop/texte/2003–012a.htm. Accessed July 27, 2015.

Joerges, Christian and Florian Rödl (2014) 'EU Commission President: Who and What Did We Actually Vote For?', VerfBlog, www.verfassungsblog.de/en/eu-kommissionspraesident-wen-und-wollten-wir-eigentlich-waehlen/. Accessed July 27, 2015.

Kaldor, Mary and Ivan Vejvoda (eds.), (1999/2002) *Democratization in Central and Eastern Europe*. London: Pinter; paperback edition (2002) London and New York: Continuum.

Katenhusen, Ines and Wolfram Lamping (eds.) (2003) *Demokratien in Europa. Der Einfluss der europäischen Integration auf Institutionenwandel und neue Konturen des demokratischen Verfassungsstaates*. Opladen: Leske und Budrich.

Krastev, Ivan (2010) 'The Other Transition', *Journal of Democracy* 21(1) January: 113–119.

Król, Marcin (2002) 'Democracy in Poland', in Mary Kaldor and Ivan Vejvoda (eds.), pp. 67–77.

Langenbacher, Nora and Britta Schellenberg (eds.) (2011) *Is Europe on the 'Right' Path? Right-Wing Extremism and Right-Wing Populism in Europe*. Berlin: Friedrich-Ebert-Stiftung.

Lavenex, Sandra (2004) 'EU External Governance in "Wider Europe"', *Journal of European Public Policy* 11(4) August: 680–700.

Milward, Alan (1992) *The European Rescue of the Nation-State*. London: Routledge.

Mudde, Cas (2006) 'Anti-System Politics', in Paul Heywood, Erik Jones, Martin Rhodes, and Ulrich Sedelmeier (eds.), *Developments in European Politics*. Basingstoke: Palgrave, pp. 178–195.

Offe, Claus and Ulrich Preuss (2006) 'The Problem of Legitimacy in the European Polity. Is Democratization the Answer?, in Colin Crouch and Wolfgang Streeck (eds.) *The Diversity of Democracy. Corporatism, Social Order and Political Conflict*. Cheltenham: Edward Elgar, pp. 175–204.

Outhwaite, William (2014) www.discoversociety.org/2014/07/01/viewpoint-the-european-commission-presidency-this-time-its-different/. Accessed July 27, 2015.

Pew Global Attitudes Project (2009) 'Two Decades After the Wall's Fall', www.pewresearch.org. Accessed July 27, 2015.

Pridham, Geoffrey (2007) 'The Effects of the European Union's Democratic Conditionality: The Case of Romania during Accession', *Journal of Communist Studies and Transition Politics* 23(2) June: 233–258.

Pridham, Geoffrey (2010) 'Change and Continuity in the European Union's Political Conditionality: Aims, Approach, and Priorities', *Democratization* 14(3) June: 446–471.

Ringen, Stein (2007) *What Democracy Is For: On Freedom and Moral Government*. Princeton: Princeton University Press.

Ringen, Stein (2010) 'Democratic Quality in America and Europe', in Jens Alber and Neil Gilbert (eds.), *United in Diversity ? Comparing Social Models in Europe and America*. Oxford: Oxford University Press, pp. 21–36.

Roberts, Andrew (2010) *The Quality of Democracy in Eastern Europe. Public Preferences and Policy Reforms*. Cambridge University Press.

Rose, Richard (2009) *Understanding Post-Communist Transformation: A Bottom Up Approach*. London: Routledge.

Rupnik, Jacques (2010) 'In Search of a New Model', *Journal of Democracy* 21(1) January: 105–112.

Scharpf, Fritz W. (1988) 'The Joint-Decision Trap. Lessons from German Federalism and European Integration', *Public Administration* 66(2): 239–78.

Schmidt, Vivien (2006) *Democracy in Europe. The EU and National Polities*. Oxford: Oxford University Press.

Schimmelfennig, Frank and Ulrich Sedelmeier (2005) 'The Politics of EU Enlargement: Theoretical and Comparative Perspectives'. In Frank Schimmelfennig and Ulrich Sedelmeier (eds.), *The Politics of European Union Enlargement: Theoretical Approaches*. Abingdon, UK and New York, USA: Routledge, pp. 3–32.

Schulz-Forberg, Hagen and Bo Stråth (2010) *The Political History of European Integration. The Hypocrisy of Democracy-Through-Market*. London: Routledge.

Sedelmeier, Ulrich (2014) 'Anchoring Democracy from Above? The European Union and Democratic Backsliding in Hungary and Romania after Accession', *Journal of Common Market Studies* 52(1): 105–121.

Shackleton, Michael (2014) 'The Election of the Commission President in 2014: What Does It Tell Us about Democracy in the European Union?', EISS 2014 Keynote speech, University of Agder, Norway. http://brage.bibsys.no/xmlui/bitstream/handle/11250/222238/ISLWP2014–4.pdf?sequence=1&isAllowed=y. Accessed July 27, 2015.

Shkolnikov, Vladimir (2009) 'Nations in Transit 2009: Democracy's Dark Year'. Washington and New York: Freedom House. https://freedomhouse.org/report/nations-transit-2009/overview-essay#.VRF5G2dFBdg. Accessed July 27, 2015.

Stråth, Bo (2011) 'Still the Europe of Milward? On the Need for a New Long-Term Historical Understanding of Today's Europe'. London: UCL European Institute Working Paper No. 1.

Van der Pijl, Kees (2006) 'A Lockean Europe? Anglo-liberalism and Its Discontents', *New Left Review* 37(Jan–Feb): 9–37.

Verdun, Amy and Osvaldo Creci (2005) *The European Union in the Wake of Eastern Enlargement. Institutional and Policy-Making Challenges*. Manchester: Manchester University Press.

von Beyme, Klaus (2005) 'Asymmetric federalism between globalization and regionalization', *Journal of European Public Policy* 12, 3, June: 432–447.

Weiler, Joseph (2001) 'Europe's *Sonderweg*', in Kalypso Nicolaïdis and Robert Howse (eds.), *The Federal Vision: Legitimacy and Levels of Governance in the US and the EU*. Oxford: Oxford University Press.

Zielonka, Jan (2006) *Europe as Empire. The Nature of the Enlarged European Union*. Oxford: Oxford University Press.

Žižek, Slavoj (2009) '20 Years of Collapse', *New York Times* November 9.

8   Out of the crisis?

The world economic crisis which broke out in the United States in 2006 has had a variety of impacts on Europe. The European Union has both amplified its impact, especially in the form of the Eurozone, and also provided some limited protection to member states. The impact on the integration process is similarly ambiguous, and its outcome impossible to predict. Wolfgang Streeck (2014) has provided the most compelling analysis of the crisis, and one which has inspired many subsequent analyses, such as those discussed later.[1] It is striking that the first two of the three main chapters of his book barely mention Europe, with the implication that the changes he describes would have taken place even if the international and transnational regime in Europe had been very different. In his account, the EU is what he calls a neoliberal transnational consolidation state, presiding over those of the member states. Postdemocracy, for Streeck, is the political superstructure of an increasingly neoliberal state form, whether inside or outside Europe. He takes a broad view in disciplinary terms, pointing up the limitations of social and political theories of crisis or democracy which abstract from political economy (Streeck, 2014: xv) and a long view of the current crisis, in the light of which the similarities across European capitalism outweigh the 'varieties' (Streeck, 2014: xixii; see also Streeck, 2012c).

The neo-Marxist crisis theories of the 1970s were right, Streeck argues, to focus on the antagonistic relations between capitalism and democratic politics. Habermas and others were, however, wrong to assume that economic contradictions could be displaced into the political and broadly cultural sphere and to direct their attention to these (Streeck, 2014: 12–13, 16).[2] At the economic level as well, capitalism 'bought time', deferring 'social conflicts, at first by means of inflation, then through increased government borrowing, next through expansion of private loan markets[3] and finally (today) through central bank purchases of public debt and bank liabilities' (Streeck, 2014: xiv). Modern governments have two constituencies: the voters and the markets. International capital now influences politics not just indirectly, by choosing to invest or not to invest in national economies, but directly, 'by financing or not financing the state itself' (Streeck, 2014: 84) Debt policy becomes international financial diplomacy (Streeck, 2014: 90). Or, one might add, in the European case, also the domestic policy of the transnational European polity.

In Streeck's analysis, then, we are not so much in late capitalism as in late democracy. Democracy loses its redistributive capacity (promise or threat, depending on how you see it) and becomes 'a combination of constitutional state and public entertainment'. Capitalism has been 'de-democratised' through the de-economisation of democracy' (Streeck, 2014: 5). Among the intellectual roots of de-democratisation are a domestic and a transnational variant. The domestic one is in the theories of 'ungovernability' which paralleled and in some respects over-lapped the neo-Marxist crisis theories of the 1970s.[4] For the transnational variant, Streeck refers to a 1939 paper by Hayek which argues for an interstate federation which would 'neutralize' (Streeck, 2014: 102) the democratic institutions of the member states. This, Streeck suggests, brushing aside what by the 1980s were merely 'remnants' of a social democratic programme in Brussels (Streeck, 2014: 104), and the 'so-called European Parliament' (Streeck, 2014: 115), is essentially the direction which the Union has taken. The circumvention and undermining of democratic institutions in member states and at the European level is not just a reaction or overreaction to the current crisis – nor, he would probably add, the result of the extension of European law in some earlier Court judgements ana-lysed by Fritz Scharpf (2012, 2013b) and Christian Joerges (Joerges and Rödl, 2008) – but something intrinsic to the 'international consolidation state' which the EU has become.

This is one dimension of the EU's amplification of the crisis: the addition of a further level of state which is no less neoliberal and even less democratic than the member states, and one which 'amplified' the boom and encouraged states and individuals to accumulate dangerous levels of debt. As Wade Jacoby (2014: 54) writes of the new member states, 'The perceived safety of EU Member States allowed private actors to increase their borrowing well above the already high flows elsewhere in post-communist Europe'. The second dimension relates spe-cifically to the Eurozone and hence, in the longer term, to the Union as a whole (leaving aside for the moment the prospect that the United Kingdom and Sweden might remain outside the eurozone, without, like Denmark, pegging their cur-rency to the euro).

The eurozone does not of itself point to a core–periphery division within the EU, since it is open eventually (in the English sense of the word for the bulk of member states, and in the conditional sense of *éventuellement* for the British and Scandinavian opters-out)[5] to all EU members. It does, however, in its present critical state, sharpen up the dilemma between closer integration to sustain the currency and, alternatively, a much more restricted set of entry criteria, perhaps to be imposed retrospectively on problem states. At both ends of this argument, Ger-many and Greece, there were calls for the respective state to opt out of the euro.[6]

At the beginning of the third postcommunist decade, it was clear, to put it crudely, that on the whole the north of Europe had crap banks (or at least hopelessly irresponsible ones)[7] and the south had crap states. (Ireland managed to have both, and many banking systems in southern Europe were also not beyond reproach.) The economic crisis seemed, however, to be under control. Then, in what would normally be the European holiday season of July and August 2011, every news agenda was full of withdrawal or expulsion from, or complete collapse of, the eurozone, of state bankruptcies, and, more optimistically, of Eurobonds and the coordination of fiscal and economic policy. Out of the vast flow of commentary, it is worth singling out contributions by Fritz Scharpf and Wolfgang Streeck. In lectures in April and May 2011, respectively, Streeck and Scharpf addressed the crisis. Streeck set it in the context of the tense relation between capitalism and democracy since 1945, focusing on the current threat to democracy as well as capitalism (Streeck, 2011: 11–12):

> In the years after 2008, distributional conflict under democratic capitalism has turned into a complicated tug-of-war between global financial markets and sovereign national states. Where in the past workers struggled with employers, citizens with governments, and private debtors with private creditors, it is now financial institutions wrestling with the same states that they had only recently successfully blackmailed into saving them from themselves.

Speaking in a university set up under the European treaties, Streeck (2011: 9) barely mentioned the local European context, presciently stressing the overall dimensions of the sovereign debt problem. Democracy, then, is 'pre-empted' by external pressures bearing on the rich countries as well as the poor. (To repeat the point made earlier, Germany and France may have robust states, but their banks are hopelessly exposed.)

Speaking a few weeks later in London, Scharpf also addressed the theme of pre-emption of democracy with reference to European Monetary Union (EMU). Lacking the high mobility of capital and labour and internal transfers normally considered necessary for an 'optimal currency union', Europe relied on short-term convergence programmes and failed to address the imbalances between member states.[8] In the postcrisis Union,

> Like the provinces or cantons in a federal state, they lose control over the instruments of macroeconomic management, and they are likely to suffer from uniform national policies that do not fit their regional economy. At the same time, however, the EU budget is minuscule in comparison to the budget of federal states, there are no European taxes and there is no European social policy to alleviate interregional imbalances. Instead, member states are expected to cope with all economic problems by relying entirely on their own policy resources ... [and] ... are subject to the intrusive supervision and potential punishment imposed by supranational authorities.
>
> (Scharpf, 2011: 31–32)

Scharpf (2011: 37) concluded that 'In the worst case . . . the attempts to save the Euro through the policies presently enacted may either fail on their own terms, or they may not only undermine democracy in EU member states but endanger European integration itself'. There were voices (including Wolfgang Streeck at the 2011 conference of Europeanists in Barcelona) suggesting that the EU had overburdened itself with its southern and some of its eastern accessions.

This, then, is a second way in which Europe, in the form of the eurozone, amplified a global crisis. On the other hand, states outside the eurozone such as the United Kingdom and Hungary also adopted damaging austerity programmes. As Steffen Lehndorf (2015: 23) puts it, 'You don't need the Troika to wreak havoc'. In postcommunist Europe, the impact was most acute in a second wave, in 2011, particularly in the Baltic States (of which only Estonia was at that time joining the eurozone), where unemployment doubled before falling back to more normal levels around the middle of the European range (EBRD, 2012; Leschke, Theodoropoulou, and Watt, 2015: 297). The postcommunist states most closely engaged with the eurozone and the outside world in general, such as Hungary, were the most affected (EBRD, 2012; Myant and Drahokoupil, 2012; Jacoby, 2014). One impact has been to put in question existing governmental trajectories, whether these are at the more strongly neoliberal end of the spectrum, as in Estonia, or more corporatist, as in Slovenia (Bohle and Greskovitz, 2012: 256–258; Lindstrom, 2015: 53–73).

Did Europe also provide some protection? Iceland certainly thought it would, applying to join the EU in the summer of 2009 and negotiating from 2010 until 2013, when it stopped pursuing its application. (What would have happened if it had been *in* the eurozone when the crisis hit is anyone's guess.) In the short term, however, any benefit the eurozone members derived from the European Central Bank guarantee of the currency and from direct support through bond purchases, accelerated disbursements of structural funds, and other measures was probably less than they could have achieved by devaluing the local currencies they had abandoned. More broadly, however, and despite appalling levels of social dislocation and emigration, it is probably true that '[t]he NMS economies are better off than they were before EU membership and better off than they would have been without membership' (Jacoby, 2014: 67). In this context, it is interesting to see that the crisis has not prevented, though it may have delayed, new accessions to the eurozone (Slovakia in 2009, Estonia in 2011, Latvia in 2014, and Lithuania in 2015), and even the political forces most opposed to current EU policies, such as Greece's Syriza and Spain's Podemos, are not calling for exit from the eurozone. At the other end of the political spectrum, the strongly neoliberal economist Anders Åslund (2010) combines a blistering critique of the European Central Bank with strong support for the expansion of the eurozone. Wolfgang Streeck's proposals amount in essence to a combination of street protest, bypassing the 'blocked channels of institutionalized democracy' (p. 223) and a new Bretton Woods regime in Europe of fixed yet variable exchange rates, allowing devaluations where necessary and retaining the euro as a secondary currency. This is hardly convincing. The toothpaste of the euro was undoubtedly spread too wide, and it would probably have been better to have left it in the tube for a bit longer, but even if it could and should be put back, it is hard to see how this could be more than the first stage of an alternative programme for the EU.

Assuming that the immediate eurozone crisis has ended, as Mario Draghi claimed on March 5, 2015, where does all this leave the EU? The most dramatic diagnosis, hinted at in my second preface to the hypothetical second edition of this book, is that the eurozone crisis is merely the tip of an iceberg which has damaged and is about to sink the entire flawed project of European integration. A weaker form of this diagnosis suggests that, while a modest degree of integration, such as the single market, was and remains worthwhile, monetary union should not have been on the agenda, or at least not so early or on such an indiscriminate basis. The last of these variants suggests the policy of disaggregating the euro into a northern (hard) and/or southern (soft) version, or cutting adrift either the southern 'problem children' or, alternatively, Germany and possibly other more robust member states. Then there is the position of the 2010–2015 UK government, which echoed Winston Churchill's view of European integration: that it would be a good idea *for them*, by endorsing further integration within the eurozone while allowing a semi-detached and more independent position outside it.

This brings us to the question which is the main concern of this chapter: the impact of the crisis on the institutional and political future of the Union. Here again there is a negative view that it has opened up a latent but now serious political division between the North (especially Germany) and the South, with anti-austerity parties or movements strongest in Greece and Spain, less so in Italy and Portugal.[9] In institutional terms, the crisis has consolidated a tendency already present in the strengthening of the European Council (which brings together heads of state and government), in the Maastricht Treaty of 1992 and the Lisbon Treaty of 2009, towards what Jürgen Habermas (2012), following Philipp Dann and Stefan Oeter, has called 'executive federalism' and Hauke Brunkhorst (2014) 'collective Bonapartism'. In a context of crisis management, Angela Merkel, with a mixture of careful and more perfunctory consultation with other heads of government or state, drove through a set of measures, often in conjunction with the European Central Bank (sidelining the Commission and the Parliament) and the International Monetary Fund. However damaging many of these policies may have been, things had to be done, and done quickly, and Merkel filled a leadership vacuum, given a lame-duck French president, Sarkozy; his successor, Hollande (a lame duck from the outset); the marginality, for various reasons, of Italy; and the pathetic irrelevance of the United Kingdom.[10]

Anthony Giddens (2014: 6) has brilliantly distinguished between what he calls EU1, the formal institutions of the Union, and EU2, the ad hoc grouping of heads of state or government in the leading member states 'where a lot of the real power lies, exercised on a selective and informal basis'. In his argument,

> Europe must choose a new future, and this time the citizens must be directly involved. The eurozone countries have to set the pace, but the states outside the euro will be affected just as much by the innovations that are made.
>
> The Union must develop an EU3 – a system conferring more dynamic leadership and political legitimacy as well as greater macro-economic stability than exists at present . . . economic federalism, now inevitable if the euro

is to be saved, has to be accompanied by political federalism in some guise or other.

(Giddens, 2014: 9, 29)

This is a third response to the crisis, one which recognises the imperative of further integration, but in a different and more democratic form. Giddens' book is full of policies for a new Europe, but merely hopeful about the possibility of mobilising a political consensus around them.

As always, the 'deepening' of the Union is linked in complex ways with the question of its 'widening'. We may have entered the decade not just of accession fatigue, but of other types of fatigue (Majone, 2014). Volker Balli has written of the thir*teen* (not the earlier thirty) 'glorious years' of the EU from 1994 to 2007, ending with the global financial crisis and leading into the subsequent crisis of the Eurozone and its periphery, and the Estonian commentator Ahto Lobjakas (2009: 43) has suggested that 'the EU's project, internationally speaking, has been in retreat since pretty much the moment in 2004 it admitted 10 mostly ex-communist new member states':

> The tragedy of the European Union is that it is a 21st century power trapped in an (early) 20th century world which in turn appears to be sliding back into the 19th century . . . The voluntary ceding and pooling of sovereignty by member states . . . has in recent years not only become increasingly unpopular with national publics within the union, but is also perceived with growing concern by many (if not all) member state governments as counter-productive in a world where power is still overwhelmingly exercised by nation states and remains fundamentally a zero-sum game.
>
> (Lobjakas, 2009: 41)

It might seem strange to see such a neorealist analysis coming from one of the smaller member states,[11] but the rationale is clear.

> What [Robert] Cooper [2003] did not seem to pay sufficient attention to in the heady days leading up to the EU's historic enlargement in 2004 was that the space round the bloc is not virgin territory, but a patchwork of states contested by another . . . imperial power.
>
> (Lobjakas, 2009: 43)

If the EU's approach to the 2004 accession states seems with hindsight politically hypercautious, though economically reckless about the implications of accession for the new member states, the EU now abuts what in Russia's version of the Monroe Doctrine is a small but important part of its 'near abroad', as well as, with Turkey's membership on the horizon, the Middle East.[12]

Whereas the Vobruba model suggests the likelihood of a *Flucht nach vorn*, a forward flight, with the accession of Turkey and perhaps Belarus, Ukraine, and Moldova, as well as the remaining parts of the Western Balkans, there is a growing version of Euroscepticism focused around a retreat to a core Europe. This is worlds away from the Gaullist Euroscepticism of the British Conservatives, but for the political, as opposed to geographical, periphery of the EU, its implications would be similar, except that the periphery would be explicitly marginalised, excluded or self-excluded from Schengen, the Eurozone, and other forms of integration. These may shift from their original construction as the eventual telos for more or less all member states to becoming the privileges of an inner circle in the north of the continent. The discussion in 2010–2011 of a voluntary or involuntary contraction to a northern Eurozone will probably not go away as long as the economic fundamentals remain as they are. Anyone who, like me, doubts whether the EU could function on such a rigidly dualistic basis has to confront the analyses of Wolfgang Streeck, Fritz Scharpf, and others.

There are essentially two different lines of argumentation here which may be coming together. The first, which was a main theme of the previous chapter and of the analysis by Bo Stråth with which it ended, is the long-standing critique of the EU's inability to develop a social policy, reinforced by a negative evaluation of the Court's developing jurisprudence in this area. Set up in the heyday of Keynesian economics and social democratic optimism, the European Economic Community (EEC) might have been expected to address the issue of a common social policy, not least because it already had one in a disguised form in the Common Agricultural Policy (CAP), which was one of the main planks of the Community and the main area of expenditure. For a number of reasons this social policy agenda did not emerge. One might be the CAP itself and its very substantial costs. Another was undoubtedly the diversity and complexity of welfare systems even in the six original member states, with many recipients of state aid relying on a cocktail of payments from a variety of public and semi-public sources; a third was the suspicion of the EEC on much of the European Left, especially continental communists and later the British Labour Party (Nairn, 1973). The last attempt to develop a social dimension was perhaps the Mitterand–Delors initiative which resulted in the European Social Charter, bitterly opposed by the British, who opted out until the return of Labour, now relatively pro-European, in 1997.

By now, neoliberal orthodoxy had undermined the ideological basis for social policy, except where it could be subordinated to market considerations. This was indeed the route taken by the European Court in a series of judgements which expanded the individual rights of mobile Europeans to the benefit systems of other member states in which they settled or worked as transborder commuters. In 1981 the Court reaffirmed a decision in 1963 that it was for the Community and not an individual member state (in this case the Netherlands) to define who counted as a 'worker' under the Rome Treaty provision for the free movement of labour. A set of further judgements set aside provisions in the law of member states restricting social security and other benefits to resident nationals. James Caporaso and Sidney Tarrow argued that decisions of this kind amounted to a re-embedding of the EU market in a new legal and political structure. In the case of a British tourist who had been mugged in Paris and had been denied the compensation to which French nationals were entitled, 'It was enough for the ECJ that Mr Cowan was a

Community citizen and that he was seeking access to services that were his right under Community law' (Caporaso and Tarrow, 2009: 608). Along with a range of anti-discrimination provisions, such as the requirement that equal pay legislation should consider not just identical work, where there was a gender division of labour, but work of equal value, this amounted to 'a much broader movement to legalization and the creation of rights.' (Caporaso and Tarrow, 2009: 603) Thus '[g]iven the institutional obstacles preventing the Council of Ministers from making social policy, most social policy in the EU is a product of the ECJ and comes in the form of market-compatibility requirements' (Caporaso and Tarrow, 2009: 603).

In a rapid response from the Max Planck Institute in Cologne, where Fritz Scharpf (2009) had presented a much more critical analysis of the situation, Martin Höpner and Armin Schäfer argued that Caporaso and Tarrow had been too selective in their focus 'on individual social rights that the ECJ grants to labor migrants and their families' (Höpner and Schäfer, 2010: 24). Other Court decisions had had the effect of restricting the right to strike and other aspects of local labour legislation, as when foreign contractors bringing in workers from another member state could evade local minimum wage provisions. Following Scharpf in stressing the diversity of member states, not just in their levels of development and prosperity but in their models of capitalism, Höpner and Schäfer (2010: 27) argue that recent developments in the EU undermine the more coordinated or institutionalised forms of capitalism characteristic of Western continental and Nordic Europe. This is reflected at the political level:

> The integration of capital and labor markets that has now come to the fore causes asymmetrical adjustment burdens. Just as the attempted creation of a uniform European market for friendly and hostile takeovers means something different *institutionally* to France than it does to great Britain, so too does the opening of service markets have other implications for high-wage economies like Germany than it does for the East European accession countries. In both cases the actors define their interests first and foremost as country-specific rather than ideologically.

The alternative to a 'common political space' might seem to be a dual or multiple political space, rather as the literature discussed in the next chapter on the European public sphere often suggests that the alternative to a common public sphere is a set of multiple and overlapping or intersecting public spheres. Scharpf (2010: 244) did not make this argument, but he did point to the difficulties of mobilising agreement at the European level to defend current economic and social policy regimes, with the consequence that 'the EU cannot be a "social market economy"':

> [G]ood Europeans need to draw a distinction between their continuing support for political and social integration in Europe on the one hand, and their unquestioning acceptance of policy choices dictated by a non-accountable judicial authority, on the other hand.

Here, as in his earlier paper, Scharpf (2010: 243) proposed a mechanism which 'would allow member governments to appeal to the judgement of their peers in the European Council in cases where European law is felt to impose unacceptably tight constraints on politically highly salient national concerns'. In other words, a watered-down version of the 1965 'Luxemburg compromise', directed this time not against Council decisions but against those of the court in . . . Luxemburg.

This suggestion, which Scharpf preferred to the judicial alternative of a European Constitutional Court made up of, say, the chief justices of member states, would still be a European-level solution, though it is easy to see that it might lead to a situation where groups of states defended common interests, rather than just local concerns such as the restriction of abortion in Ireland or of alcohol sales in Sweden. This might be branded as special pleading by a sub-group of member states resistant to the idea that the fundamental economic policies and structures of member states should be coordinated according to the will of the majority. This social democratic or coordinated economy perspective (since, as Höpner and Schäfer noted in the passage quoted earlier, tends to cut across left–right divisions) was compatible with the two-speed integrationist approach formulated initially, as we saw earlier, by Schäuble and Lamers in 1994 and taken up by Joschka Fischer (2000), as well as by others such as Habermas. But this, as I have argued earlier, risks institutionalising a binary divide in what is currently a Europe of, as Delors once put it, variable geometry.

Proposals of the kind discussed earlier bring together three interconnected sets of problems: the failure of the EU to develop a social policy, its failure to address inequalities between member states, and its failure to develop an adequate political structure. Hauke Brunkhorst (2014b: 160) calls for an 'end to the cold war of the nations through transnationalisation of the democratic class struggle'.[13] In this perspective, the European Parliament might come to balance out the excesses of 'rule by judges' (Brunkhorst, 2014a: 164). This depends in turn on whether something like a European identity develops further, in the course of successive political events such as those through which we have lived since 2007, and earlier ones such as the Constitution debate (Statham and Trenz, 2013). As Klaus Eder (2011: 42) has suggested,

> . . . collective identity in Europe is still in a process of becoming, and instead of pre-empting a "European identity" we should look at the process and the factors that shape the robustness of the meaning of the events happening in its course.

The next chapter addresses some of these issues.

For the moment, we are left with the paradox of a European Union with an expansionist dynamic whose every expansion threatens further overstretch and whose most successful moves towards greater integration, Schengen and the euro, seem to be going sour. At the same time, its core member states in the industrial West are more and more dependent on the rest. Never has the regulation of global capitalism been more urgent, but the leading players are all handicapped in one way or another: the United States by economic deficit and political deadlock, which resulted in the downgrading in August 2011 of its credit rating; China by the simmering political conflicts which will one day undermine its political dictatorship (if this is not reformed earlier); and the EU by its inability to coordinate its economic and foreign policies. The rule of thumb always used to be that the pace of European integration depended on the strength of economic prosperity and of geopolitical threat (from the USSR). With prosperity gone for the foreseeable future, it remains to be seen whether the threats both from Russia and from a more aggressive China (or one engulfed in civil war), or a United States captured by Tea Party Republicans and/or withdrawing into isolationism, concentrate the European mind.[14]

Notes

1 See also the excellent review of the German original by Colin Crouch (2013).
2 Habermas (2013: 138) readily concedes this: 'Today we confront not (any longer) a legitimation crisis, but a solid (*handfest*) economic crisis'.
3 A process aptly described by Colin Crouch (2009) as 'privatised Keynesianism'.
4 For a comparative discussion, see Schäfer (2009).
5 Only the United Kingdom is solidly 'out' for the moment. Sweden is officially obliged to join at some point; Denmark is not, but has pegged its krone to the euro. Both envisage future referendums on joining, whereas the United Kingdom is currently flirting with one on membership of the Union itself.
6 As Lehndorf (2015: 9) points out, 'When one considers that Greece's share in the EU's economic output was at that time 1.8 per cent – it is now even smaller – it beggars belief that the announcement [of revised figures for public debt and the budget deficit] set off an avalanche that brought the European Monetary Union to the brink of collapse'.
7 As Offe (2015) summarises the situation: 'Banks enjoy a somewhat miraculous second-strike capability: After having contracted heavy losses from reckless investments, they emerge stronger than before, because the credit they supply is now more in demand'.
8 See the appendixes to Scharpf's paper, comparing Germany with the GIPS countries (here Greece, Ireland, Portugal, and Spain).
9 Historically, of course, these countries had a good deal in common with the later postcommunist accessions; Louka Katseli (2001: 85–86) gave a very similar analysis of their trajectories. More recently, they have been competitors for structural funds, and their relative prosperity, even after the crisis broke, has made postcommunist member states like Slovakia unwilling to support aid packages.
10 The critique by Ulrich Beck (2013), whose early death is a terrible loss to European sociology, seems to this extent unfair.
11 See Schöpflin (2009).
12 Giddens' explicit defence of federalism for the Union is accompanied by a call for serious discussion and 'closure' on the issue of 'where its ultimate borders are likely to lie' (Giddens, 2014: 204). For him, this would include Turkey but probably not (any more of) the former Soviet republics (except perhaps Moldova).
13 It has been suggested that the complex policy-making structure of the EU poses particular difficulties for social democracy, since '[c]ontrol of the market and capitalism

has always required both a strong central authority and a strong political force capable of pursuing policies that are different from the market's' (Moschonas, 2009: 173; see also Meyer and Rutherford, 2012, and, for a broader focus on social policy and social democracy, Offe, 2015).

14   The plethora of studies of integration contrasts with the virtual absence of systematic refection on possible disintegration. For a stimulating exception, see Vollaard (2014).

Bibliography

Åslund, Anders (2010) *The Last Shall Be First. The East European Financial Crisis*. Washington, D.C.: Peterson Institute for International Economics.

Beck, Ulrich (2013) *German Europe*. Cambridge: Polity.

Bohle, Dorothee and Béla Greskovits (2012) *Capitalist Development on Europe's Periphery*. Ithaca and London: Cornell University Press.

Brunkhorst, H. (2014a) 'Collective Bonapartism – Democracy in the European Crisis', *German Law Journal* 15(6). www.germanlawjournal.com/index.php?pageID=11&art ID=1658. Accessed July 27, 2015.

Brunkhorst, H. (2014b) *Das doppelte Gesicht Europas*. Frankfurt: Suhrkamp.

Caporaso, James and Sidney Tarrow (2009) 'Supranational Institutions and the Transnational Embedding of Markets', *International Organization* 63(Fall): 593–620.

Cooper, Robert (2003) *The Breaking of Nations*. London: Atlantic Books.

Crouch, Colin (2013) 'The Debtor State', *European Journal of Sociology* 54(3): 477–484.

EBRD (2012) *Transition Report. Cross-Border Integration – An Important Response to the Crisis*. London: European Bank for Reconstruction and Development.

EBRD (2013) *Transition Report. Stuck in Transition?* London: European Bank for Reconstruction and Development.

Eder, Klaus. 'Europe as a narrative network. Taking the Social Embeddedness of Identity Constructions Seriously', in Sonia Lucarelli, Furio Cerutti, and Vivien A. Schmidt (eds.), *Debating Political Identity and Legitimacy in the European Union*. London: Routledge, pp. 38–54.

Fischer, Joschka (2000) 'Vom Staatenverbund zur Föderation – Gedanken über die Finalität der europäischen Integration' ("Humboldt-Rede", 12. Mai 2000). www.europa. clio-online.de/site/lang__de-DE/mid__11373/ItemID__17/40208215/default.aspx and www.cvce.eu/en/obj/speech_by_joschka_fischer_on_the_ultimate_objective_of_ european_integration_berlin_12_may_2000-en-4cd02fa7-d9d0-4cd2-91c9- 2746a3297773.html. Accessed July 27, 2015.

Giddens, A. (2014) *Turbulent and Mighty Continent. What Future for Europe?* Cambridge: Polity.

Habermas, J. (2012) *The Crisis of the European Union. A Response*. Cambridge: Polity.

Habermas, J. (2013) *Im Sog der Technokratie*. Frankfurt: Suhrkamp.

Habermas, J. (2014) '"Für ein starkes Europa" – aber was heißt das?' *Blätter für deutsche und internationale Politik* 3(March): 85–94.

Hale, T., D. Held and K. Young (2013) 'Gridlock: From Self-reinforcing Interdependence to Second-order Cooperation Problems'. *Global Policy* 4(3) September: 223–235.

Hayek, F.A. (1939) 'The Economic Conditions of Inter-state Federalism', *New Commonwealth Quarterly*. V (2, Sept.): 131–149; reprinted in Hayek FA (1948) *Individualism and Economic Order*. Chicago: The University of Chicago Press, pp. 255–272.

Höpner, Martin and Armin Schäfer (2010) 'Polanyi in Brussels? Embeddedness and the Three Questions of European Economic Integration', MPIfG Discussion Paper 10/8. Cologne: Max Planck Institute for the Study of Societies.

Jacoby, Wade (2014) 'The EU Factor in Fat Times and in Lean: Did the EU Amplify the Boom and Soften the Bust?', *Journal of Common Market Studies* 52(1): pp. 52–70.

Joerges, C. and Rödl, F. (2008) 'Das soziale Defizit des europäischen Integrationsprojekts', *Kritische Justiz* 41(2): 149–165.

Katseli, Louka (2001) 'The Internationalization of Southern European Economies', in Heather D. Gibson (ed.), *Economic Transformation, Democratization and Integration into the European Union*. Basingstoke: Palgrave, pp. 75–118.

Lehndorf, Steffen (2015) 'Europe's Divisive Integration – An Overview', in Steffen Lehndorf (ed.), *Divisive Integration. The Triumph of Failed Ideas in Europe – Revisited*. Brussels: ETUI, pp. 7–37.

Leschke, Janine, Sotira Theodoropoulou, and Andrew Watt (2015) 'Towards Europe 2020? Austerity and New Economic Governance in the EU', in Steffen Lehndorf (ed.), pp. 295–329.

Lobjakas, Ahto (2009) *The Limits of Europe*. Tallinn: Estonian Foreign Policy Institute.

Majone, Giandomenico (2014) *Rethinking the Union of Europe Post-Crisis: Has Integration Gone Too Far?* Cambridge: Cambridge University Press.

Meyer, Henning and Jonathan Rutherford (eds.) (2012) *The Future of Social Democracy. Building the Good Society*. Basingstoke: Palgrave Macmillan.

Moschonas, G. (2009) 'Reformism in a "Conservative" System: The European Union and Social Democratic Identity', in J. Callaghan et al. (eds.), *In Search of Social Democracy. Responses to Crisis and Modernisation*. Manchester: Manchester University Press, pp. 168–192.

Myant, Martin and Jan Drahokoupil (2012) 'International Integration, Varieties of Capitalism and Resilience to Crisis on Transition Economies', *Europe-Asia Studies* 64(1) January: 1–33.

Nairn, Tom (1973) *The Left Against Europe*. Harmondsworth: Penguin.

Offe, Claus (2015) *Europe Entrapped*. Cambridge: Polity.

Schäfer, Armin (2009) 'Krisentheorien der Demokratie: Unregierbarkeit, Spätkapitalismus und Postdemokratie', *dms – der moderne Staat – Zeitschrift für Public Policy, Recht und Management* 1: 159–183.

Scharpf, Fritz W. (1988) 'The Joint-Decision Trap. Lessons from German Federalism and European Integration', *Public Administration* 66(2): 239–78.

Scharpf, Fritz W. (2009) 'Legitimacy in the Multilevel European Polity', *European Political Science Review* 1(2): 173–204.

Scharpf, Fritz W. (2010) 'The Asymmetry of European Integration or Why the EU Cannot Be a "social market economy"', *Socio-Economic Review* 8: 211–250.

Scharpf, Fritz (2011) 'Monetary Union, Fiscal Crisis and the Preemption of Democracy', London School of Economics: LEQS Annual Lecture Paper, May.

Scharpf, Fritz W. (2012) 'Perpetual momentum: directed and Unconstrained?', *Journal of European Public Policy* 19(1): 127–139.

Scharpf, Fritz W. (2013a) 'Monetary Union, Fiscal Crisis and the Disabling of Democratic Accountability'. In A. Schäfer and W. Streeck (eds.), *Politics in the Age of Austerity*. Cambridge: Polity Press, pp. 108–142. (Also published as MPIfG Discussion Paper 11/11, PDF).

Scharpf, Fritz W. (2013b) Legitimacy Intermediation in the Multilevel European Polity and Its Collapse in the Euro Crisis. In K. Armingeon (ed.), *Staatstätigkeiten, Parteien und Demokratie. Festschrift für Manfred G. Schmidt*. Wiesbaden: Springer VS, pp. 567–596. (Also published as MPIfG Discussion Paper 12/6, PDF).

Schöpflin, György (2009) *The Small States of Europe and Large Whirlpools: The Implications of a Multi-Polar World*. Tallinn: Estonian Foreign Policy Institute.

Statham, Paul and Hans-Jörg Trenz (2013) *The Politicization of Europe. Contesting the Constitution in the Mass Media*. London: Routledge.

Streeck, Wolfgang (2011) 'The Crises of Democratic Capitalism', *New Left Review* 71(September-October). www.newleftreview.org/?page=article&view=2914. Accessed July 27, 2015.

Streeck, Wolfgang (2012a) 'Markets and Peoples', *New Left Review* 73(January–February). www.newleftreview.org/?page=article&view=2939. Accessed July 27, 2015.

Streeck, Wolfgang (2012b) 'Wolfgang Streeck – Germany', *European Societies* 14(1): 137–139.

Streeck, Wolfgang (2012c) 'Varieties of What? Should We Still Be Using the Concept of Capitalism', in Julian Go (ed.) *Political Power and Social Theory*, 23, 311–321.

Streeck, Wolfgang (2014) *Buying Time: The Delayed Crisis of Democratic Capitalism*. London: Verso.

Vollaard, Hans (2014) 'Explaining European Disintegration', *Journal of Common Market Studies* 52(5): 1142–1159.

9 Europeanisation and the European Union

The concept of Europeanisation, though of relatively recent origin (if twenty-five years or so is recent), is fairly well entrenched in the literature, though a book review (Van den Bergh, 2009: 437) suggests that 'the Europeanization literature may not have come of age yet', and a major handbook opens rather disarmingly with the observation that '[t]he concept of Europeanization may have been, and perhaps still is, essentially contested as to its usefulness for the study of European politics' (Vink and Graziano, 2007: 3). It has, however, also been used more broadly to describe transnational societal and cultural processes, for example, by the anthropologists John Borneman and Nick Fowler (1997) and, more substantially, by Adrian Favell and Virginie Guiraudon (2011). In their introduction, Favell and Guiraudon (2011: 14–15) note that none of the very substantial comparative works in the later twentieth century on Western European state structures, political economy, welfare state regimes, and so on

> . . . give any credence to the impact of the European Union, or look for an underlying Europeanization of European society influenced or structured by the EU. There was, in short, no clear thought about the emergence of a distinctive European society (in the singular), even if some of the work hinted at convergent European social structures.

This is also absent, they argue, from most specialist work on the EU, dominated as it is by political science, international relations, and economics.[1] As well as focusing on institutional and policy questions, they suggest (Favell and Giraudon, 2011: 20), 'EU scholars should be asking how the emerging EU institutional complex changes or does not change the sources of social power and its distribution among live European actors'. Their book usefully covers these two areas, focusing on class and social and geographical mobility (and firms and markets) on a European scale, as well as, in the second half, examining politics in and oriented to the EU institutions.

Like globalisation, Europeanisation can refer either to a state or a process; some accounts of globalisation therefore prefer to describe the former as globality, for which the equivalent would be the clumsy term 'Europeanness'; we can probably do without 'Eurality'. It would be hard to deny that the terms globalisation and Europeanisation refer to observable processes in the contemporary world, and they often seem to overlap in their observable manifestations. Thus the globalisation of, say, the insurance market, may substantially mean in Europe its Europeanization.

We have learned, I think, to ask in relation to globalisation, what it is that is said to be globalised. Is it the globe? Is it social relations or sectors such as the one just mentioned? Is it national states? Whereas the globalisation literature often *slides* towards the last of these, asking about the implications of globalisation for 'us' in Germany, Britain, or wherever,[2] many globalisation theorists would see this as a rather old-fashioned and parochial way of thinking. In relation to Europeanisation, however, there often seems to be an automatic assumption that it *means* the Europeanisation of domestic political systems.[3] If I am right about this, it may just be a contingent feature of the way the term has been used so far, or it may be a symptom of a broader scaling-down of supranational ambitions. As I suggested in an earlier paper on European intellectuals (Outhwaite 2009), there may be a kind of Dutch auction in much thinking about Europe, where we start by asking whether there is a European society, or if not that, perhaps at least a Europe-wide civil society, and then retreat to a conception in which there may not be a European civil society but perhaps at least a European public sphere, and finally, if disappointed in that expectation,[4] to the theme of my earlier paper: whether at the *very* least we can talk about a smallish number of transnationally recognised European intellectuals, including social theorists.[5]

This is what is captured in the metaphor of the half-full or half-empty glass, or that of 'now you see it, now you don't'. It is hard not to find oneself vacillating between a relatively upbeat account of these matters and a more sober or pessimistic one. Howard Davis (2009: 267), in his excellent afterword to the volume in which that paper was published, suggested that I was too pessimistic in focusing on media structures:

> [T]he health of the European public sphere does not depend on, and should not be judged on, the extent of convergence in media regulation or the trans-frontier integration of markets . . . the evidence will neither be found in the media system increasingly dominated by the commercial imperative nor in the life-world dominated by the imperative to entertain, but in the space between where opportunities arise for intellectuals and their publics to act.
>
> (p. 267)

For Klaus Eder (2005: 341–342), too, an emergent public sphere and demos are evolving together:

> A transnational public . . . exists in Europe as a cross-cutting of elite publics, citizens' publics and popular publics, related to each other by some supranational institutional environment . . . A European public is not a chimera but a thing that already turns up in critical times [he mentions Habermas' intervention in the Iraq war protest] . . . A transnational public sphere . . . is one which

is no longer tied to a reified body of people such as the nation, but to a latent demos that can be there when time requires it.

This, then, to change the metaphor again, is the conceptual fence I sit on, along with, I think, quite a lot of other commentators on the European scene. Let me say a bit more about the structure of the fence. A number of people would say that, like God, we should content ourselves with a less ambitious project – in our case, that of mapping transnational practices rather than talking in grandiose terms about societies, civil societies, or public spheres. These include, for example, Gerard Delanty and Chris Rumford (2005), Rumford (2003), and Volker Balli (2009), who has powerfully argued that the EU polity itself should be understood as a structure of agreements and regulations, in a mood of 'new sobriety'/neue Sachlichkeit. My inclination is to take the other route, of seeing how much mileage one can get out of relatively traditional concepts such as state (or polity) and society (or civil society) in relation to *la chose européenne*.

Let me start with society. We should, I think, recognise that Durkheim is dead: our conceptions of society have to be less concretistic, more anchored in practices of sociation (Vergesellschaftung) at many different levels, including that of Europe as a region or the EU and its extensionally similar avatars (Schengenland, the eurozone, the European Economic Area, etc.) as a socio-political structure. The mechanisms of this sociation would include, for example, the euro and the increasingly dense intra-European transport links (faster trains, more and cheaper air routes, etc.) – even the (horribly bureaucratised) Bologna process in higher education. So we have a common currency, gradually extending to almost all the Union, and a common borderless space (except, of course, for the United Kingdom and Ireland). Neil Fligstein (2008: 2) records his surprise that Europeans, even those in the forefront of European-scale projects, are so unaware of the extent to which European society is a reality. As Adrian Favell (2009: 177) points out in relation to freedom of movement, '[T]he European Union is a unique space . . . there is nothing like this kind of politically constructed post-national space anywhere else on the planet'.

To this level of society there corresponds a level of state or polity somewhere between the national states and the level at which Martin Shaw and others have identified the beginnings of a global state. The EU polity, despite its catastrophic deficit in democratic legitimacy (Outhwaite, 2010), increasingly displays the attributes of a state, trumping national state authority through EU law and centralised powers (as in the Open Skies case). As the international lawyer Jan Klabbers (2011) has pointed out, both the US Supreme Court and the European Court of Justice (ECJ) resist any outside influences on their respective polities. (This, of course, raises important issues of the relation between globalisation, here in the form of cosmopolitan international law and Europeanisation.) The success of legal integration within the limits of a system which will always be conflictual (Nickel 2009), makes up in some respects, though not of course those of democracy and civil society, for the pathetic weakness of political integration.

European levels of state and society can be seen to interact and reinforce one another. It is because there are elections to the European Parliament that we get some limited attention, even in the United Kingdom, to EU matters. Farmers, whom one expects to be relatively isolated from the great world outside, are in fact more attentive than most of us to the politics of Brussels because of the Common Agricultural Policy (CAP). The euro makes Europeans of us all, unless we happen to live on the Anglo-Scandinavian periphery or, for the moment, in many of the newer member states.

Neil Fligstein (2008) focuses on the class slope of Europeanisation. There *is* a European society: 'Europe-wide social fields are being built where people and organizations from different countries come routinely to interact' (p. 9). And there *are* Europeans, but these form a small minority. '[T]here exists a European society for the group of educated, mobile people who are middle or upper-middle class' (p. 206). The 'Euro-clash' (pp. 217–218) from which the book takes its title is that between two intersecting trends: one towards closer integration and the other towards a defensive focus on the nation-state, mobilising those who have lost out in the processes of globalisation and Europeanisation.[6] Once again, the globalisation of recruitment to elite positions in business, universities, or sport tends, in the European region, to mean its Europeanisation. Adrian Favell (2011: 59) conducted two major complementary studies. One was a quantitative study based on 5000 telephone interviews with intra-EU migrants across Western Europe (Britain, France, Germany, Italy, and Spain), who make up a proportion of the total population in low single figures: 2.7% in the United Kingdom and France, 2.1% in Germany, and just over 1% in Spain and Italy. The only countries with substantially higher proportions are Belgium (6.4%), Ireland (9.6%), and nearly a quarter in Luxemburg. Recchi and Favell (2009) found that their respondents were substantially upper and upper-middle class in origin.[7]

> Upper and upper middle-class movers reach their highest number in Italy; around 45 per cent of British, French and Germans in Italy are drawn from classes I-II. Only Italians and Spanish in Germany (about 45 and 60 per cent respectively from class V-VII are exceptions to this rule, fitting in larger numbers with the traditional immigrant profile as low-skilled or manual workers.
> (Favell, 2011: 63–64)

Favell (2008) also conducted a qualitative study based on sixty interviews and participant observation of mobile young and youngish professionals in London, Brussels, and Amsterdam, pioneering 'Euro-stars' living in 'Euro-cities'.[8] Although many had improved their material life-chances, especially women moving from Southern Europe, and they mostly welcomed the cosmopolitan experience, they often encountered administrative and cultural obstacles even in these ostensibly highly cosmopolitan and globalised cities. Favell (2011: 74) summarises this as follows:

> Home countries of origin and foreign countries of residence alike have their way of re-asserting their norms, value systems and social hierarchies over the

lives of these pioneers. They see their experiences and opportunities being *re*-nationalized by the weight of mainstream lives lived in national structures; they are often caught out on a limb in their life choice, out of time and place in terms of both the peers they left back home, and the natives living and working around them.

Even the very substantial numbers of migrants from postcommunist EU states, who have benefited massively from freedom of movement in the early 2000s, have often stayed only for a few years, returning as the 2008 recessions hit Western and Eastern Europe. On the other hand, enough people have left some of the smaller states, such as the Baltic States, to create a serious demographic problem which is only now being realised. At the two extremes of postcommunist Europe, parts of Eastern Germany are becoming seriously depopulated, while very large numbers of Russians say that they would rather live abroad, as many are now doing (Narizhnaya, 2013).

We are still only in the early stages of developing accounts of Europe's social structures comparable to what is routinely available in most national states.[9] Juan Díez Medrano (2011: 34–35) usefully suggests looking at transnational processes along three dimensions: identity, strong trans-European ties, and political mobilization. Among the ties, he focuses in particular on the two extremes of capital ownership and intermarriage. Citing Rodríguez et al (2006), who find rather little evidence of cross-European as opposed to global or national investment,[10] he notes their claims for the existence in the financial sectors in Germany and Belgium of 'something akin to a "European" cluster of companies coordinating their investment strategies . . . it is precisely in this region that citizens identify most frequently as Europeans'. This is not just found at the heartland of European integration since the 1950s,[11] but is also the focus of work by Steffen Mau (2010), Jochen Roose (2010), and others on cross-border socialisation. As for intermarriage, Díez Medrano (2011: 38–39) notes the relatively high level of Anglo-Spanish marriages, reflecting the fact that the British, while largely abjuring a European identity, are prominent among those travelling to Spain for holidays or to live. Although intermarriage rates are low in Europe, between 1996 and 2007 'the odds that a Spaniard will marry another European have doubled or more in this period'. Despite straws in the wind like these and some evidence of Europeanised political mobilisation (Guiraudon 2011), Díez Medrano (2011: 46) ends up stressing what he neatly calls 'the enduring salience of the national'.

Mau and Verwiebe (2010: 286) suggest two elements of 'stratification through Europeanisation'. First, the 'emergence of new groups': EU elites (central and local civil servants and lobbyists) and Europeanised milieus such as Erasmus students; transnational elites and migrants (including retirement migration); and beneficiaries of EU transfers such as underdeveloped regions, agriculture, and fisheries. Second, 'effects on social conditions': marketisation creating pressure on uncompetitive industries, regions, and workers; 'spatialisation of social inequality' (regional and centre-periphery); and 'diffuse effects' such as freedom of movement and transnational consumption and payment systems, including the common currency. Regional integration

... increases income inequality as it drives welfare state retrenchment and pushes the adoption of market-oriented policies as well as fiscal austerity ... regional integration is associated with economic convergence among the Member States, but also with increased income inequality within national societies.

(Mau and Verwiebe, 2010: 291)

They cite the innovative work of Jason Beckfield (2006, 2009). As for the subjective dimension of inequalities, Delhey and Kohler (2006: 132) show that many Europeans have quite a developed understanding of other European countries as reference groups in their thinking about inequalities: 'By and large, the respondents' ratings reflect quite realistically the positions of countries in the GDP league table'. Mau and Verwiebe (2010: 352) conclude their analysis with the observation that

... Europe's social structure now is more than the sum of its parts: it is an emergent, discrete macro-societal formation. Important preconditions and driving forces of its emergence lie, on the one hand, in its common values, traditions and shared history ... and, on the other hand, in the politically initiated integration process, which affects large sectors of society.

A very substantial amount of work has been done on the topic of European identity, which was a regular question in the Eurobarometer polls from 1973 to 2007 and from time to time since then. The 1973 Copenhagen summit produced a paper on 'European identity', defined as being based on a 'common heritage' and 'acting together in relation to the rest of the world'. As Bo Stråth (2002) has suggested, the appeal to identity has in some ways replaced appeals to the notion of integration as a self-evident good.[12] The EU's Eurobarometer tracked identity for a long time, tending only to show that a European identity came well after regional or national ones for most Europeans. The national differences were more interesting, with Britons and Turks least likely to affirm a European identity and Germans, along with Italians and other southern Europeans, much more positive in their responses. Exposure to intra-European mobility through exchanges or migration had, unsurprisingly, a reinforcing effect.

Klaus Eder in particular has worked substantially on this topic, partly in conjunction with Bernhard Giesen and Willfried Spohn (see Maier and Risse, 2003). Much of the earlier work tended to focus on the topical issue of European Union citizenship, which had been put on the policy agenda by the Maastricht Treaty and subsequent actions in the 1990s. This is, in fact, the focus of Eder and Giesen (2001). As they argue in their concluding chapter (p. 266), citizenship can be seen as the 'foundation myth of a new European collective identity'; '[t]he democratic discourse on citizenship has become the transnational master-narrative of democratic self-organization in Europe' (2001: 264). The citizenship theme has subsequently become more muted, perhaps because the EU's citizenship policy was itself so half-hearted,[13] but the related theme of identity remains a major focus of work. Here Giesen tends to stress shared values in a Durkheimian way, whereas

Eder places more emphasis on conflict and dissensus. In his own chapter in the edited book, Eder (2001: 230) brings out the diversity of European culture:

> Although the code of cultural traditions in Europe represents a contradictory mixture of incompatible traditions, it obviously furthermore fulfils social-integrative functions . . . it follows that it is not the internal cohesion of a cultural code which makes social integration possible . . . What integrates is the fact that traditions are good for communication. Traditions are good in order to represent identity and difference.

It is not possible, he emphasizes, simply to Europeanize a national form of consciousness: 'For Europe is no longer as obvious as the nation has been'.[14] At a European level, the only realistic option is a minimalist conception of identity, which is constantly reshaped. Echoing Renan's remark about *national* consciousness, Eder (2001: 238–239) writes: '[T]he making of identity becomes daily political business'.

In a later volume, edited with Willfried Spohn, Eder returned to this theme via a discussion of the critiques of the concept of identity which, as he recalls, Adorno (19: 151) called 'the prototype of ideology'.[15] Addressing the fraught issue of 'core' versus 'peripheral' Europeans, Eder (2005: 205) concludes that 'the emerging transnational European society needs even more collective identity than national societies or any non-modern societies, because it is a system of social relations where social relations are mediated more than ever by cultural techniques'. As he writes a little later in the chapter (p. 207), 'there is no such "thing" as a collective identity or a collective memory – these concepts rather grasp a moment in a permanent struggle of naming'.

In another essay, Eder (2008: 33) refers to Europe as a 'transnational space of cultural differences'. In implicit contrast to Habermas, he stresses that he does not understand

> . . . a post-national situation in the sense that the national age is being replaced by a post-national age. Rather, I take the evolutionary view of emerging structures that are added to existing ones while changing their function.[16]

In the transnational situation of contemporary Europe, cultural differences are increased by migration, by the reaffirmation of ethnic identities, and, most importantly, by the fact that 'the nation has itself become a case of cultural differences within an emerging transnational community; national sentiments have become normal cultural difference' (Eder, 2008: 42).

The scene is set for 'an increase in symbolic struggles' (Eder, 2008: 44). The most promising possible outcome is one involving a 'transnational unity of differences':

> In the transnational situation there is no longer a people on top of class, nation or ethnicity; there are rather a series of people (*demoi*) who identify at times

with class, with nation or with ethnicity. The idea of a hierarchy of identifica-
tions is to be replaced by the idea of a network of cross-cutting identifica-
tions. These many *demoi* are held together by the reliability of an institutional
framework they have accepted by voluntary agreement and which guarantees
everybody the maximum fairness in real life.

(Eder, 2008: 46)

A recent volume to which Eder also contributed brings together the themes of
European identity and political legitimacy which, as one of the editors notes, have
often been discussed in isolation from one another (Lucarelli, 2011: 203). They
are clearly distinct, in that one could have a strong European identity without
supporting a particular political expression of it like the EU, but equally clearly
interrelated.[17] Vivien Schmidt (2011: 16–17) makes this point more fully and goes
on to relate it to her own model of the problematic interrelation between EU and
national politics. As we saw earlier, she sees a partial remedy in the extension of
debate about EU matters at the level of the member states:

[T]he EU depends on national elites *saying* what the EU has been *doing* for
the building of a sense of *being* European.
    But . . . national political elites have also been in the business of *saying*
what the nation state has been *doing* in their efforts to reinforce a national
sense of *being*, in particular, in light of the encroachments of European
integration.

(Schmidt, 2011: 27)

The problem, then, is the one discussed in the two previous chapters, that '[if]
EU citizens have little sense of identity in the EU and increasingly question its
legitimacy, then would politicizing the EU necessarily have the effect of building
legitimacy or of further undermining it?' (Schmidt, 2011: 34).

Eder (2011), like Schmidt, stresses the narrative dimension, in which his sociological realism and his focus on practices, including discursive practices, come
out strongly.[18] He insists that one should not reduce identity to measurable identi-
fications. An identity is something more sedimented:

A collective identity is a semantic property of the social relations among
a defined set of people. The set of people we are dealing with are the EU
citizens. The thing that these EU citizens share is the national citizenship
narrative.[19]

It therefore becomes an empirical question whether networks of European citizens will develop strong narratives around political and other issues at a European
level.

We can only wait for future events – for further opposition to the Lisbon
Treaty, for weak performances on the stage of foreign or migration policy – to

tell us about the robustness of the story that makes a political community and one day might also provide it with a collective identity.

(Eder 2011: 51)

A political identity cannot, in other words, be fabricated, in the way criticised by Furio Cerutti in his contribution to the same book. Cerutti deconstructs a Commission call for research on identity which

> . . . could assess how official identity symbols (such as the EU flag, the anthem, the EU slogan, the passport, the Euro, the '.eu' internet domain name, city branding like Brussels Capital of Europe or European capital of culture, commemoration days, artistic festivals or scientific events), and personal experiences with the European Union are present in the citizen's everyday life.

(Commission, 2009; Cerutti, 2011: 3–4)

To see the EU concocting a set of pseudo-national symbols as though it were a new state like South Sudan is not very convincing:

> It is only when the peoples and the elites in the EU and national institutions perceive that they are affected by the same choices, thus having a common road to follow, that they can take significant steps forward in identifying with each other and the institutions. In this sense, the creation of the euro was the most promising step forward in the past decades, both financially and symbolically.

(Cerutti, 2011: 5)

Albrecht Sonntag, in the same volume, also notes 'the counterproductive side effects of the EU's use of political symbols'. Nor, Cerutti argues, does one need to assume, like the German Federal Constitutional Court in its decision of 2009 on the Lisbon Treaty, that the EU would need 'a uniform [einheitlich] European people' to count as a legitimate subject of legislation, with the implication 'that, since this will not happen in Europe for at least a few decades, there will never be a democracy in Europe, or the EU quasi-polity can only be a-democratic' (Cerutti, 2011: 8).

These misunderstandings do, however, point to the importance of what Cerutti calls 'subjectivity' or 'a phenomenological approach to European identity' (Cerutti, 2011: 12–13):

> For the EU, legitimacy cannot but be what I call 'substantial legitimacy', which includes legitimacy in the Weberian sense (affinity to one of the acceptable models of good governance) made effective by good performances and supported by a sense of identity that (also) expresses itself through symbols and shared narratives. The problem is how this can work against the background of a sovereign power divided between member states and union, and

a conventional wisdom about legitimacy that sees it as a feature exclusive to the democratic nation state.

One indirect way of approaching issues of European identity deserves special mention: it is another inevitably imprecise but often-asked question about trust in other nationalities. Jan Delhey (2007: 255) used this approach to address the question of social cohesion in the EU. It relates, he notes, to an argument made by Karl Deutsch et al (1966: 17):

> The populations of different territories might easily profess verbal attachments to the same set of values without having a sense of community that leads to political integration. The kind of sense of community that is relevant for integration . . . turned out to be rather a matter of mutual sympathy and loyalties; of 'we-feeling', trust and mutual consideration; of political identification in terms of self-images and interests; of mutually successful predictions of behaviour and of cooperative action in accordance with it.

In an earlier paper Delhey (2005: 15) stressed the use of this measure: Not only would the EU as a whole be more cohesive, the more EU citizens trust one another, but '[i]f the "others" were trusted as much as one's own compatriots, the social barriers between the nations would have dissolved, and the sign "nationality" would no longer be a significant one in the European social space'. The successive EU enlargements have, by definition, increased the geographical distance between members: Have they also increased social distance as measured by (mis)trust? Delhey (2007: 273) concludes from an analysis of Eurobarometer surveys that distance tends indeed to reduce trust, though common borders have no observable effect in the opposite direction.

> The integrative effect of enlargement depends on the extent to which acceding nations differ from the present club members in three main dimensions: level of modernization (mechanisms: prestige), cultural characteristics (mechanisms: similarity) and power in the international system (mechanisms: perceived threat).

Turkey is therefore particularly suspect for other Europeans, being poor, Muslim, and large; Bulgaria and Romania were also relatively untrusted both by EU-15 citizens and by those in the 2004 accession round. On the positive side, there is a general increase in levels of trust, and this tends to increase with length of EU membership. There are, however, variations: 'For example, the Germans now trust the Poles less but trust the Czechs and Hungarians more than they did the Italians in the 1970s' (Delhey, 2007: 267).

On the related issue of support for free movement of workers within the EU, which, of course, was a fundamental principle from the beginnings of the European Community, it is alarming to note that, according to the European Values

Survey of 1999–2000, only three states (Sweden, Netherlands, and Denmark) had a majority rejecting the suggestion that 'If jobs are scarce, employers should give priority to [nationals] over immigrants' (Halman, 2001: 69). The average in the EU-15 was a third, and in the 2004–2007 accession states barely over 10%. Interestingly, Ukraine and Russia had figures twice those of the EU postcommunist states. Florian Pichler (2009: 725) argues, however, that the apparent East/West difference is explained by structural factors, primarily gross domestic product (GDP) and 'sociopolitical culture'. Cosmopolitanism is better measured without reference to identity, since cosmopolitans may be strongly or weakly attached to locality and national state.

An Arena Working Paper by Hans-Jörg Trenz (2009) lends support to Eder's approach to European identity, bringing together the constitutional debates in the European Union from 2002 to 2007 with issues of identity and democracy. Rather than postulating a European identity 'as the basic infrastructure of a European democracy', Trenz (2009: 1) suggests that it should be seen rather 'as a contingent by-product of entering into democratic practice'. In an approach which I discuss more fully later in this chapter in relation to the public sphere, Trenz examines the way in which the issues were framed in two quality newspapers in France and two in Germany. He found that in both countries in the debates up to 2005 instrumental justifications (in terms of power politics, interests, or problem solving) were much more prominent (close to 50%) than those invoking rights and democracy (around a third in Germany and a quarter in France) or identity and values (only 17% in Germany and 27% in France). Where it was used, identity language was diverse and fragmented; Trenz speaks of an 'identitarian Babel'.

Discussions of European identity do in fact tend to merge into questions about the existence of a European public sphere. Here, as in the case of research on identity, 'Frankfurt' critical theory has substantially shaped the debates. As Michał Krzyżanowski, Anna Triandafyllidou, and Ruth Wodak (2009: 1) note, Habermas' *Structural Transformation of the Public Sphere* was a major influence, especially after it finally appeared in English in 1989, followed by a paper by Nancy Fraser (2007, 2014) on 'Transnationalizing the Public Sphere'. Work at Bremen by the late Bernhard Peters and others (Peters, 2008; Wessler et al, 2008) and by Paul Statham, who earlier collaborated with Eder on social movements and the media, has been particularly prominent. One of the most recent and perhaps the most substantial study, that by Statham and Ruud Koopmans, covering seven West European states, illuminates not just the public sphere but many other areas of EU politics and civil society. In his own chapter in the volume, Statham (2010: 292) concludes soberly that

> . . . European civil society is . . . not only marginal compared with national civil society and the European executive, but also compared with globally operating NGOs . . . the substance of the European Union's public sphere "deficit" consists in the over-domination by elite actors of Europeanized debates.

Rather than trying to arouse a largely dormant European civil society, or to increase the powers of a European Parliament which is inevitably remote from most voters, Statham (2010: 306) suggests

> ... that the supranational European institutions holding power would be better off strengthening their communicative links to citizens and seeking legitimacy through national parliaments and media, rather than engaging in another round of top-down efforts to engage a remote and inattentive citizenry.

This would bring European Union politics into line with a well-established finding of studies of European media. As Koopmans (2007: 185) comments, the weakness of a supranational media presence in Europe means that 'one therefore arrives naturally at a "Europeanization" approach . . . that focuses on the domestic aspect of European integration – in this case, the ways in which European integration affects debates in national news media'. Michał Krzyżanowski, Anna Triandafyllidou, and Ruth Wodak, in a volume concerned with a series of 'crisis moments' in late-twentieth- and early twenty-first-century Europe, also stress the pervasive 'national filter' through which issues affecting Europe are presented.[20] The approach Statham suggests would probably work better in continental Europe than in the more detached countries of Scandinavia, let alone the United Kingdom.[21]

A related issue which is increasingly attracting attention is so-called 'Euroscepticism'. The term is slightly misleading, since it refers not so much to scepticism about particular policies or prospects as to a more wholehearted rejection of integration and/or the main directions of policy in the European Union.[22] Research has tended to focus on party politics, and in particular the question of whether Euroscepticism functions more as a resource drawn on contingently and opportunistically by parties or as a more fundamental structuring feature of politics in Europe. There is certainly a tendency for fringe or peripheral parties of the left and right to adopt a Eurosceptical stance, but as Statham et al (2010: 2712) point out, the only core parties in their sample of seven countries generating a 'hard' level of Eurocriticism are the British Conservatives and the conservative Swiss People's Party (SVP): 'committed Euroscepticism at the core of party systems is basically limited to two conservative parties in Britain and Switzerland'.[23] They conclude that '[w]hat we are perhaps witnessing is the beginning of a process in which criticism of Europe becomes normalized within national party politics'.[24] This work supports an analysis presented by Hooghe and Marks (2008) of the shift 'from permissive consensus to constraining dissensus'. They focus on the gap between elite and mass support for the EU, with elites uniformly in the mid-80s to mid-90s and public support running, in the extreme cases, at under half that level.[25] It is not, they argued, that European publics have become significantly more Eurosceptical. 'The decisive change is the elite has had to make room for a more Eurosceptical public'[26] (Hooghe and Marks, 2008: 9). In other words,

European politics has become multi-level in a way that few, if any, anticipated. The European Union is no longer isolated from domestic politics; domestic politics is no longer isolated from Europe. The result is greater divergence of politically relevant perceptions and a correspondingly constricted scope of agreement.

(Hooghe and Marks, 2008: 14)

The left/right division has traditionally been viewed as a relatively easy basis for compromise, as compared to regional or religious cleavages, but, as the authors point out, 'left/right conflict over European issues is not the same as left/right conflict over national policies because the scope for economic redistribution is throttled in Europe' (Hooghe and Marks, 2008: 15).

Consequently, left/right conflict at the European level is about social regulation, rather than redistribution. This alienates the radical left which regards the European Union as a one-sided capitalist project endangering social protection at the national level. Social democrats also wish to protect national welfare regimes from a European joint-decision trap, but see virtues in co-ordinating fiscal policy at the European level and in building a 'citizens Europe'.

(Hooghe and Marks, 2008: 16)

It is therefore not the left–right dimension which shapes choices on European issues, but Herbert Kitschelt's libertarian/authoritarian dichotomy, which they had earlier reformulated as green/alternative/libertarian (*gal*) versus traditionalism/authority/nationalism (*tan*). The *tan*s are by no means always also 'black',[27] in the sense of Christian Democratic or, more broadly, conservative: indeed, conservative parties in Western Europe tend to divide or even split on the European issue. British Conservatives are divided; the German Christlich-Demokratische Union (CDU) is more pro-EU than its Bavarian ugly sister, the Christlich-Soziale Union (CSU); the Gaullists are split on the question. Further right, there is, however, a clear association.

Tan parties, such as the French Front National or the Austrian Freiheitliche Partei, reject European integration because they believe it weakens national sovereignty, diffuses self-rule and introduces foreign ideas. They oppose European integration for the same reasons that they oppose immigration: it undermines national community.

(Hooghe and Marks, 2008: 18)

Earlier in Western Europe, it was often left parties that were suspicious of European integration; the British Labour Party was a strong example (Nairn, 1973). In postcommunist Europe, there is still an association between the Left (both re-badged communist parties and newly founded left parties) and Euroscepticism.

'In Western Europe, the mobilization of national identity and of left concerns about the loss of national protection is expressed in different parties; in Eastern Europe, they are fused' (Hooghe and Marks, 2008: 18). As they note, 'The debate on Europe has been framed by opponents of European integration, i.e. populist *tan* parties, nationalists in conservative parties, and radical left parties' (Hooghe and Marks, 2008: 21).

There is, then, a built-in tendency for European politics to undermine the willingness to compromise on which it so much depends at the level of the EU. The authors point in particular to referendums as a source of conflict and note that 'Referendums are not easily forgotten' (Hooghe and Marks, 2008: 20). One might add that the EU, like the weather, is intrinsically more likely to attract criticism than approbation, as reflected in low levels of public (as distinct from elite) support. To quote Ivan Krastev (2011),

> There is a paradox that we know from the countries of the former Yugoslavia and the Soviet Union: that while the younger generation is much more European-minded than the previous one, it is less interested in defending the European Union. It takes the EU for granted; defending it makes no sense to them.

It is perhaps for reasons such as this that Eurobarometer phrased one of its standard questions in such stark terms: 'How would you feel if you were told tomorrow that the EU had been scrapped?'[28] Even then, the 2004 result had 43% 'indifferent' as against 39% 'very sorry' and 13% 'very relieved'. The major Western European countries are all close in their responses over time, except that Italians are much more prone to say 'sorry' and Britons much less (Rother and Langner, 2004: 11). On the question of disenchantment with the European Union, Trenz and de Wilde (2009) offer a useful overview, concluding that Europe has not become 'an ethically charged notion in pan-European public discourses'.[29]

Such public discourses are indeed hard to find at a European level. If one looks at media structures across Europe, print and electronic media have experienced opposite developments: concentration in the first case; massive diversification in the latter. In both, however, ambitious projects of Europeanization in the 1970s tended to be abandoned or scaled down in the latter part of the twentieth century. Morley and Robins (1995: 52) noted, for example, 'the retreat of many of the entrepreneurial enthusiasts of "European" satellite television, away from their original pan-European ambitions, towards a revised perspective which accepts the limitations and divisions of separate language/cultural markets in Europe'. There is also no genuinely European newspaper, published in the major languages, unless one counts the monthly *Le monde diplomatique*. (*The European* [1990–1998], published only in English and owned for most of its brief life by the notorious Robert Maxwell, made a poor showing compared to the *Herald Tribune, Financial Times*, or *Economist*.)[30] More discouraging still, perhaps, is the abandonment of automatic syndication of articles in mainstream newspapers, as opposed to the production of specialised cosmopolitan editions such as *Le*

Monde's weekly/monthly in English or the *Guardian Weekly*. As Timothy Garton Ash, someone who deservedly benefits more than most from transnational syndication, commented in *The Guardian* (5.14.09, p. 27) in an article on European foreign policy, 'This column . . . may appear in translation in a number of European newspapers, but even that will be patchy and unusual'.

A recent survey of transnational media in Europe draws a useful distinction between

- European pan-regional media, such as Euronews, launched in 1993 on a transnational public service broadcasting base and transmitting in the major West European languages; this however is highly dependent on second-hand material and very uneven in its European reach.[31]
- Global media, such as *Le monde diplomatique* or CNN International.
- International media, such as the Franco-German ARTE, created in 1991 and now broadening out across Europe, but with most of its viewers coming from France and to a lesser extent Germany.[32] *Baltic Times*, with its headquarters in Riga, is an Eastern European example.
- National media with a transnational mission, such as Deutsche Welle (broadcasting TV in English and Spanish as well as German and most recently also in Arabic), BBC World, and France 24, which broadcasts in English as well as French, but is solidly and explicitly French in its basis and orientation.

Brüggemann and Schulz-Forberg (2009: 7012) display these various media thus in relation to their ideal types. Viewing/readership figures in Europe in 2006–2007 are given in Table 9.1 (Brüggemann and Schulz-Forberg, 2009: 706):[33]

The authors conclude: 'While European transnational communication space is growing and attracting influential elite audiences, the role of transnational media in reaching out to the broader European public remains very modest' (Brüggemann and Schulz-Forberg, 2009: 707; cf. Adam, Berkel, and Pfetsch, 2003: 70; also Eriksen, 2005). As Koopmans (2007: 185) comments, the weakness of a supranational media presence in Europe means that 'one therefore arrives naturally at a "Europeanization" approach . . . that focuses on the domestic aspect

Table 9.1

Deutsche Welle TV	5.3 million per week
BBC World	0.8 million per day
Arte	c.15 million per day (4.9m. in Germany and 9.3m. in France)
Euronews	3.6 million per day
European Voice	15,600 copies (weekly), plus daily web version
Financial Times	0.2 million daily
The Economist	0.4 million weekly
Time	0.4 million weekly
CNN International	1.6 million per day
Eurosport	22 million per day

of European integration – in this case, the ways in which European integration affects debates in *national* news media'.

Those taking a sceptical view of the existence of a European public sphere, particularly media theorists, have tended to conclude that Europe has not got past first base. Marianne van de Steeg (2002: 499–500) cites three typical examples from Philip Schlesinger (1995: 25–26), Peter Graf Kielmansegg (1994: 27–28), and Dieter Grimm (1995: 294–295).[34] For Kielmansegg and Grimm, linguistic division more or less rules out the possibility of Europe forming a communicative community. Schlesinger sets the stakes fairly modestly as 'the minimal establishment of a European news agenda as a serious part of the news-consuming habits of significant European audiences who have begun to think of their citizenship as transcending the level of the nation-state'. He goes on, however, to suggest that

> . . . even a multilingual rendition of a single given European news agenda is more likely to be diversely "domesticated" within each distinctive national or language context . . . than it is likely to reorient an audience towards a common European perspective.

And what for Schlesinger is a hypothesis becomes for Grimm a matter of definition:

> A Europeanized communication system ought not to be confused with increased reporting on European topics in national media. These are directed at a national public and remain attached to national viewpoints and communication habits. They can accordingly not create any European public nor establish any European discourse.

As van de Steeg argues, this is both theoretically and empirically dubious. Theoretically, it overlooks the ways in which a communicative community may not just be the product of an existing substantive community but may help to bring it into existence.[35] Empirically it seems to rule out interesting elements of Europeanisation within existing national media structures. As she shows in a modest but suggestive study of the discussion in 1989 to 1998 of the prospects of EU eastern enlargement in four European weeklies, there are significant differences between the four. Whereas *Der Spiegel* and the *New Statesman* tended to relate most clearly to their respective national frameworks, the Spanish *Cambio 16* reprinted articles from similar German, Italian, and French journals, and the Dutch *Elsevier* engaged more directly with pan-European debates. The *New Statesman* stands out for its relative lack of attention to the concrete implications of enlargement for the EU's institutions and procedures (van de Steeg, 2002: 514–515).

Hartmut Wessler et al (2008) provide a more substantial comparison over a longer time period, 1982–2003, which comes to similar results. The authors avoided specifically European themes like that studied by van de Steeg; their own detailed case studies of newspapers in France, Britain, Austria, Germany, and Denmark concern military intervention and genetically modified food. For these two cases, they compared a right-centre and a left-centre paper in each country. The differences in relation to Europeanisation were, however, not significant, so their broader investigation of Europeanisation confined itself to one from each country: *Le Monde, The Times, Frankfurter Allgemeine, Die Presse*, and *Politiken*. The authors distinguish usefully between 'vertical Europeanization', a focus on EU policy and governance, and 'horizontal Europeanization', by which they mean the openness of national media to situations, voices, and approaches elsewhere in Europe.[36] This suggests (pp. 56–57) four elements of Europeanization:

1   *Comprehensive Europeanization.* This pattern combines high levels of vertical and horizontal Europeanization, that is, close monitoring of EU governance and intensive discursive integration between European countries.
2   *Segmented Europeanization.* This means vertical but not much horizontal Europeanization. Nationally segmented public spheres pay more attention to Brussels but not to each other.
3   *Europeanization aloof from the EU.* This would mean horizontal without vertical integration. Here, an increasingly intensive communicative exchange takes place between European neighbours, but no more attention is paid to the EU as such.
4   *A parochial public sphere.*

The five papers vary interestingly along these dimensions, as presented on page 63 of their text.

Le Monde stands out for the thoroughness of its coverage of the EU but pays little attention to analyses from elsewhere in Europe; the other four differ little in the degree of their EU coverage but differ sharply in their openness to other European countries. Even discounting references from Germany, *Die Presse* stands out in the volume of its quotations from other European countries (p. 67); *The Times* is predictably the most parochial.

There are clearly interesting issues here about what determines the degree of Europeanisation of national and, for that matter, regional media. (We may expect *The Times*, a right-wing paper published in a large insular state with delusions of grandeur, to pay little attention to the outside world, but the position of *Politiken* is perhaps more surprising.)[37] The overall picture is of what the authors call segmented Europeanisation, in which national media converge independently in the quality of their approach to the EU and to other issues but pay relatively little attention to other aspects of the rest of Europe apart from those foregrounded by the EU.

Perhaps we need to ask why we might *want* more of a European public sphere. One reason might be that invoked by Habermas and Derrida in their appeal against the invasion of Iraq. Europe here appears as a regional and, in aspiration at least, a value platform. This does not, however, get us very far, since their campaign was, for good reasons, part of a *worldwide* movement of revulsion against the war. A more substantial reason would be to have a base to mobilise European opinion on a European scale around issues concerning Europe as a geographical region and/or a political community. Here, however, we fall into the black hole well described by Vivien Schmidt (2006) and discussed in previous chapters: the misfit between the levels of the European polity and the levels at which decisions are taken.

Schmidt's analysis was followed in 2008 by at least two important contributions taking a similar line. One is the influential article by Hooghe and Marx (2008), discussed earlier. The second, a substantial book by Richard Münch (2008, 2010), analysed what he called 'the dialectic of transnational integration and national disintegration', concluding that Europe is headed towards an individualistic liberal constitutionalism much more like the United States than the traditional (or, more precisely, late nineteenth to late twentieth century) European welfare state. Focusing particularly on the impact of the European Court, reinforced at a political level by the 'Open Method of Coordination' (OMC) between member states, Münch (2010: 152–153) identified a process in which individuals and corporations are 'freed' from the constraints or protections of local or national regulation, whereas the OMC releases member states themselves from local and European democratic control, resulting in a degradation of politics towards right-wing extremism.

We are therefore confronted by a ridiculous and disgraceful situation in which elections to the European Parliament – a parliament whose members repeatedly assure us, with some justification, that it provides a more useful basis for policy making than those of the member states – take the form of a (usually midterm) national pseudo-election. The 2014 election was a substantial improvement, since it also involved the indirect election of the Commission president, preceded by hustings, notably three large meetings in Maastricht, Florence, and Brussels, which were no less substantial than many of those in national elections. Even then, David Cameron contested the legitimacy of the procedure, and this dimension of the election was occluded in many member states, particularly, of course, the United Kingdom. In the Parliament itself, one can see EU politics either as a half-full chamber of deliberative democracy (Eriksen and Fossum, 2000; Neyer, 2003) or as a half-empty one of distasteful horse trading, or what De Gaulle called 'tractations'.

It is arguably this situation which should concern us as national and European citizens, rather than the defective state of the European public sphere. But the two issues are interrelated, and this suggests a possible focus both for analysis and for policy. Eurobarometer (EB) and other surveys consistently show that European voters are less keen on joint decisions within the EU on issues concerning health and welfare, education, taxation, and pensions, which are otherwise central to their concerns.[38] EB 76 (Autumn 2011: p. 76), has less than a quarter supporting decisions at the EU level on pensions and only slightly more on taxation and welfare,[39] as against over three quarters on fighting terrorism and around two thirds on environmental, defence, and foreign policies (Finland, followed at some distance by Sweden and the United Kingdom, diverge from the consensus in wanting national decision making for defence and foreign affairs). EB 74 (Autumn 2010) has two thirds favouring national decisions on education. EB 68 (Autumn 2007: 110) lists the highest and lowest national scores for support for European-level action. Not surprisingly, it is the least well-provided countries such as Portugal,

Cyprus, and Greece where support for a common approach is strongest, and the Nordic countries and Netherlands where it tends to be weakest, with a marked dispersion on all these dimensions between, for example, a high of 68% and a low of 8% for health and social security.

Here then, there seems a prima facie case for a strong EU policy initiative to take these issues in hand and to level up rather than down. It has to be said that most of the relatively little literature I know on the subject is extremely sceptical about the prospects of such a policy focus. Leibfried and Pierson's excellent edited volume on European social policy largely amounts in the end, I think, to showing that, to put it crudely, there isn't one and there is unlikely to be one, with the editors trying in their conclusion to give as upbeat an analysis as possible. As they note, however, the disparities in the proportion of resources allocated to social spending are massive (Leibfried and Pierson, 1995: 32). It is true that the national states have incompatible systems and that to rock this boat might seem unwise, but it might be a way of breathing some life into an EU politics which otherwise threatens to deteriorate into irrelevance, except as the object of xenophobic demagogy.[40]

There is, however, a further reason why we might be concerned with the public sphere as a value in itself rather than as a means to other political ends, however important. This concerns the levels at which public communication takes place. At a time when the EU has moved, however falteringly, towards multilevel governance, the media forums which observe them, no less than the parliamentary assemblies which might control them (in the continental sense, of course, of the word control), have become, if anything, *more* national. Not only is there no European newspaper; regional newspapers in the United Kingdom and elsewhere, including those of potential national states such as Scotland, are under serious threat. In thinking about these issues, it is probably helpful to look back at the history of European nationalism. What we need, arguably, are Andersonian imagined communities at supranational, national, and subnational levels, intersecting with and enriching one another. We seem, however, rather unlikely to get them.

* * *

Conclusion

European studies have been immeasurably enriched by late-twentieth-century social theory oriented to themes of modernity, globalisation, and cosmopolitanism, as well as by notions of governance and Europeanisation emerging more directly from the mainstream literature.[41] As Hans-Jörg Trenz (2008a: 19) suggests in a splendid recent overview, we need to ask 'whether European integration is to be understood in terms of continuity or in terms of discontinuity of the project of modernity . . . [and] . . . how Europeanization is linked to more encompassing processes of globalization'. And this is a challenge which sociology, broadly understood, is particularly well fitted to meet, despite its late arrival on the scene of European studies. In a chapter in Favell and Guiraudon's book on the sociology of the European Union, Trenz (2011: 213) concludes: 'European society is not simply the other side of EU governance to be addressed and domesticated by EU institutions. It is, above all, an emergent reality, indicating a major reconfiguration of the European social, political, economic and cultural space'. The sociological classics, he notes, have a contribution to make. Max Weber's sociology is 'helpful to understand the dynamic aspects of European integration as a modern form of political order that expands around a bureaucratic apparatus in constant search of legitimacy' (Trenz, 2011: 195). What Weber called 'rule by officials' (Beamten-herrschaft) – a pejorative term distinct from his value-free concept of bureaucracy – clearly exists in an extreme from that at the EU level. Whereas in Germany after 1918 Weber had wanted to balance rule by officials with the charismatic element provided by a directly elected president, the EU has produced a pale imitation in the elected presidency of the European Council, choosing one of the most faceless potential candidates, Herman van Rompuy, to inaugurate the post. (Donald Tusk has since developed a slightly more substantial profile.)

Emile Durkheim, the other founding father of sociology (counting Marx here as a grandfather), pioneered the theme of integration with his distinction between 'mechanical' and 'organic' solidarity.[42] In what was probably a deliberate inversion of the usual associations of these terms, he identified mechanical solidarity with 'simple' societies whose members mostly did the same things (for example, hunting and gathering), and organic solidarity with the interdependence of members of societies with a complex division of labour.[43] Trenz goes on to discuss the relevance of two more recent theorists, Michel Foucault and Pierre Bourdieu, with Foucault illuminating in particular the 'disciplinary' practices of EU regulation and security policies and Bourdieu the accumulation and use of social capital by Europeanised elites and mobile professionals (the 'Eurostars' studied by Adrian Favell [2008]. More recently, Didier Georgakakis (2012) has edited a major book developing a Bourdieusian approach to the 'Eurocrats', and David Spence and I have outlined the relevance of the work of Luc Boltanski and his collaborators (Outhwaite and Spence, 2014). Bourdieu inspired some of the most important work on postcommunism by Ivan Szelényi and others.[44] His influence can be seen in other work on the EU by Niilo Kauppi (2012) and Frédéric Mérand (2011a, 2011b).

Foucault has indeed been a source of some major work on the EU, for example, the study by William Walters and Jens Henrik Haahr (2005). Walters and Haahr creatively apply Foucault's model of governmentality to give a distinctive critical edge to the question of how Europe is governed. In terms of EU studies, their analysis connects with, for example, the work by Andrew Barry (2001) and Giandomenico Majone (1996). 'By foregrounding regulatory practice they are able to convey something of the uniqueness of the EU: *how* it is able to govern extended social and economic spaces without possessing anything like the administrative apparatus or financial capacity of a nation-state' (Walters and Haahr, 2005: 14; see also 138–139)[45] Foucault's stress on the collection of information and the representation of the territory in the governmental *imaginaire* illuminates their analysis of Jean Monnet's practice in the European Coal and Steel Community, where the *bilan* yields a *vue générale* of the industries. The regulated freedom of movement within the EU combines freedom and surveillance in a manner which invites a Foucauldian approach, as does, in a different way, the 'benchmarking' practices involved in the Open Method of Coordination (and, as we have seen, the accession process) (Walters and Haahr, 2005: 138–139).[46]

Foucault has, then, a good deal to offer in the study of an entity like the EU, which relies so much on 'soft' or 'capillary' power rather than the traditional mechanisms of state authority and its exercise. A Foucauldian approach is also prominent in the analysis of EU territorial or spatial policy, notably in a book by Ole B. Jensen and Tim Richardson (2003).[47] Transport networks and the creation of larger or smaller transborder regional entities, such as the North Sea region or the Danish/Swedish Øresund region, respectively, can be seen, they argue, to embody the pursuit of what they call a monotopia, a single European space:

> [W]e might conceptualise the emerging field of European spatial policy discourse as an attempt to produce a new framework of spatialities – of regions within member states, transnational mega-regions, and the EU as a spatial entity – which disrupts the traditional territorial order, and destabilises spatialities within European member states.
>
> (Jensen and Richardson, 2003: 44)[48]

The theme of territorial representation is discussed more fully in the appendix; for the moment I am concerned with the power of this unifying discourse as it confronts environmentalist objections and those of regions or cities marginalised or ignored by big European projects. Jensen and Richardson (2003: 254–255) suggest that the northern, eastern, and southern peripheries of the enlarged EU might collaborate to encourage

> . . . a more nuanced policy approach to places and peripherality. However, the risk is that divergent regional positions will not be able to achieve this, and that the core/urban hegemony in the EU spatial policy will prevail. If this happens the survival of locally constructed places in Europe appears unlikely as anything other than rundown backward spaces, or exotic and 'authentic' communities.

The beginnings of a serious normative *political* theory of the EU, as anticipated by Deirdre Curtin (1997), can be found in the work of Richard Bellamy and Dario Castiglione (2000, 2003), Heidrun Friese and Peter Wagner (2002, 2006) and, more recently, in an edited book by Jürgen Neyer and Antje Wiener (2010). For Friese and Wagner (2002: 351), the inadequacy of a purely technocratic or 'output' legitimation of the emergent European polity points to the need

> . . . to envisage a Europe that can provide "input legitimation", in Scharpf's terms, but contra Scharpf,[49] that has a "European people" as the ultimate source of authority, in Grimm's terms but contra Grimm, and that shows

"relations of association" that can sustain high levels of trust and solidarity, in Offe's terms but contra Offe.[50]

As they note, this requires us to reconnect historical sociology and political philosophy, which had drifted apart in the second half of the twentieth century (Friese and Wagner, 2002: 343). The process of European integration can be understood in the terms of republican political philosophy as 'the deliberate founding of a polity' (Friese and Wagner, 2002: 353), but this still leaves open the question of what, if anything, is specifically European about such a polity. An answer, they suggested, could be found in a 'specifically European form of modernity' – more solidaristic and less individualistic than that found, for example, in North America.[51]

The wide-ranging volume edited by Neyer and Wiener contains valuable chapters by authors discussed earlier in this book, notably Beck and Grande who develop their ideas on empire, and Erik Eriksen. Eriksen's notion of a 'stateless vanguard', together with Neil Walker's chapter on sovereignty and Andreas Føllesdal's summary discussion of federalism, reopen fundamental issues which had lain somewhat dormant since the exchange in 1998 between the European Court judge Federico Mancini and Joseph Weiler. Mancini (1998: 41) had argued uncompromisingly for a federal EU, 'ridding the Union of the last . . . vestige of its original constitution: the essentially international nature grafted onto its policy-making machinery'. Weiler (1998: 62) responded equally vigorously that we should 'just forget about a European State and start thinking . . . about . . . democracy'.

> I am concerned that the boundary between Europe and non-Europe is plenty deep and does not need a further deepening, which a European State would surely bring about.
>   Being conservative and old-fashioned, I prefer the banal status quo of a Supranational Community to the bold new world of another State.
>
> (Weiler, 1998: 60)

Weiler undoubtedly won on points, and Justice Mancini's federalism looks even less sober now than it did at the time, yet as Føllesdal points out, 'federal ideas and elements,' notably the relation between levels glossed over by the principle of subsidiarity, continue to be highly relevant. The EU, particularly in its legal architecture, may have affinities with (other) international organisations, but it remains, more importantly, something like a polity. And law, as Habermas and others have insisted, demands democratic legitimation.

Notes

1 See Delhey (2005) and Delanty and Rumford (2005).
2 More generally, of course, regional integration has long been seen as a response to globalisation (see, for example, Behr, 2004: 153). My thanks to my colleague Hartmut Behr for a copy of his paper and his comments on an earlier version of this section.

3 See, for example, Goetz and Sahling (2008: 4), '[T]here is broad agreement that Europeanisation stands for the consequences of European integration as they are observable within the member states of the European Union (and beyond)'. Héritier (2005: 199–200) distinguishes three senses of the term but then focuses on one of them: '[T]he impact of . . . EU policy measures on the existing policies, political and administrative processes, and structures of member states'. See also the classic overview by Olsen (2002).

4 It is, of course, a simplification to pose the issue simply as one of the existence or non-existence of a European public sphere. As Thomas Risse (2002: 1–2) and others have suggested, it makes more sense to distinguish between different types of public spheres and different dimensions of 'transnationalness'. For a more optimistic analysis, see, for example, Trenz and Eder (2004) and Risse (2014).

5 Richard Münch (1999: 249), for example, suggested that the bearers of a European identity will primarily be 'the elites of top managers, experts, political leaders and intellectuals'. Fligstein (2008) also emphasises this aspect.

6 See also Hix (2008) for a more detailed and nuanced account of EU political cleavages.

7 Class categories here are the Erikson, Goldthorpe, Portocarero scale, as used in the European Social Survey. On mobility within the EU, see http://ec.europa.eu/eurostat/statistics-explained/index.php/Migration_and_migrant_population_statistics; also Recchi (2015).

8 Cities like these *are* exceptional, as noted by Andreotti and Le Galès (2011: 88) in their study of elites: 'Lyon, Milan and Madrid in our selection represent dynamic, relatively large and international European cities, although they do not display quite the same global features as Paris or London'. In Milan, for example, 'our interviewees do not mention many international connections . . . Similarly, in Madrid or Lyon, belonging to international networks was also relatively limited . . . by contrast, most Parisians mention two or three foreign friends with whom they have regular exchanges' (Andreotti and Le Galès, 2011: 93–94).

9 One of the most interesting recent contributions is work by Ovsey I. Shkaratan and Gordey Yastrebov. Yastrebov (2010) suggests that in a statist society like Russia, and perhaps in other postcommunist states (Shkaratan and Yastrebov (2010: 2) there is a differentiation between East Central Europe and 'eastern Christian societies (Russia, Ukraine, Bulgaria, Romania, Georgia)' and the stratification hierarchy 'is most likely to resemble a rigid system of relatively isolated *estates*, which originate from power ranks, rather than the hierarchy of *classes*, which originate from the general distribution of labour and property relations'. This is reflected in looser associations between education, occupation, and income and lower subjective and objective measures of meritocracy. A 2011 special issue of *European Societies* (13(3)) addresses issues of career mobility in Western Europe.

10 For a different emphasis, see Fligstein (2011).

11 Though also of historical antagonisms. I sometimes wondered why KLM commuter flights from Amsterdam to Germany featured announcements in Dutch and English but never, in my experience, in German.

12 See also Schulz-Forberg and Stråth (2010: 40–43).

13 For a comprehensive discussion, see Shaw (2007); also Shaw, Bellamy, and Castiglione (2006). Barbara Einhorn (2006) uses the term in the broader sense of Eder and Giesen's volume. For an interesting angle on EU and national citizenship, see Joppke (2010) and Recchi (2015: 107–122).

14 Eder is closer than most critical theorists to functionalist as well as evolutionary forms of analysis; see Trenz and Eder (2004) and Eder and Trenz (2007).

15 Eder also discusses the critique by Brubaker and Cooper (2000).
16 Habermas (2011: 45–46) has more recently offered a much more muted defence of European postnationalism. He insists that a 'supranational commonwealth' (Gemeinwesen) like the EU should not be understood as 'a kind of *incomplete* federal republic' and that the national states 'are not only historical actors on the way to the civilising of the core of force (Gewaltkern) in political authority, but *lasting* achievements and living forms of an "existing state of justice" (Hegel)'.
17 There is then the further question, answered affirmatively by Dieter Fuchs in his chapter, of whether a sense of identity conduces to support for further integration. However, '[t]he question concerning the integration ideals can only be addressed by elite and public discourses. The results of these discourses require the scope of European identity to be left entirely open. And as long as this is the case, the question of whether a strong or weak identity is required will also remain open' (Fuchs, 2011: 73).
18 See also Eder (2006).
19 Eder (2011: 42). As he notes (p. 41, n. 8), this is an approach pioneered by Karl Deutsch.
20 Krzyżanowski, Triandafyllidou, and Wodak (2009: 262). As they also note (p. 268), 'the international character of the European Public Sphere does not support the conception of Europe as an ethically charged notion in pan-European public discourses'. See also Hepp et al (2012).
21 Statham's stress (p. 286) on the peculiarity of UK discourse on the EU is fully documented in the rest of the study, which covered five other member states (France, Germany, Italy, Netherlands, and Spain) and one nonmember, Switzerland.
22 As Statham et al (2010: 273) note, '[G]rowing criticism of Europe is not coterminous with emergent Euroscepticism. Significantly high Eurocriticisms among Dutch center parties in our sample were actually indicative of a normalized Europhile party politics'.
23 See also their Table 10.4, p. 264. One should probably now add the UK Independence Party and perhaps also the *Front National*.
24 p. 272. For an interesting analysis of the gender gap in support for the EU, with women expressing lower levels of support than men in a wide variety of member states, see Liebert (1997); also Banducci and Netjes (2003).
25 Hooghe and Marks (2008: Fig. 4, p. 11). Those of the EU-15 with the greatest gap between elite and mass support are (in increasing order) France, the United Kingdom, Belgium, Finland, Austria, Germany, and Sweden.
26 As Karp, Banducci, and Bowler (2003: 279) showed in relation to the EU-15, there is a clear relationship between perceptions of the benefits of EU membership and the actual level of net financial transfers, with Germany and Sweden at the bottom and Ireland and Greece at the top. The Dutch are more positive than their objective position would suggest: the British, predictably, less so.
27 The 'Black and Tans' were a special force of the Royal Irish Constabulary, responsible for state terrorism in the last years of British rule in Ireland.
28 The French and German versions are a little more muted, referring to 'disparition' and 'Scheitern'.
29 See also Hooghe and Marks (2008). Their Figure 4, p. 11, shows the gap between roughly constant elite support in 1996 across the member states and a 50% difference in popular support ranging from Ireland to Sweden, whereas their Figure 3 shows the decline in support from around 46% in the mid-1980s to the high 30s in 2003–2005.

30 *The Economist* sells more than twice as many copies in the rest of Europe as it does in the United Kingdom, and over twice as many again worldwide. *The Financial Times* also sells twice as many in the rest of Europe and slightly more again in the rest of the world (Brüggemann and Schulz-Forberg, 2009: 705). The *European Daily* remains apparently at a programmatic stage.

31 (Brüggemann and Schulz-Forberg, 2009: 703). For postcommunist Europe, one could add *Transitions Online* (TOL), based in Prague, which claims 7000 subscribers and, plausibly enough, a substantially larger number of readers. (Subscribers can forward articles from the site to others.)

32 In print, this is paralleled by *Lettre International*, first published in France in 1984 and describing itself as 'Europas Kulturzeitschrift', which has a home base in Germany and editions in several languages.

33 To these one might add *Transitions Online*, with 7000 subscribers, and *Baltic Times*, with a weekly circulation of 12,000 in 2009 and a claimed 150,000 readers of the print and/or online versions (website, accessed 3.23.15).

34 Another would be Jürgen Gerhards.

35 Although she does not discuss intellectuals explicitly, van de Steeg's conception of the public sphere is loaded in that direction; she defines it as 'consisting of actors who debate in public a topic which they consider to be in the public interest, i.e. of concern to the polity'. More importantly, a media analysis of this kind would be highly relevant to assessing the structural opportunities for Europeanizing intellectuals. There are, of course, parallels with Habermas' position on these issues and, more specifically, with his dispute with Grimm. Also with Ulrich Beck and Edgar Grande's more speculative argument in *Cosmopolitan Europe* that a reflective and cosmopolitan conception of Europe can to some extent escape the dilemmas of in/out, us/them, nation-state/federation. The undeniable elitism of the EU is here given a positive spin: the EU embodies the paradox of a civil society *from above* aiming to establish one from below (Beck and Grande, 2004: 196). More optimistically, they suggest, the concept of European civil society offers the EU the opportunity of opening up a transnational space in such a way that it organises itself.

36 For an earlier version of this distinction framed in slightly different terms, see Koopmans and Erbe (2004).

37 See, however, Favell (2008: ix–x).

38 On the harmonisation of welfare state regimes, see, for example, Busch (2011); also the excellent volume edited by Alber and Gilbert (2010) of comparative studies within the EU and with the United States.

39 EB 74 (Autumn 2010: 56), has two thirds favouring national decisions on education. In relation to the crisis, EBs 79n and 80 recorded stable responses to the question about whether remedies should best come from the EU (22%) or the national governments (21%–22%).

40 See, for example, Marlier and Natali (2010) and, for the postcommunist region, Vanhuysse (2006a, 2006b), Offe (2009), and Fuchs and Offe (2009). Alber and Gilbert (2010: 415) conclude their edited volume: 'Looking at the data displayed here . . . it is difficult to see how the European countries form part of a common social model'. A number of chapters in their book point in particular to the differences between the continental Western European states (with the Nordic and Southern European ones as relatively generous and mean outliers, respectively) and the Anglophone and postcommunist ones.

41 Several excellent chapters in Rumford (2009) are concerned with this.

42 Mau and Verwiebe (2010: 276, citing Heidenreich [2006: 44]), suggest that national social and employment policies are comprehensive and grounded in mechanical solidarity, whereas European-level ones are limited and relate to organic solidarity.

43 Richard Münch (2008) develops this Durkheimian (and later functionalist) theme.

44 See in particular Eyal, Szelényi, and Townsley (1998) and other work discussed in Outhwaite (2007); also the fascinating account of a Bourdieusian 'practitioner' in Chechnya in Derlugian (2005).

45 As they note later, '[T]he European Commission relies heavily on "elite capture" and the formation of extensive networks which reach well beyond its institutional boundaries' (Walters and Haahr, 2005: 29).

46 As Neil Walker (2006: 548) points out in a classic paper on sovereignty (which was, of course, one of Foucault's bugbears), '[T]he recent development of the Open Method of Coordination is in some measure at least in response to the indeterminacy and contestation of jurisdictional boundaries between state and EU . . . The OMC responds by side-stepping the hard questions of competence and substituting for a compartmentalised decision-making hierarchy an inclusive policy cycle which lacks any authoritative end-point'.

47 I am grateful to Chris Rumford for drawing my attention to these books; see his introduction to Rumford (2009). In a related vein, Erik O. Eriksen, whose theoretical affiliations are more Habermasian, speaks of an EU 'deliberative epistocracy' (Eriksen, 2009: 168–177).

48 The EU's insistence that essentially unitary states like Poland and England (as distinct from the United Kingdom) should develop more or less artificial regional entities is a striking example.

49 It is surely no longer the case, even if it was in 1999, that effective European policy 'is limited to certain policy areas of relatively low political salience in which its legitimacy is not really in doubt' (Scharpf, 1999: 203; cited by Friese and Wagner [2002: 349]).

50 Offe (1998) had expressed doubts, restated in Offe (2003, 2005), whether Europe could sustain a level of solidarity in the context of social policy comparable to that in national states. See also Offe (2009, 2015).

51 Wagner (2012) develops this argument more fully.

References

Adam, S., B Berkel, and B Pfetsch (2003) 'Media Opportunity Structures – A Brake Block for the Europeanisation of Public Spheres?' www.EUROPUB.COM. Accessed July 27, 2015.

Alber, Jens and Neil Gilbert (eds.) (2010) *United in Diversity? Comparing Social Models in Europe and America*. Oxford: Oxford University Press.

Andreotti, Alberta and Patrick Le Galès (2011) 'Elites, Middle Classes and Cities' in Adrian Favell and Virginie Guiraudon (eds.), *Sociology of the European Union*. Basingstoke: Palgrave, pp. 76–99.

Balli, Volker (2009) *Power and Gestalt of Political Concepts. A Study of the Emergence, Nature and Self-Understanding of the European Union Polity*. Ph.D. thesis, EUI.

Banducci, Susan and Catherine Netjes (2003) 'Gender, Supra-National Institutions and European Integration', ECPR Conference, Marburg.

Barry, Andrew (2001) *Political Machines: Governing a Technological Society*. London and New York: Athlone Press.

Beck, Ulrich and Grande, Edgar (2007) 'Cosmopolitanism: Europe's Way out of Crisis', *European Journal of Social Theory*, 10(1): 67–85.

Beckfield, Jason (2006) 'European Integration and Income Inequality', *American Journal of Sociology* 71: 964–985.

Beckfield, Jason (2009) 'Remapping Inequality in Europe. The Net Effect of Regional Integration on Total Income Inequality in the European Union', *International Journal of Comparative Sociology* 50(5): 1–24.

Behr, Hartmut (2004) 'Globalisierung als Motor regionaler Integration? Untersuchungen zum Selbstverständnis des "Akteurs EU", *Zeitschrift für Politik ZfP*, Heft 2: 135–154.

Bellamy, Richard and Dario Castiglione (2000) 'Democracy, Sovereignty and the Constitution of the European Union: The Republican Alternative to Liberalism', in Z. Bankowski and A. Scott (eds.), *The European Union and Its Order*. Oxford: Blackwell, pp.170–190.

Bellamy, Richard and Dario Castiglione (2003) 'Legitimizing the Euro-"Polity" and Its "Regime". The Normative Turn in EU Studies', *European Journal of Political Theory* 2(1): 7–34.

Borneman, John and Nick Fowler (1997) 'Europeanization', *Annual Review of Anthropology* 26: 487–514.

Brubaker, Rogers and F Cooper (2000) 'Beyond "Identity"', *Theory, Culture and Society* 29: 1–47.

Brüggemann, Michael and Hagen Schulz-Forberg 'Becoming Pan-European? Transnational Media and the European Public Sphere, *International Communication Gazette*, 71(8): 693–712.

Busch, Klaus (2011) 'Das Korridormodell – Relaunched. Ein Konzept zur Koordinierung wohlfahrtsstaatlicher Politiken in der EU.' *Internationale Politikanalyse*. Berlin: Friedrich-Ebert-Stiftung.

Cerutti, Furio (2011) 'How Not to (Mis)understand Political Identity in the European Union', in Sonia Lucarelli, Furio Cerutti, and Vivien A. Schmidt (eds.), *Debating Political Identity and Legitimacy in the European Union*. London: Routledge, pp. 3–154.

Curtin, Deirdre (1997) *Postnational Democracy. The European Union in Search of a Political Philosophy*. Dordrecht: Kluwer.

Davis, Howard (2009) 'Conclusion. Revisiting the Concept of the Public Intellectual', in Christian Fleck, Andreas Hess, and Stina Lyon (eds.), *Intellectuals and Their Publics*. Farnham: Ashgate, pp. 261–270.

Delanty, Gerard and Chris Rumford (2005) *Rethinking Europe: Social Theory and the Implications of Europeanization*. London: Routledge.

Delhey, Jan (2005) 'Das Abenteuer der Europäisierung. Überlegungen zu einem soziologischen Begriff europäischer Integration und zur Stellung der Soziologie zu den *Integration Studies*', *Soziologie* 34(1): 7–27.

Delhey, Jan (2007) "Do Enlargements Make the European Union Less Cohesive? An Analysis of Trust between EU Nationalities," Journal of Common Market Studies 45: 253–279.

Delhey, Jan and U. Kohler (2006) 'From Nationally Bounded to Pan-European Inequalities? On the Importance of Foreign Countries as Reference Groups', *European Sociological Review* 22(2): 125–40.

Derlugian, Georgi (2005) *Bourdieu's Secret Admirer in the Caucasus: A World-System Biography*. Chicago: University of Chicago Press.

Deutsch, Karl et al. (eds.) (1966) *International Political Communities*. Garden City: Anchor Books.

Díez Medrano, Juan (2011) 'Social Class and Identity' in Adrian Favell and Virginie Guiraudon (eds.), *Sociology of the European Union*. Basingstoke: Palgrave, pp. 28–49.

Eder, Klaus (2005) 'Remembering National Memories Together: The Formation of a Transnational Identity in Europe', in Klaus Eder and Willfried Spohn (eds.), *Collective Memory and European Identity*, Aldershot, Ashgate, pp. 187–220.

Eder, Klaus (2006) 'Europe's Borders. The Narrative Construction of the Boundaries of Europe', *European Journal of Social Theory* 9: 255–271.

Eder, Klaus (2008) 'Symbolic Power and Cultural Differences: A Power Model of Political Solutions to Cultural Differences', in Per Mouritsen and Knud Erik Jørgensen (eds.). *Constituting Communities. Political Solutions to Cultural Conflict*. Basingstoke: Palgrave.

Eder, Klaus (2011) 'Europe as a Narrative Network. Taking the Social Embeddedness of Identity Constructions Seriously', in Sonia Lucarelli, Furio Cerutti, and Vivien A. Schmidt (eds.). *Debating Political Identity and Legitimacy in the European Union*. London: Routledge, pp. 38–54.

Eder, Klaus and Bernhard Giesen (eds.) (2001) *European Citizenship. Between National Legacies and Postnational Projects*. Oxford: Oxford University Press.

Eder, Klaus and Hans-Jörg Trenz (2007) 'Prerequisites of Transnational Democracy and Mechanisms for Sustaining It: The Case of the European Union', in Beate Kohler-Koch and Berthold Bittberger (eds.), *Debating the Democratic Legitimacy of the European Union*. Lanham: Rowman and Littlefield, pp. 165–188.

Einhorn, B. (2006) *Citizenship in Contemporary Europe*. Basingstoke: Palgrave; 2nd edn 2010.

Eriksen, Erik Oddvar (2005) 'An Emerging European Public Sphere', *European Journal of Social Theory* 8(3): 341–363.

Eriksen, Erik Oddvar (2009) *The Unfinished Democratization of Europe*, Oxford: Oxford University Press.

Eriksen, Erik Oddvar and Fossum, J. E. (eds.) (2000) *Democracy in the European Union – Integration through Deliberation?*. London: Routledge.

Eyal, G., Szelényi, I. and Townsley, E. (1998) *Making Capitalism Without Capitalists : Class Formation and Elite Struggles in Post-Communist Central Europe*. London: Verso

Favell, Adrian (2008) *Eurostars and Eurocities. Free Movement and Mobility in an Integrating Europe*. Oxford: Blackwell.

Favell, Adrian (2009) 'Immigration, Migration and Free Movement in the Making of Europe', in Jeffrey T. Checkel and Peter J. Katzenstein (eds.), *European Identity. Cambridge*: Cambridge University Press, pp. 167–189.

Favell, Adrian and Virginie Guiraudon (eds.) (2011) *Sociology of the European Union*. Basingstoke: Palgrave.

Fligstein, Neil (2008) *Euro-Clash. The EU, European Identity, and the Future of Europe*. New York: Oxford University Press.

Fligstein, Neil (2011) 'Markets and Firms' in Adrian Favell and Virginie Guiraudon (eds.), *Sociology of the European Union*. Basingstoke: Palgrave, pp. 100–124.

Fraser, Nancy (2007) 'Transnationalizing the Public Sphere. On the Legitimacy and Efficacy of Public Opinion in a Post-Westphalian World', *Theory, Culture & Society* 24(4): 7–30.

Fraser, Nancy et al. (2014) *Transnationalizing the Public Sphere*, ed. Kate Nash. Cambridge: Polity.

Friese, Heidrun and Peter Wagner (2002) 'The Nascent Political Philosophy of the European Polity', *Journal of Political Philosophy* 10(3): 342–364.

Friese, Heidrun and Peter Wagner. (2006) 'European Political Modernity', in Ralf Rogowski and Charles Turner (eds.), *The Shape of the New Europe*. Cambridge: Cambridge University Press, pp. 61–86.

Fuchs, Dieter (2011) 'European Identity and Support for European Integration', in Sonia Lucarelli, Furio Cerutti, and Vivien A. Schmidt (eds.), *Debating Political Identity and Legitimacy in the European Union*. London: Routledge, pp. 55–192.

Fuchs, Susanne and Claus Offe (2009) 'Welfare State Reform in the Enlarged European Union: Patterns of Reform in Postcommunist States', in Chris Rumford (ed.), *The SAGE Handbook of European Studies*. London: SAGE, pp. 420–441.

Georgakakis, Didier (2012) *Le champ de l'Eurocratie: Une sociologie politique du personnel de l'UE*, Paris: Economica.

Goetz, Klaus and Meyer-Sahling, Jan-Hinrik (2008) 'The Europeanisation of National Political Systems: Parliaments and Executives', *Living Reviews in European Governance* 3(2).

Grimm, Dieter (1995) 'Does Europe Need a Constitution?', *European Law Journal* 1(3): 282–302.

Guiraudon, Virginie (2011) 'Mobilization, Social Movements and the Media' in Adrian Favell and Virginie Guiraudon (eds.), *Sociology of the European Union*. Basingstoke: Palgrave, pp. 128–149.

Habermas, Jürgen (2011) 'Wie demokratisch ist die EU? Die Krise der Europäischen Union im Licht einer Konstitutionalisierung des Völkerrechts', *Blätter für deutsche und internationale Politik*, 8: 37–48.

Halman, Loek (2001) *The European Values Study: A Third Wave. Source Book of the 1999/2000 European Values Study Surveys*. Tilburg: WORC.

Heidenreich, Martin (ed.) (2006) *Die Europäisierung sozialer Ungleichheit*. Frankfurt: Campus.

Hepp, A., M Brüggemann, K Kleinen-von Königslöw, S Lingenberg, and J Möller (2012) *Politische Diskurskulturen in Europa. Die Mehrfachsegmentierung europäischer Öffentlichkeit*. Wiesbaden: VS Verlag für Sozialwissenschaften.

Héritier, Adrienne (2005) 'Europeanization Research East and West: A Comparative Assessment', in Frank Schimmelfenning and Ulrich Sedelmeier (eds.), *The Europeanization of Central and Eastern Europe*. Ithaca: Cornell University Press, pp. 199–209.

Hix, Simon (2008) *What's Wrong with the European Union and How to Fix it*. Cambridge: Polity.

Hooghe, Liesbet and Gary Marks (2008) 'A Postfunctionalist Theory of European Integration: From Permissive Consensus to Constraining Dissensus', *British Journal of Political Science* 39(1): 1–23.

Jensen, Ole B. and Tim Richardson (2003) *Making European Space. Mobility, Power and Territorial Identity*. London: Routledge.

Joppke, Christian (2010) 'The Inevitable Lightening of Citizenship', *European Journal of Sociology* 51(1): 9–32.

Karp, Jeffrey, Susan Banducci and Shaun Bowler (2003) 'To Know It is to Love It? Satisfaction With Democracy in the European Union', *Comparative Political Studies*, 36(3): 271–292.

Kauppi, Niilo (ed.) (2012) *A Political Sociology of Transnational Europe*. Colchester: ECPR Press.

Kielmansegg, Peter (1994) 'Läßt sich die Europäische Gemeinschaft demokratisch verfassen?', *Europäische Rundschau* 22(2): 23–33.

Klabbers, Jan (2011) 'The European Union in the Global Constitutional Mosaic', in Neil Walker, Jo Shaw, and Stephen Tierney (eds.), *Europe's Constitutional Mosaic*. Portland: Hart, pp. 287–307.

Koopmans, Ruud (2007) 'Who Inhabits the European Public Sphere? Winners and Losers, Supporters and Opponents in Europeanised Political Debates', *European Journal of Political Research* 46: 183–210).

Koopmans, Ruud and Jessica Erbe (2004) 'Towards a European Public Sphere? Vertical and Horizontal Dimensions of Europeanised Political Communication', *Innovation* 17 (2): 97–118.

Krastev, Ivan et al (2011) 'The EU: The Real Sick Man of Europe?', *Eurozine*, August 5. www.eurozine.com/articles/2011–08–05-vienna-en.html. Accessed July 27, 2015.

Krzyżanowski, Michał, Anna Triandafyllidou, and Ruth Wodak (eds.) (2009) *European Public Sphere and the Media: Europe in Crisis*. Basingstoke: Palgrave.

Leibfried, Stephan and Paul Pierson (eds.) (1995) *European Social Policy*. Washington, D.C.: Brookings.

Lucarelli, Sonia (2011) 'Debating identity and Legitimacy in the EU: Concluding Remarks', in Lucarelli, Cerutti, and Schmidt (eds.), pp. 193–206.

Maier, Matthias L. and Thomas Risse (eds.) (2003) 'Final Report of the Thematic Network "Europeanization, Collective Identities and Public Discourses (IDNET)"', Robert Schuman Centre for Advanced Studies, EUI 2003. www.eui.eu/DepartmentsAnd Centres/RobertSchumanCentre/Research/ArchivedProjects/Idnet/Index.aspx. Accessed March 22, 2015.

Majone, Giandomenico (1996) *Regulating Europe*. Routledge Research in European Public Policy. London: Taylor & Francis.

Mancini, Federico (1998) 'Europe: The Case for Statehood' *European Law Journal*, 4(1): 29–42.

Marlier, Eric and David Natali, with Rudi van Dam (eds.) (2010) *Europe 2020: Towards a More Social EU?* Brussels: Peter Lang.

Mau, Steffen (2010) *Social Transnationalism. Lifeworlds beyond the Nation State*. London: Routledge.

Mau, Steffen and Roland Verwiebe (2010) *European Societies. Mapping Structure and Change*. Bristol: Policy Press.

Mérand, Frédéric (2011a) 'Governance and State Power: A Network Analysis of European Security', *Journal of Common Market Studies*, 49(1): 121-47.

Mérand, Frédéric (2011b) *European Security since the Fall of the Berlin Wall*. Toronto: University of Toronto Press.

Morley, David and Kevin Robins (1995) *Spaces of Identity. Global Media, Electronic Landscapes and Cultural Boundaries*. London: Routledge.

Münch, Richard (1999) Europäische Identitätsbildung', in R. Viehoff and R.T. Segers, *Kultur, Identität, Europa*. Frankfurt: Suhrkamp.

Münch, Richard (2008) *Die Konstruktion der europäischen Gesellschaft. Zur Dialektik von transnationaler Integration und nationaler Desintegration*. Frankfurt: Campus. Abridged as Münch 2010.

Münch, Richard (2010) *European Governmentality: The Liberal Drift of Multilevel Governance*. London: Routledge.

Nairn, Tom (1973) *The Left Against Europe*. Harmondsworth: Penguin.

Narizhnaya, Khristina (2013) 'Russians Go West', *World Policy Journal*: Spring. www.worldpolicy.org/journal/spring2013/russians-go-west. Accessed July 27, 2015.

Neyer, Jürgen (2003) 'Discourse and Order in the EU: A Deliberative Approach to Multi-Level Governance', *Journal of Common Market Studies* 41(4): 687–706.

Neyer, Jürgen and Antje Wiener (2010) *Political Theory of the European Union*. Oxford: Oxford University Press.

Nickel, Patricia Mooney (2009) 'Network Governance and the New Constitutionalism', *Administrative Theory & Praxis* 29(2): 198–224.

Offe, Claus (1998) 'Demokratie und Wohlfahrtsstaat: Eine europäische Regmeform unter dem Streß der europäischen Integration', in Wolfgang Streeck (ed.), *Internationale Wirtschaft, nationale Demokratie*. Frankfurt: Campus, pp. 99–136.

Offe, Claus (2003) Is There, or Can There Be, a 'European Society'?, in Ines Katenhusen and Wolfram Lamping (eds.), *Demokratien in Europa. Der Einfluss der europäischen Integration auf Institutionenwandel und die Zukunft des demokratischen Verfassungsstaates*. Opladen: Leske und Budrich.

Offe, Claus (2005) 'The European Model of "Social" Capitalism: Can It Survive European Integration?', in Max Miller (ed.). *Worlds of Capitalism. Institutions, Governance and Economic Change in the Era of Globalization*. London: Routledge, pp. 146–178.

Offe, Claus (2009) 'Epilogue: Lessons Learnt and Open Questions. Issues of Welfare State Building in Post-Communist EU Member States,' in Alfio Cerami and Pieter Vanhuysse (eds.), *Post-Communist Welfare Pathways. Theorizing Social Policy Transformations in Central and Eastern Europe*. Basingstoke: Palgrave, Chapter 13.

Offe, Claus (2015) *Europe Entrapped*. Cambridge: Polity.

Olsen, Johan (2002) 'The Many Faces of Europeanization', *JCMS*, 40(5): 921–952.

Outhwaite, William (2007) 'Bourdieu and Postcommunist Class Formation', www.socresonline.org (12, 6, autumn). Accessed July 27, 2015.

Outhwaite, William (2009) 'European Society and the European Intellectual', in Christian Fleck, Andreas Hess, and Stina Lyon (eds.), *Intellectuals and Their Publics*. Farnham: Ashgate, pp. 59–68.

Outhwaite, William (2010) 'Legality and Legitimacy in the European Union', in Chris Thornhill and Samatha Ashenden (eds.), *Legality and Legitimacy: Normative and Sociological Approaches*. Baden-Baden: Nomos, pp. 279–290.

Outhwaite, William and David Spence (2014) 'Luc Boltanski in Euroland', in Simon Susen and Bryan Turner (eds.), *The Spirit of Luc Boltanski*. London: Anthem, pp. 425–444.

Peters, Bernhard, edited by Hartmut Wessler (2008) *Public Deliberation and Public Culture. The Writings of Bernhard Peters, 1993–2005*, Basingstoke: Palgrave Macmillan.

Pichler, Florian (2009) '"Down-to-Earth" Cosmopolitanism: Subjective and Objective Measurements of Cosmopolitanism in Survey Research', *Current Sociology* 57(5): 704–732.

Recchi, Ettore (2015) *Mobile Europe. The Theory and Practice of Free Movement in the EU*. Basingstoke: Palgrave Macmillan.

Risse, Thomas (2002) 'How Do We Know a European Public Sphere When We See One?', IDNET workshop, EUI. http://web.fu-berlin.de/atasp/texte/pi5s1otn.pdf. Accessed July 27, 2015.

Risse, Thomas (2014) 'No Demos? Identities and Public Spheres in the Euro Crisis', *Journal of Common Market Studies* 52(6): 1207–1215.

Rodríguez, Jospe, Julián Cardenas, and Christian Oltra (2006) 'Redes de poder económico in Europa', *Sistema* 194: 3–44.

Roose, Jochen (2010) *Vergesellschaftung an Europas Binnengrenzen. Eine vergleichende Studie zu den Bedingungen sozialer Integration*. Wiesbaden: VS Verlag.

Rother, Nina and Tanja Langner (2004) 'Dimensions of Identification with Europe: Secondary Analysis of Comparative Surveys', PIONEUR Working Paper No. 8, February.

Rumford, Chris (2003) 'European Civil Society or Transnational Social Spaces', *European Journal of Social Theory* 6(1): pp. 36–37.

Rumford, Chris (ed.) (2009) *Sage Handbook of European Studies*. London: SAGE.

Scharpf, Fritz (1999) *Governing in Europe: Effective and Democratic?* Oxford: Oxford University Press.

Schlesinger, Philip (1995) Europeanisation and the Media: National Identity and the Public Sphere. Arena 7 Working Paper. www.arena.uio.no/publications/working-papers1995/95_07.xml. Accessed July 27, 2015.

Schmidt, Vivien (2006) *Democracy in Europe. The EU and National Polities*. London: Oxford University Press.

Schmidt, Vivien (2011) 'The Problems of Identity and Legitimacy in the European Union: Is More Politics the Answer?', in Sonia Lucarelli, Furio Cerutti, and Vivien A. Schmidt (eds.), *Debating Political Identity and Legitimacy in the European Union*, London: Routledge, pp. 16–37.

Schulz-Forberg, Hagen and Bo Stråth (2010) *The Political History of European Integration. The Hypocrisy of Democracy-through-market*. London: Routledge.

Shaw, Jo (2007) *The Transformation of Citizenship in the European Union. Electoral Rights and the Restructuring of Political Space* Cambridge: Cambridge University Press.

Shaw, Jo, Richard Bellamy, and Dario Castiglione (eds.) (2006) *Making European Citizens*. Basingstoke: Palgrave.

Shkaratan, Ovsey and Gordey Yastrebov (2010) 'Russian Neo-Etacratic Society and its Stratification: Discovering Real Social Groups', *Journal of Communist Studies and Transition Politics*, 26(1): 1–24.

Statham, Paul (2010) 'What Kind of Europeanized Public Politics?', in Ruud Koopmans and Paul Statham (eds.), *The Making of a European Public Sphere. Media Discourse and Political Contention*. New York: Cambridge University Press, pp. 277–306.

Stråth, Bo (2002) 'A European Identity. To the Historical Limits of a Concept', *European Journal of Social Theory* 5(4): 387–401.

Trenz, Hans-Jörg (2009) 'In Search for Popular Subjectness. Identity Formation, Constitution Making and the Democratic Consolidation of the EU', Arena Working Paper No. 7, April.

Trenz, Hans-Jörg (2011) 'Social Theory and European Integration', in Adrian Favell and Virginie Guiraudon (eds.), *Sociology of the European Union*. Basingstoke: Palgrave, pp. 193–213.

Trenz, Hans-Jörg and Klaus Eder (2004) 'The Democratising Dynamics of a Public Sphere: Towards a Theory of Democratic Functionalism', *European Journal of Social Theory* 6: 5–25.

Trenz, Hans-Jörg and Peter de Wilde (2009) 'Denouncing European Integration. Euroscepticism as Reactive Identity Formation', Arena Working Paper No. 14, September.

van de Steeg, Marianne (2002) 'Rethinking the Conditions for a Public Sphere in the European Union', *European Journal of Social Theory* 5(4): 499–519.

Van den Berg, Casper (2009) Review of *The Europeanization of British Politics* – Edited by I. Bache and A. Jordan, *Journal of Common Market Studies* 47(2) March: 437–438.

Vanhuysse Pieter (2006a) *Divide and Pacify. Strategic Social Policies and Political Protests in Post-Communist Democracies*. Budapest: Central European University Press.

Vanhuysse Pieter (2006b) 'Czech Exceptionalism? A Comparative Political Economy Interpretation of Post-Communist Policy Pathways, 1989-2004', *Sociologický časopis/ Czech Sociological Review*, 42(6): 1115–1136.

Vink, Maarten and Graziano, Paolo (eds.) (2007) *Europeanization. New Research Agendas*. Basingstoke: Palgrave.

Wagner, Peter (2012) *Modernity*. Cambridge: Polity.

Walker, Neil (2006) 'Late Sovereignty in the European Union', in Walker (ed.), *Relocating Sovereignty*. Aldershot: Ashgate, pp. 521–550. First published in 2003.

Walters, William and Jens Henrik Haahr (2005) *Governing Europe. Discourse, Governmentality and European Integration*. London: Routledge.

Weiler, Joseph (1998) 'Europe: The Case Against the Case for Statehood' *European Law Journal*, 4(1): 43–62.

Wessler, Hartmut et al (2008) *Transnationalization of Public Spheres*. Basingstoke: Palgrave Macmillan.

10 Appendix on territoriality

One way of judging how far Europeans are beginning to think in terms of a single European society is to examine our use of broad regional concepts of the kind which are familiar in the United States: the East, the West, the South, the Midwest, New England, and so on. Joel Garreau (1981), a US journalist since turned law professor, offered a more interesting list of 'nine nations':

- New England (expanded north to include parts of Canada)
- The Foundry, the industrial square stretching from New York to the Great Lakes and including the Toronto area
- Dixie (the southeast, including most of Florida)
- The Breadbasket, the central and prairie belt, again reaching into Canada
- Mexamerica, from the Texan coast to Southern California
- Ecotopia (the rest of the Pacific Coastal belt)
- The Empty Quarter (apparently a Saudi term for a similarly unpopulated area): all the rest except for
- Quebec and
- The Islands (of South Florida and the Caribbean)[1]

A popular work by a US journalist based in Frankfurt (Delamaide, 1995) took up this theme and discussed emergent 'superregions' in Europe, based on a model drawn up by the European Commission for *Europe 2000* (1991).[2] Hartmut Kaelble, in a series of Berlin conferences and most recently in a special issue of the *Journal of Modern European History* (Wirsching et al, 2011); Göran Therborn (1995, 2006,); and Michael Mann (1998, 2006, 2011)[3] have all addressed these issues in one way or another, and they have been a prominent feature not just in human geography and regional studies (!) but in the historiography of Europe, where there has been talk of a 'spatial turn', especially in Germany, after 1989 (Troebst, 2003: 183 & n. 52).[4] The EU has, of course, been central to much macro-regional planning, with a host of initiatives of which the more practical include long-distance roads, such as the E80 running from Lisbon to Eastern Turkey, or waterways such as the Rhine-Main-Danube. As noted earlier, Jensen and Richardson (2003) see this as the attempt to construct a frictionless European space, a 'monotopia'.

This book has been mainly concerned with the East/West division and with degrees of 'Easternness' (see also Outhwaite, 2011), but one effect of what I call the uniting of Europe since 1989 and 2004/2007 (Outhwaite, 2010) is the relativisation of East/West in favour of North/South and other polarities.[5] As we have seen, the ongoing financial crisis of European states has revived long-standing North/South stereotypes, though now in a postgeographical sense in which the 'South' includes Ireland and Iceland, and probably soon the United Kingdom.

A brief list of European macro-regions would include the following:

1 'Eastern' in the sense of postcommunist Europe[6]
2 Northern or Nordic Europe
3 Central Europe
4 The Danube Basin
5 The Balkans
6 Mediterranean Europe
7 Atlantic Europe
8 Alpine Europe

The first of these had, and the second retains, a substantial political component. Politically even the democratic EU member states in the West of postcommunist Europe are as divided as can be, with opposition to Russia particularly strong in the Baltic States and a full spectrum of economic policies from neoliberal Estonia to more corporatist Slovenia.

Nordic Europe has been less mouvementé, at least in the recent past. The concept of Norden has a long history (Sørensen and Stråth, 1997), and Lee Miles (2010: 184) writes that '[i]n many ways, the Nordic region . . . represents an exemplary example of a region with many homogenous and common features uniting its component states'. The Nordic Council, an assembly of parliamentarians and ministers from the five Nordic states and the autonomous regions of Greenland, the Faroes, and Åland, has existed since 1952, thus coeval with the European Coal and Steel Community (ECSC), and introduced a free-travel zone and other common measures. Within the region, there are, of course, significant north–south differences and the linguistic division between Finnish and the mutually intelligible Scandinavian languages. The North, of course, may now be taken to include at least the Baltic States, and a looser notion of a Baltic Europe forms a third European macro-region.

Here we begin to cut across state boundaries, and the history of the Hanseatic League becomes relevant. The Hansa, sometimes described as 'the European Union of the Middle Ages'(Aust and Schmidt-Klingenberg, 2003: 89), had agencies as far to the north as Novgorod and Bergen and as far west as London, as well as centres inland in, for example, Breslau and Kraków. Similarly, a contemporary notion of a Baltic Europe would include parts of Germany, Poland, and Russia and perhaps Belgium, The Netherlands, and the east coast of England and Scotland. (In Gateshead, across the river from Newcastle, is the multistorey Baltic Exchange building, now an arts centre.) The United Kingdom is linked to Norway by the North Sea speckled with oil rigs and itself part of a North Sea Region, including most of England and Scotland, the Netherlands, and parts of Sweden, Denmark, Norway, and Germany (Jensen and Richardson, 2003).

The European Union may be said to have upstaged or '*aufgehoben*' regional groupings of this kind and, in particular, links between Nordic Europe (especially Sweden and Finland) and the Baltic States. As Marko Lehti (2010: 135) briskly puts it, 'Following EU membership, the Balts no longer want to become Nordic'. He goes on to quote the Latvian foreign minister's comment that 'the success of today's Europe lies in its regions, but the Nordics are not any more seen as the only partner'. The Baltic States were, of course, previously part of the Soviet Union and may return to a more continental focus, depending on developments in Russia, Belarus, and Ukraine. In East Central Europe, the Visegrád group was similarly relativised by the EU membership of first its component parts and then of Romania and Bulgaria, which are now included. Similarly, dyadic relations such as those between the United Kingdom and Ireland have been reshaped by EU membership, though these countries continue to maintain a free-travel zone outside Schengen.

The EU adopted in 2009 a 'Baltic Strategy' which is, it emphasises, 'the first time that a comprehensive Strategy, covering several Community policies, is targeted on a "macro-region"' (http://ec.europa/regional_policy/cooperation/baltic.) It is also, Lehti (2010: 138) notes, 'the first regional-based programme that is focussed solely in EU territory'. The Baltic Strategy is therefore intended to be complementary to the earlier 'Northern Dimension', which like the Barcelona Process in relation to the Mediterranean, was concerned with 'external cooperation' with nonmembers – in this case Russia. More recently, the EU has also launched a Strategy for the Danube Region, which includes not just the member states in the region and the Western Balkans (apart from Kosovo and Macedonia), but also Moldova and Ukraine.[7] With 115 million people living in the region thus defined, it would count as one of the larger macro-regions.[8]

The 'Balkans', like 'Mitteleuropa', is a term with a disturbing history (and this may be part of the motivation for drawing the 'Danube region' so broadly). As Spyros Economides (2010: 113) writes,

> Contemporary definitions of 'the Balkans' have changed, especially because of the relationship with the EU. The consensus is that the 'modern Balkans' are made up of Albania, Bulgaria, Greece, Romania, Turkey and Yugoslavia (and its successor states).

'Western Balkans' seems to have become entrenched as an alternative to the more cumbersome 'former Yugoslavia and Albania' or the slightly vague 'southeast Europe'. As Economides (2010: 116) notes, the definition of the Western Balkans as Yugoslavia minus Slovenia plus Albania marked out a '*policy-relevant region*' of potential member states.

The Western Balkans, now including Slovenia, also form part of a broader Southern or even 'Mediterranean' Europe, if one includes the Adriatic with the

Mediterranean rather as we included the North Sea with the Baltic. The EU has been more than usually chaotic in its conceptualisation of the Mediterranean region and its proliferation of initiatives, of which Sarkozy's was one of the most recent. More interesting in relation to the Mediterranean is the idea of a 'red' or 'hot' banana, running from Barcelona to Rome, to complement or even replace the 'blue banana' of earlier European industrial and postindustrial activity.

The Alpine region identified by Delamaide is also discussed by Daniele Caramani (2010). Although it is centred around a non-EU state, Switzerland, it became in 2001 the object of an EU initiative, the 'Alpine Space Programme', one of fourteen such programmes of the European Regional Development Fund and running from the three southeastern regions of France to Slovenia and Austria. Caramani agrees with Michael Keating (2005: 67) that the Alpine region has

> . . . not developed those middle-range transnational spaces that could lift questions out of the local context while not taking them all the way to Europe. There is nothing like the Nordic area or the British Isles.

The dominant political cultures of the region, Caramani suggests, are suspicious of integration in the form promulgated by the EU while attracted to 'an *alternative* form of integration' (Caramani, 2010: 94) which stresses the defensive aspects of European integration against external threats.[9]

The last region, 'Atlantic Europe', is a good deal more diffuse, stretching from Portugal to the North Cape of Norway.[10] Historically identified with transatlantic trade, notably the slave trade, it probably has little significance any more except in relation to the fishing industry and the environmental threats which this faces. The issue of coastlines does, however, raise an issue in relation to countries which adjoin two or more seas. In the case of the Baltic and the Mediterranean, the response has generally been to offer a generous definition which would make, for example, Portugal a Mediterranean country and Norway a Baltic one. France and Spain are special cases, with Atlantic as well as Mediterranean coasts; Russia has, of course, at least four.

How seriously should we take these European macro-regions? Their institutional status is clearly varied, as we have seen. Depending on the topic of investigation, the number and location of regions will vary. In the case of migration, for example, Mau and Verwiebe (2010: 126) distinguish seven regional 'subsystems in the European migration space': Scandinavia, the Central/Northwest (United Kingdom, Ireland, France, Benelux), Central (Germany, Austria), Mediterranean (Spain, Greece, Cyprus), Central/East (Hungary, Czech Republic, Slovenia, Poland), East/Southeast (Romania, Bulgaria, Slovakia), and the Baltics. In some regions, such as the Baltic States, cooperation efforts have declined, partly due to the fact that policy coordination at the EU level makes this less imperative (Bult, 2010). Keating's criterion mentioned earlier seems a useful one to apply. As Jensen and Richardson show, there are clearly serious concerns to be raised about the European Union's territorial policies, no less than about those of member states. More fundamentally, the mythical dimension of metageographies like these can be questioned (Lewis and Wigen, 1997).[11] Most Europeans probably operate with a fairly flexible North/South and East/West mental map, though one which has always been politically inflected, locating Greece in Western Europe, formerly communist Prague east rather than west of Vienna, and so on. As Johann Arnason (2003: 221, col. 2) writes, 'the inherited notions of East and West should be ranked with the problems rather than the premises of historical sociology'. Yet, he goes on, since there *was* something like a 'rise of the West', 'notwithstanding the basic defects of dichotomizing theories, they can . . . serve to illustrate a deep-rooted and recurrent challenge to an alternative model that is still in the making'.

These regions are, of course, 'imagined' in Benedict Anderson's sense of imagined communities; as Dariusz Gafajczuk (2011) has written in relation to central Europe, 'what is missing in accounting for space as a geopolitical *territory* is . . . the much more fluid *landscape* of identity in its raw density'. What *is*, I think, happening is that we are thinking more often on a continental scale, with fewer mental limits. A weekend trip from Western Europe to Tallin no longer seems exotic, and many European workers are commuting long distance, as from Poland to Britain. We may not know quite where we are going, but we Europeans are on the move.

Notes

1 For a more recent geographical account, see Enloe and Seager (2011).
2 Churchill (1951: 636) in 1943 (on a train in Turkey) envisaged a postwar 'instrument of European government . . . The units forming this body will not only be the great nations of Europe and Asia Minor as long established, but a number of confederations formed among the smaller states, among which a Scandinavian Bloc, a Danubian Bloc, and a Balkan Bloc appear to be obvious'. Of the effects of 1989, Delpeuch (1994: 23) wrote: 'In this redrawing of European geography, the Baltic again becomes a lake, and France a Finistère' (my translation).
   See also Götz (2010: 91–92).
3 See Mann (2011: 58): 'I've been impressed by the way in which macro-regions influence welfare regimes and varieties of capitalism. The Anglophones, Nordics, Continental Europeans (with Mediterranean countries separating somewhat from their northern neighbours in recent years), Latin Americans, East Asians – and there may be more, too – manifesting distinctive trajectories of development'.
4 See also Koselleck (2000) and the work of Ed Soja. John Agnew (1989: 9) had earlier criticised what he called 'the devaluation of place in social science'. On the emergence of the notion of historical regions in the late nineteenth century, see Faber (1979) and the 2011 special issue of the *Journal of Modern European History* 9(1); on the French debates, see also Chartier (1980). One of the less savoury theorists of the *Grossraum* was, of course, the Nazi Carl Schmitt.
5 On North-South, see, for example, Bourdieu (1980).
6 This is the only point at which my list diverges from Delamaide's. His 'Slavic Federation' consists of Belarus, Ukraine, and Russia. See also Chapter 3.
7 This was discussed at a recent seminar at University College London organised by the European Institute and the Hungarian Embassy: www.ucl.ac.uk/european-institute/highlights/danube.

8 Population figures are, of course, fluid for regions of this kind. Kęstutis Girnius (2011: 33) gives the Baltic region 50 to 80 million inhabitants, but a hinterland brings the total up to more like 230 million.

9 A comparison with the Nordic countries would be interesting here, as part of a more differentiated approach to 'euroscepticism'. (On this, see, for example, Beichelt (2011); also the centre run at Sussex University by Alex Szczerbiak and Paul Taggart and a new network within the Universities Association for Contemporary European Studies (UACES) framework.)

10 A narrower version of Atlantic Europe focuses on the United Kingdom and Ireland (known in the former but not the latter as the 'British Isles') and their relationship with North America (Gamble, 2010).

11 The authors provide a cautious defence of an alternative, including an interesting comparison between Europe and India (Lewis and Wigen, 1997: 170 and 273 n. 41) and some stimulating reflections on Central Asia (Lewis and Wigen, 1997: 176–181). More controversial is their macro-region including Russia, the Caucasus, and Southeast Europe, on the grounds that if Russia, stretching as it does to the Pacific, is distinguished from Europe, it is 'difficult to argue' that Slavic and/or Orthodox parts of Europe should not be included with it (Lewis and Wigen, 1997: 187 and 273 n. 38). It is significant that they do not mention the European Union except in passing.

References

Agnew, John (1989) 'The Devaluation of Place in Social Science', in John A. Agnew and James S. Duncan (eds.) *The Power of Place: Bringing Together Geographical and Sociological Imaginations*: Boston: Unwin Hyman, Chapter 2.

Arnason, Johann (2003) 'East and West: From Invidious Dichotomy to Incomplete Deconstruction', in Gerard Delanty and Engin F. Isin (eds.), *Handbook of Historical Sociology*. London: Sage, Ch. 15, pp. 220–234.

Aust, Stefan and Schmidt-Klingenberg, Michael (eds.) (2003) *Experiment Europa. Ein Kontinent macht Geschichte*. Stuttgart: Deutsche Verlags-Anstalt.

Beichelt, Timm (2011) 'Vom Nutzen der EU-Skepsis für Europas Integration', *Berliner Republik*. (www.b-republik.de). Accessed July 27, 2015.

Bourdieu, Pierre (1980) 'Le Nord et le Midi: Contribution à une analyse de l'effet Montesquieu', *Actes de la recherche en sciences sociales* 35(November): 21–25.

Bult, Jeroen (2010) *A Bicycle Getting Rusty: Some Thoughts on Baltic Cooperation*. Tallinn: Estonian Foreign Policy Institute.

Caramani, Daniele (2010) 'Alpine Europe', in Kenneth Dyson and Angelos Sepos (eds.), *Which Europe? The Politics of Differentiated Integration*. Basingstoke: Palgrave Macmillan, pp. 83–98.

Chartier, Roger (1980) 'Science sociale et découpage régional', *Actes de la recherche en sciences sociales* 35(November): pp. 27–36.

Churchill, Winston (1951) *The Second World War*, vol. 4: *The Hinge of Fate*. London: Cassell.

Commission of the European Communities, Directorate-General for Regional Policy (1991) *Europe 2000: Outlook for the Development of the Community's Territory*. Brussels and Luxemburg.

Delamaide, Darrell (1995) *The New Superregions of Europe*. New York: Penguin.

Delpeuch, Jean-Luc (1994) *Post-communisme: L'Europe au défi. Chronique pragoise de la réforme économique au coeur d'une Europe en crise*. Paris: L'Harmattan.

Economides, Spyros (2010) 'Balkan Europe', in Kenneth Dyson and Angelos Sepos (eds.), *Which Europe? The Politics of Differentiated Integration*. Basingstoke: Palgrave Macmillan.

Enloe, Cynthia and Joni Seager (2011) *The Real State of America Atlas: Mapping the Myths and Truths of the United States*. London: University of California Press.

Faber, Karl-Georg (1979) 'Geschichtslandschaft – Région historique – Section in History. Ein Beitrag zur vergleichenden Wissenschaftsgeschichte', *Saeculum* 30(1): 4–21.

Favell, Adrian and Virginie Guiraudon (eds.) (2011) *Sociology of the European Union*. Basingstoke: Palgrave.

Gafajczuk, Dariusz (2011) 'Resonant Typographies: Central Europe's Paradoxical Middle', *Theory, Culture & Society* 29(3) May: 52–71.

Gamble, Andrew (2010) 'Anglo-America and Atlantic Europe', in Kenneth Dyson and Angelos Sepos (eds.), *Which Europe? The Politics of Differentiated Integration*. Basingstoke: Palgrave Macmillan, pp. 99–111.

Garreau, Joel (1981) *The Nine Nations of North America*, Boston: Houghton Mifflin.

Girnius, Kęstutis (2011) 'The Baltic Sea Region', in *Europa Regional Surveys of the World: Central and South-Eastern Europe*. Abingdon: Routledge, pp. 33–38.

Goodin, Robert E. and Charles Tilly (eds.) (2006) *The Oxford Handbook of Contextual Political Analysis*. Oxford: Oxford University Press.

Götz, Norbert (2010) 'Rationalities of European Integration: Legitimisation and Communalisation', in Sven Eliason and Nadezhda Georgieva (eds.), *New Europe. Growth to Limits?* Oxford: Bardwell Press, pp. 91–106.

Jensen, Ole B. and Tim Richardson (2003) *Making European Space. Mobility, Power and Territorial Identity*. London: Routledge.

Keating, Michael (2005) 'Regionalism in the Alps; Subnational, Supranational, and Transnational', in D. Caramani and Y. Mény (eds.), *Challenges to Consensual Politics: Democracy, Identity, and Populist Protest in the Alpine Region*. Brussels: P.I.E. – Peter Lang, pp. 53–69.

Koselleck, Reinhart (2000) 'Raum und Geschichte' (1986), in Koselleck, *Zeitschichten. Studien zur Historik*. Frankfurt: Suhrkamp, pp. 78–96.

Lehti, Marko (2010) 'Baltic Europe', in Kenneth Dyson and Angelos Sepos (eds.), *Which Europe? The Politics of Differentiated Integration*. Basingstoke: Palgrave Macmillan, pp. 126–141.

Lewis, Martin and Kären E. Wigen (1997) *The Myth of Continents. A Critique of Metageography*. Berkeley and Los Angeles: University of California Press.

Mann, Michael (1998) 'Is There a Society Called Euro?', in R. Axtmann (ed.), *Globalization and Europe*. London: Pinter.

Mann, Michael (2006) 'Globalization, Macro-Regions and Nation-States', in Gunilla Budde, Sebastian Conrad and Oliver Janz, (eds.), *Transnationale Tendenzen, Theorien. Jürgen Kocka zum 65. Geburtstag*. Göttingen: Vandenhoeck & Ruprecht, pp. 21–31.

Mann, Michael (2011) *Power in the 21st Century. Conversations with John A. Hall*. Cambridge: Polity.

Mau, Steffen and Roland Verwiebe (2010) *European Societies. Mapping Structure and Change*. Bristol: Policy Press.

Miles, Lee (2010) 'The Nordic Countries and the Fourth EU Enlargement', in Lee Miles (ed.), *The European Union and the Nordic Countries*. London: Routledge, pp. 61–76.

Outhwaite, William (2010) 'Europe at 21: Transitions and Transformations since 1989', LEQS Discussion Paper Series No. 18, London: LSE.

Outhwaite, William (2011) 'Postcommunist Capitalism and Democracy: Cutting the Post-communist Cake', *Journal of Democratic Socialism* 1(1, October: 1–23. http://demo craticsocialism.net/. Accessed July 27, 2015.

Sørensen, Øystein and Bo Stråth (eds.) (1997) *The Cultural Construction of Norden*. Oslo: Scandinavian Universities Press.

Therborn, Göran (1995) *European Modernity and Beyond. The Trajectory of European Societies 1945–2000*. London: Sage.

Therborn, Göran (2006) 'Why and How Place Matters', in Robert E. Goodin and Charles Tilly (eds).

Therborn, G. (2011) *The World. A Beginner's Guide*. Cambridge: Polity.

Troebst, Stefan (2003) 'Introduction: What's in a Historical Region? A Teutonic Perspective', *European Review of History* 10(2): 173–188.

Vassiliev, Boyko (2010) 'The Region No One Could Name', *Transitions Online*, 4.22.10.

Wirsching, Andreas, Göran Therborn, Geoff Eley, Hartmut Kaelble, and Philippe Chassaigne (2011) 'The 1970s and 1980s as a Turning Point in European History?', *Journal of Modern European History (JMEH)* 9(1): 8–26.

Index

.

For Product Safety Concerns and Information please contact our EU
representative GPSR@taylorandfrancis.com
Taylor & Francis Verlag GmbH, Kaufingerstraße 24, 80331 München, Germany

www.ingramcontent.com/pod-product-compliance
Lightning Source LLC
Chambersburg PA
CBHW070243290326
41929CB00046B/2403

* 9 7 8 0 3 6 7 8 7 0 6 6 9 *